AF328892

INDIA'S HISTORIC BATTLES

INDIA'S HISTORIC BATTLES

From Alexander the Great to Kargil

KAUSHIK ROY

PRIMUS BOOKS

An imprint of Ratna Sagar P. Ltd.

Virat Bhavan
Mukherjee Nagar Commercial Complex
Delhi 110 009

Offices at

CHENNAI LUCKNOW
AGRA AHMEDABAD BANGALORE COIMBATORE
DEHRADUN GUWAHATI HYDERABAD JAIPUR JALANDHAR
KANPUR KOCHI KOLKATA MADURAI MUMBAI
PATNA RANCHI VARANASI

First published 2004
Revised edition 2020

ISBN: 978-93-89755-74-9 (paperback)
ISBN: 978-93-89755-75-6 (POD)

Published by Primus Books

Laser typeset in Adobe Garamond Pro
by Guru Typograph Technology
Crossings Republic, Ghaziabad 201 009

Contents

Preface to the New Edition   vii

Preface to the First Edition   ix

List of Abbreviations   xi

Map: Decisive Battles Fought in India   xii

Introduction: Battles in Indian History   1

1. *Phalanx* against *Rathas* and *Hastis*: The Battle of Jhelum, 326 BC   8

2. Crescent Over Hindustan: The Second Battle of Tarain, AD 1192   27

3. The Men on Horseback: The First Battle of Panipat, 21 April 1526   47

4. Chance in History: The Second Battle of Panipat, 5 November 1556   59

5. Abdali's Organ Pipes: The Third Battle of Panipat, 14 January 1761   70

6. Red Phoenix Rising: Buxar, 23 October 1764   83

7. The Tiger Caged: The Siege of Seringapatam, 4 May 1799   95

8. Open Fire: The Battle of Assaye, 23 September 1803   106

9. *Dal Khalsa's* Last Chance: Ferozeshah, 21–2 December 1845   118

10. Under Siege: Lucknow, 1857–1858   130

11. Mousetrap: Imphal and Kohima, March–July 1944   143

12. Mission Impossible? Kargil, May–July 1999   154

Conclusion: Towards Armageddon or the
End of Battle?   165

Bibliographical Essay   171

Glossary   179

Bibliography to the New Edition   185

Index   189

Preface to the New Edition

IN 2004, I WROTE this book in an attempt to popularize military history of India. However, the book soon went out of print; despite the fact that no paperback edition came out. In 2018, on a sunny day in the Department of History, Jadavpur University while chatting about other things, my ex-student cum friend Sanmitra Ghosh asked me to publish this book once more. I must admit that I had completely forgotten about this book till that time. In the last one and half decade after the publication of this volume, I have moved away from battles of India to warfare in Eurasia. I am grateful to Sanmitra for reviving my interest in *India's Historic Battles*.

I have kept the revisions to a minimum, corrected some errors and added a few things in the light of present research. However, while revising the text, I found that taking into account all the recent studies will mean writing a new book. Hence, the changes which have been made are mostly minimal and an attempt has been made to retain the original flavour of this small monograph. However, it must be noted that this present book is a new expanded edition and partly original. Those who want to pursue further studies on Indian battles will find the new bibliography useful. Names of the cities in India are always changing. I have retained those names which are most common among both the foreigners and Indians.

Lastly, military history has been my bread and butter. And my interest in military history is credited to my father. He generated the passion for armies and warfare in my mind by telling me bed time stories about Imphal-Kohima and Normandy during my childhood days. The arrangement was that I would not go to sleep till my father told me at least one war story; be it about the Tiger tanks at Kursk or the Japanese in Singapore. It is a strange coincidence that my father who wanted to pursue military history was a civil engineer from Jadavpur University, where I work at present.

Kolkata   KAUSHIK ROY

Preface to the First Edition

IN THE COURSE OF our everyday routine, little do we realize how much the context in which we live has been shaped by organized violence with its twin elements of blood and death. If the results of the battles of Tarain, Panipat, Buxar, Assaye and so on had been different, then we would have been living in a different sort of world. We also fail to take into account how much of our ordinary life and customs have been shaped by the army—the chief instrument of organized violence. Take for instance, the case of baggy trousers. American paratroopers during the Second World War first used it. Face powder and make-up most women use were introduced by the senior officers of the *Ancien Regime's* French army. The officers used make-up and face powder to hide the scars they had acquired while fighting. Nevertheless, the Indian academic's attitude towards military history remains indifferent.

From my childhood, I have been interested in matters military. By following the policy of 'beg and buy', I have built up a collection of books on military history. While doing a doctorate on the Sepoy army there was considerable pressure to integrate the military subject with wider social and political issues. Some historians who were unaware of military theories advised me to use Michel Foucault and Antonio Gramsci while writing military history. Indian historians doubt the autonomy and validity of historical studies of armies and warfare. The tradition of Jadunath Sarkar and Jagadish Narayan Sarkar has been forgotten under the pressure of Marxism and Postmodernism. I have always wanted to write a book on battles. Thanks to Anuradha Roy for allowing me to write one. Endnotes are deliberately avoided in order to make the volume reader-friendly.

Thanks to Suhrita for bearing with me while I was writing this book.

Let us turn our attention to the 'dark forces' which have shaped our destiny.

List of Abbreviations

BSF	Border Security Force
C3	Command, Control and Communications
CIA	Central Intelligence Agency
COAS	Chief of Army Staff
IAF	Indian Air Force
IAS	Indian Administrative Service
INA	Indian National Army
IPS	Indian Police Service
LoC	Line of Control
PAF	Pakistan Air Force
PoK	Pakistan Occupied Kashmir
RAF	Royal Air Force

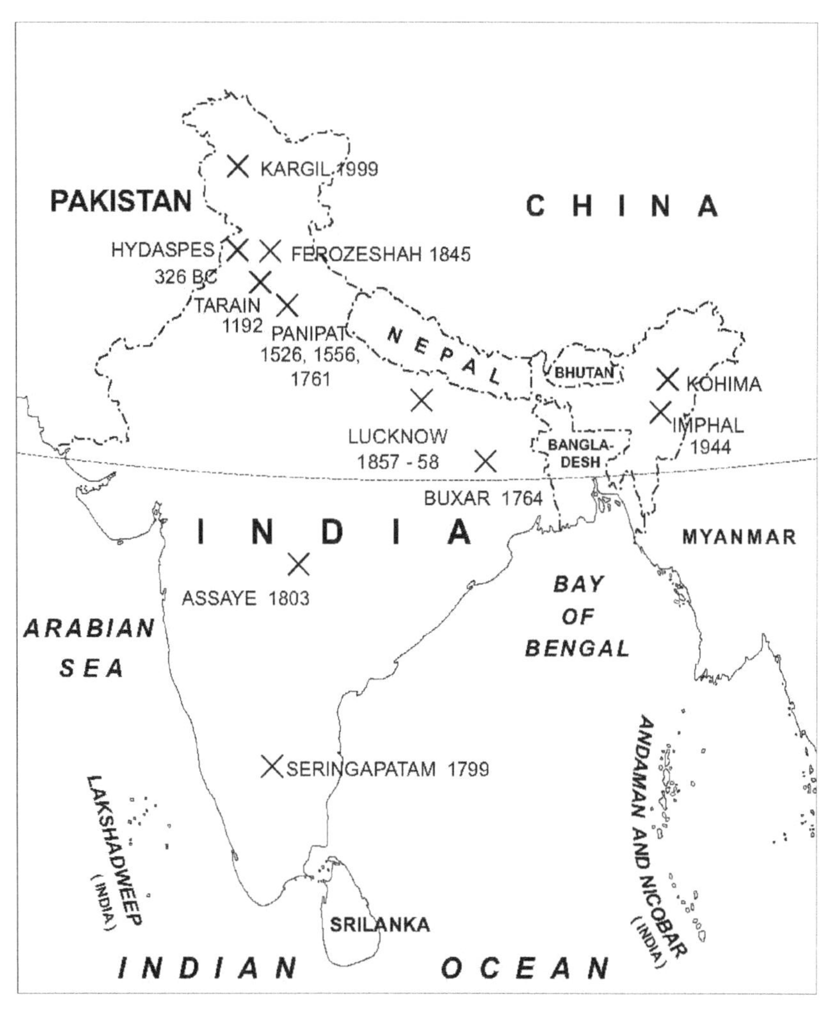

MAP: Decisive Battles Fought in India

Introduction

Battles in Indian History

'What is the battle? It is a struggle by the main force . . . it is a struggle for real victory, waged with all available strength . . . of the strategic budget, important battles may be considered its gold and silver.'

—CARL VON CLAUSEWITZ

To THE NINETEENTH-CENTURY Prussian military philosopher, Clausewitz, battles constitute the central focus of warfare. Clausewitz, in his magnum opus, *On War*, compares war with commercial transactions: decisive engagement in the battlefield is 'currency', the backbone of any financial transaction. About 2,000 years before the emergence of this Prussian military officer cum philosopher, Kautilya, the political theorist of ancient India, linked the successful conduct of battles with national survival.

Scholars like Martin van Creveld dispute the central role of battles in warfare. They argue that instead of set piece encounters between armies on a single day at a particular place; sporadic, decentralized, long-term pinpricks by guerrillas make more impact. The guerrillas' aim is not so much to attack the armed forces of the enemy as to harass them by cutting their supply lines and communications. This sort of combat is known as guerrilla warfare by the British and *Kleinkrieg* by the Germans.

But is guerrilla warfare really more decisive? The two greatest practitioners of guerrilla warfare were the Roman senator Maximius Fabius and the Chinese warlord Mao Tse Tung. Guerrilla warfare, which was known among the Romans as the Fabian strategy, failed to annihilate Hannibal's army. Both Fabius and Mao accepted the importance of decisive battles. Both advocated that at the preliminary stage, using guerrillas would significantly weaken the enemy, then the enemy army (*scbwerpunkt* in the Clausewitzian framework) could be annihilated more easily in an encounter battle.

In the Indian context, the Marathas, who practised mobile guerrilla warfare with light cavalry from the mid-sixteenth century, failed to exterminate the Mughals and the British. In desperation, from the mid-eighteenth century, the Marathas attempted to learn the techniques of decisive battles. But by then, it was too late.

Scholars like Correlli Barnett and Paul Kennedy assert that wars are not decided by decisive battles. More strategic is attritional warfare: waging war over a long period resulting in the economic exhaustion of the enemy. *Ermattungstrategie*, as this is termed, can successfully be implemented only by a state with strong economic and demographic muscles. After all, a great deal of money is required to deploy better weapons and large number of troops for a long period. The ancient Athenian admiral Thucydides, in his history of the Peloponnesian War, points out the importance of wealth in waging war successfully. Following Thucydides, Paul Kennedy, analysing the military history of the modern period, equates industrial prowess with military capability. One of the greatest practitioners of modern warfare, Napoleon Bonaparte, used to say 'God favours the side with bigger battalions.'

However, historical facts do not tally with this sort of economic and demographic determinism. In the fourth century, the Huns, who were nomadic mounted archers from Central Asia, and then the Mongols during the thirteenth century, repeatedly defeated the economically dynamic agrarian bureaucratic empires of Rome, Persia and Hind. In the industrial era, Prussia, with a weak economy and sparse population, dominated Europe because of the excellence of its General Staff in planning and conducting decisive battles. During the Second World War, the Axis powers, with comparatively weaker demographic and economic resources, were on the point of winning global hegemony. And as this book will show, in India, both the Rajput states of the early medieval era and the Mughal successor states in the eighteenth century, despite possessing greater demographic and economic potential, failed against the steppe nomads and the East India Company, respectively.

Warfare has always been important in India's historical evolution. Till 1947, armies not only consumed the biggest chunk of the government's revenue but were also the biggest government employers. The point to be remembered, however, is that battles constitute only one, though probably the most important, aspect of warfare.

This volume will concentrate on decisive battles that shaped the course of Indian history. Despite the importance of decisive battles in India's evolution, we lack a book that covers the entire span of India's historical military landscape. Colonel G.B. Malleson wrote a book titled *The Decisive Battles of India* in 1883. Malleson analysed thirteen battles fought between 1745 and 1849 which enabled the British to establish their Indian empire. After Malleson, the doyen of Indian historians, Jadunath Sarkar, in his *Military History of India* (1960), studied the twenty battles that allowed Alexander, and later the Central Asian nomads, to conquer India.

Taking into account recent researches, especially in the fields of technology, military theory and demography, this book is an attempt to provide a glimpse of twelve great battles that have decided the fate of the subcontinent. I have moved across space and time quite freely because cross-continental analysis brings out the elements of commonality as well as uniqueness of the big battles fought in India. Serious researchers will find this volume a starting point, and to aid them, a bibliographical essay is included. But the book's main audience is the general reader interested in military affairs.

The British military theorist Major General J.F.C. Fuller's statement that military hardware accounts for 99 per cent of the battle is certainly an overstatement. But while the technology of killing is important, a man equipped with a weapon does not automatically become a soldier. Men with arms need to be trained and then commanded. To win big battles, in the terminology of the ancient Chinese military philosopher Sun Tzu (500 BC), 'heaven born commanders' are required.

Each chapter analyses the nature of weapons used, the level of leadership exhibited and the soldiers' experience of battles. The book also takes into account *Kriegsfuhrung*, or the art of deploying military assets before fighting battles. In English, this translates as military strategy. After strategy comes tactics. The actual disposition of men and weapons in the battlefield and the art of commanding them in the heat of battle is known as tactics, which is derived from the Greek word *taktika*. The consequences of each battle provide the connecting link with the next chapter and I also attempt to compare events, tactics and outcomes in battles separated by space and time.

The categorization of a particular battle as 'big' on the basis of political, technological and demographic angles is always open for debate. It depends largely on the writer's opinion. For example, a battle could be regarded as decisive if the latest technology is displayed. The Second Battle of Tarain (AD 1192) falls in this category as for the first time India experienced lethal mounted archery on a large scale. Massive slaughter of human beings in a confined space (battlefield) within a short time can also be the indicator of a significant battle. Hence, Clausewitz's categorization of a big battle as '*schlacht*' which literally means butcher's slaughtering. Following Clausewitz, the Russians categorize an encounter as a *bitva* (big battle), if a lot of combatants and non-combatants lose their lives. The Third Battle of Panipat in 1761 proved to be a *schlacht* for the Marathas. In the space of seven hours, and within a 7 mi. radius, many thousands were wiped out from the face of the earth.

Battles fought between 1750 and 1850 occupy bulk of the space in this book. This is because that period witnessed the origin of modern warfare with its twin elements of infantry and artillery. The combat at Kargil in 1999 offers a glimpse of future battles: the technology of the twenty-first century and the way it might be used. Hence Kargil is included under the bracket of a decisive battle.

'No other human activity', emphasises Clausewitz, 'is so continuously or universally bound up with chance. And through the element of chance, guesswork and luck come to play a great part in war.' I have given counter-factual scenarios for most of the battles I write about, to show how often luck and chance decided the course of history. Parallel imageries are constructed on 'ifs' and 'buts', but offer a check to determinism in history. Despite the focus of the structuralists on long term factors and E.H. Carr's caricature of chance as 'Cleopatra's nose', a crucial factor in war remains the role of unforeseen.

This book does not consider naval battles: India being a continental landmass, the reach of naval power has always been limited. In 1534, the Portuguese ocean-going fleet wiped out a combined Gujarati-Ottoman fleet at Diu near the coast of Gujarat. Since the Portuguese lacked a strong army, the effect of Portuguese military power on the course of Indian history was minimal. Right from the late seventeenth century, the British had reigned supreme in the Indian Ocean. However, only when the Company created a strong land force in the second half of the eighteenth century, were the British able to project power over the subcontinent. Pure aviation war like the Battle of Britain or 'strategic bombing', as Europe had experienced during the Second World War is yet to occur in Indian skies. But from the 1940s, air power supported land power during two great battles fought in India: Imphal-Kohima (1944) and Kargil (1999). I have, therefore, included these battles in this volume.

My first chapter brings out the superiority of the Greek *phalanx* over Indian *rathas* in the plains of Punjab in May 326 BC. For the first time in Indian history, the gateway of India was opened to foreigners. This trend was to continue. After the Greeks, the Huns and the Arabs tried to invade India but their invasions petered out along the north-west frontier.

It fell on Central Asian Islamic Turks to carry out a full-scale invasion of India in the twelfth century. The Central Asian nomadic armies deployed a revolutionary weapon system comprising composite bow-armed mounted archers. By integrating the mobility of a cavalry with the firepower of bows, the nomadic horse archers were able to alter the 'speed of battle'. They destroyed the elephant-centric Rajput armies. This is the theme of the second chapter.

The potency of horse archery registered a quantum jump when light artillery (known as artillery of the stirrups among the Turks) was integrated with mounted archers. A young Turkish warlord named Zahir-ud-din Babur achieved this revolutionary synthesis. Thus, in the single afternoon of 21 April 1526 as the third chapter shows, Babur was able to decimate the Sultanate army at Panipat, which resulted in the foundation of the Mughal Empire.

In spite of Albert Einstein's assertion to the advocates of Quantum mechanics that God does not play dice, God at times does play dice. The role of the contingent in shaping the course of Indian history becomes evident in the fourth chapter. On 5 November 1556, in the historic field of Panipat, an Afghan army led by the Hindu general Hemu surrounded the Mughal force. A chance arrow killed Hemu and the near-victorious Afghan army started dissolving. But for Hemu's death, there would have been no Akbar the Great; without Akbar there would have been no *mansabdari* system and without the *mansabdari* system, the agrarian crisis would have never occurred. This very crisis in late seventeenth century resulted in the rise of the Marathas.

The Marathas, as successors of the Mughals, tried to secure the traditional 'scientific frontier' of India which ran through Kabul-Kandahar-Ghazni. This led to a tussle with the Afghans under Ahmad

Shah Abdali. The fifth chapter depicts the destruction of the Maratha light cavalry by the concentrated firepower of Abdali's *zamburaks*, again at the fateful field of Panipat, in 1761.

The Maratha collapse at Panipat enabled the East India Company's *lal paltan* to establish a bridgehead at Bengal. It is said the Bourbons learnt nothing, forgot nothing, but the case of the Indian rulers was worse. They learnt nothing but forgot everything. Despite the repeated failures of Indian cavalry against the disciplined infantry of the Company, the Nawab of Awadh relied on the 'men on horseback'. The story of Buxar where on 23 October 1764, the Company's western-modelled infantry wiped out a numerically superior Indian cavalry force is told in the sixth chapter.

While the *feranghis* were expanding in east India, Haidar Ali emerged as the strongman of south India. His cavalry ravaged the Company's possessions in the Madras Presidency. Under his son Tipu Sultan, a shift occurred within the Mysore military machine from mobile warfare based on the cavalry armies to positional warfare centred on fortresses. This came about from the influence of the 'Vauban School', made up of French officers expert in the art of fortification; it encouraged Tipu to build 'impregnable forts'. The strongest fort was constructed at Tipu's capital in Seringapatam. The art of capturing forts with the help of heavy artillery manned by engineers and sappers could be termed 'scientific war'. The seventh chapter describes the conduct of this sort of war by the British in Mysore in 1799.

The British took about half a century to crush military resistance in north and south India. This enabled the Marathas to reorganize themselves in the aftermath of the Panipat disaster and they attempted to make a comeback in the subcontinent's game of power politics. The eigth chapter depicts the Maratha military failure against the British. They could not make up their mind whether to fight with an infantry equipped with firearms as the Europeans did, or to continue their traditional scorched earth policy with their cavalry. This ambivalence resulted in their destruction in 1803 in Assaye at the hands of the 'Greatest Sepoy General', the Duke of Wellington.

After the Marathas, the last check on the British were the Sikhs. Ranjit Singh modelled a European force, the *Dal Khalsa*, with the help of ex-Napoleonic officers. It clashed with the Company's sepoy army at Ferozeshah. On 21 December 1845, the *Dal Khalsa* had actually won against the Company's *lal paltan*, with the Governor-General and the Commander-in-Chief on the point of being captured. The course of India's history was dancing on the edge of an abyss. But Sikh politicians undid what Sikh soldiers had achieved. The ninth chapter shows how treachery within the Sikh high command enabled the British to metamorphose defeat into victory.

The summer of 1857 was an ironical time for the Company, when the *lal paltan* that had won India for the British turned against their white masters. The 'rebels' were cooped up within the Red Fort of Delhi and then in Lucknow. The tenth chapter portrays how superior technology in the form of siege artillery and Enfield rifles enabled the British to retrieve the situation. But it was touch and go. If the 'rebels' had managed to launch a mobile guerrilla counterattack throughout the subcontinent, it could well have been a case of 'game over' for the British.

As killing machines in the third dimension made an appearance, the twentieth century witnessed the emergence of air-land battle—a new form of warfare. The eleventh chapter shows the twin cities of Imphal-Kohima becoming a burning cauldron for the British-led Indian army. The Japanese and the Azad Hind Fauj had surrounded Imphal and Kohima. At that critical juncture British air power intervened. While the Dakotas dropped food, the Spitfires provided fire-support. Air power turned the tide of battle in favour of the Raj.

Even after Independence, the Indian army remained embedded in colonial tradition. Towards the end of the twentieth century, it suddenly woke up, when faced with a new kind of battle at Kargil. Kargil could be regarded as a sort of 'Limited War' under a nuclear umbrella. As the last chapter shows, Kargil was an amalgamation of high-tech insurgency and low-level conventional war. India's failure at Kargil will continue to have disastrous consequences for Kashmir in particular, and India in general.

Regardless of social, political, economic and cultural factors the trajectory of history is occasionally shaped by mass organized violence, i.e. war. Despite the determined talk of peacekeeping and disarmament, warfare has been endemic in history and will remain so in the near future. In this book, I attempt to sum up India's military experience through some of the battles that have been fought here.

1

Phalanx against *Rathas* and *Hastis*

The Battle of Jhelum, 326 BC

IN THE DARK of night, men and horses huddled together, groping their way forward in heavy rain. Flashes from occasional lightning were reflected on the bright bronze helmets of the ghost-like white-skinned men armed with swords and spears trying to cross the river Jhelum in a violent thunderstorm. The soldiers who melted away in the dark of night were from Alexander's victorious Macedonian army, attempting to invade India.

Alexander became the ruler of Macedonia in 336 BC having murdered his father Philip. Immediately after crowning himself, the young king conquered the whole of Greece. The famed Spartan army and Athenian navy crumbled before Alexander's military genius. After establishing his hegemony in Greece, Alexander undertook the invasion of the greatest empire of his time: the Persian Empire. He legitimized his mania for conquest by claiming that he was taking revenge on behalf of Greece against the Persian Emperor Xerxes' invasion of Attica which had occurred around 480 BC. In truth, it was the greed for wealth, power and prestige that drove Alexander towards Persia. The Persian Empire stretched from Turkey to Afghanistan. It took three great battles to destroy the Persian army. In his triumphant progress, Alexander reached Afghanistan in 327 BC. The Greek geographers travelling with him informed their 'mad King' that he had reached the 'end of the world'. Beyond Indus, the geographers believed, there was nothing but the vast sea. Saddened by this news, Alexander mourned to his soldiers that there were no more places left for him to conquer. But then, local Persian officials told him about the land to the east of the Indus named *Indika*; they spoke of its fabulous wealth, gigantic cities and powerful maharajahs. Alexander's instinct told him that the local Persians knew more than Greek geographers carrying astrolabes. Alexander decided to add *Indika* to his empire. In early 326 BC, the Macedonian steamroller began its inexorable advance from Kabul towards river Indus. At that time, the Nanda Empire comprised of Orissa, Bihar, Madhya Pradesh and Uttar Pradesh. Punjab was under several small kings who were fighting among themselves. When Ambhi, the king of eastern Gandhara, heard of Alexander's advance he made peace with the invaders. If the great Persian Empire had crumbled to dust against the Macedonians, Ambhi reasoned, a small kingdom in Punjab could hardly measure sword with them. But Ambhi's neighbour Paurava, whom the Greeks called Porus, the ruler of the land between the Jhelum and the Chenab, decided to dispute Alexander's advance. Paurava took up position on the bank of river Jhelum (referred to as Hydaspes by the Greeks). Thus, the stage was set for one of the greatest battles of all times which the Greeks called the Battle of Hydaspes and the Indians, the Battle of Jhelum.

FROM RITUALISTIC WARFARE TO
REAL WARFARE

Conflict between nomadic tribes and settled agrarian communities has always been frequent. The land of the nomads in ancient times stretched from the Dnieper River in the west up to the Altai mountains in the east. The rising nomadic population could not sustain themselves through hunting and gathering in the semi-arid steppe land. In contrast, agrarian communities were able to generate a significant amount of surplus. The nomadic tribes started raiding the agriculturists of Mesopotamia and the Nile Valley. Herodotus writes about the repeated raids by the Scythian nomads from south Russia into Persia and in the Balkan. The nomadic incursions also spilled over to India.

As the nomadic tribes, i.e. the Indo-Aryans, entered India, they supplanted the original inhabitants of the subcontinent, who were the Dravidians. Having defeated the aboriginal inhabitants of India, the invading tribes fought amongst themselves over the spoils of war. The earliest information we have about the conflict between the Aryan tribes of India is of the *Dasarajna* or the Battle of Ten Kings which occurred in 1900 BC on the banks of the Ravi. A confederate force, actually an amalgam of several tribes under the leadership of Purukusta, was encamped on the riverbank. The ruler of the Bharata tribe, Sudas, crossed the river and attacked them. Since the crossing of the river by Sudas was unexpected, Purukusta's force was defeated. It was principally an infantry encounter as the armies at that time were composed mainly of *paiks*.

Cultural conventions laid down certain rules for combat which resulted in ritualized warfare known as *Dharmayuddha*. *Dharmayuddha* tended to reduce the lethalness of combat. Wounded soldiers and frightened warriors, keen to surrender, were not to be harmed. The use of barbed and poisoned arrows was prohibited, as were night attacks and ambushes. Sleeping enemies were not supposed to be attacked. The warriors were warned that mean, deceitful and cruel behaviour was forbidden in the battlefield. Individual duels among the leaders of the opposing tribes, who were of equal rank and equipped with similar arms, constituted the chief feature of such warfare. The clan leaders fought against each other with spears made of bronze and copper. Meanwhile, a melee ensued among the *paiks*. They were not supposed to challenge the tribal chiefs. Originally, the *paiks* used *gadas* and wore armour made of horn and skin. The infantry tactic was to hit the enemy soldiers' heads with the *gadas*. Gradually, *gadas* were replaced by spears as they had greater reach. The spears were also more lethal than the *gadas—gadas* were somewhat blunt weapons while the sharp ends of spears could make puncture wounds on the enemy. Along with spears, which were weapons for close combat, long-distance weapons like copper-tipped arrows came to be used. The death of the clan leader signified the defeat of his tribe.

By 1200 BC, a transition occurred from 'inter-tribal ritualised warfare' towards 'real war'. This shift from *Dharmayuddha* to inter-state 'real warfare' was partly due to the transition of the pastoral nomadic Aryan tribes into settled agrarian communities. With the passage of time, the nomadic tribes settled down into the newly conquered land as agriculturists and formed communities known as *janapadas*. Each *janapada* under its tribal leader known as *rajan* held sway over a particular tract of land. The *janapadas* were precursors to the state. The practice of agriculture generated a sense of territorial sovereignty among the *janapadas*. Gradually, the *rajans* became hereditary rulers known as rajas and their chief functions became tax collection and defending their respective *janapadas*. The brahmins assisted in revenue collection and the kshatriyas constituted the military followers of the rajas. Inter-*jana* warfare became common as the *janapadas* fought amongst themselves in their attempts to extend the territories under their control. The spread of agriculture had generated a hunger for fertile land. While ritualized tribal warfare aimed at raiding for women and animals—especially, cows in case of India—inter-*jana* war was geared to the subjugation of enemy territory. Inter-*jana* warfare was the first step towards inter-state warfare since the principal objective was the permanent annexation of enemy territory after annihilating the enemy force.

Technological changes also accelerated the genesis of inter-*jana* warfare. The *janapadas* discovered iron and initially used it for making ploughs that made way through the virgin forest of north India for the spread of cultivation. Later, iron was also used for making swords and spears. Iron was stronger than bronze and available in larger quantities. Thus, not only did iron weapons replace bronze weapons, the easy availability of iron also enabled the arming of larger numbers of men. With agricultural prosperity and large populations, by 1100 BC, the size of armies varied between 30,000 and 60,000. Thus, the scope of destruction of warfare registered a jump.

Similarly, in Greece around 700 BC, with the rise of polis like Thebes, Sparta and Athens, collective fighting became common. Single combat among renowned chiefs had been the hallmark of earlier Greek warfare. Now, each foot soldier, termed a hoplite, carried a concave shield or hoplon and a short spear. The hoplon was carried on the upper left arm and the spear was held in an overhand grip. The hoplite infantry could be categorized as heavy infantry since they were protected thoroughly with bronze greaves for their arms, breastplates for the chest, and helmets to protect head, cheek and neck. The clash of such infantry was called hoplite warfare.

Similar to *Dharmayuddha*, there was something ritualistic about hoplite warfare. Such warfare occurred only during the spring and the summer. After a formal declaration of war, the polis sent their hoplites. Both sides agreed to fight a short decisive engagement in the farmland surrounding their countryside. Ambushes and night attacks were considered unfair and dishonourable. Quick manoeuvres to surprise the enemy were not attempted; instead the armies met on a field previously agreed upon by both the parties. The hoplites formed a line eight-men deep and this formation was called a *phalanx*. The hoplites in the *phalanx* were also termed *phalangites*. When the opposing *phalanxes* collided, the *osthismos*, or battle, began. The hoplites pushed their opposite numbers with spears and shields. After a head on assault, one side broke and fled. Unwritten cultural rules as well as the inherent limitations of existing tactics and technology prevented the victors from pursuing the defeated. However, the hoplites with their heavy armour just could not run to eliminate the retreating foes. Further, if the victorious hoplites broke ranks in order to catch the retreating enemy soldiers, then they themselves were vulnerable to a counter-charge. Philip of Macedon changed the rules of the game.

After all, the hoplites were part-time soldiers. Being farmers, they took up arms only during emergencies. Tilling their land sometimes had to take precedence. They could not, therefore, remain under arms permanently or go far away for battles. Hence, hoplite armies were incapable of long-distance protracted campaigning. Philip recruited in his army men whose job was full time soldiering, ready to fight anywhere at any time. Philip raised the combat effectiveness of the *phalanx* by increasing its depth from eight rows to twelve rows and by introducing the *sarissa*. The *sarissa* was actually a lengthened hoplite spear, a pike. The Peloponnesian War in the fifth century BC showed the Greeks the importance of cavalry and light infantry. Philip, therefore, took great care to integrate a heavy cavalry and light infantry into his force structure.

Back in India, inter-*jana* warfare gradually gave rise to the *Chaturanga Sena*. One of the components of the *Chaturanga Sena* was the *paiks*. However, disciplined armoured infantry of the type that had emerged in Europe did not exist in ancient India. Till 300 BC, the core of the *Chaturanga Sena* was the *ratha* (chariot) made of wood and leather. The Rig Vedic Aryans used *rathas* which were actually horse-drawn chariots. While two horses pulled each small *ratha*, the bigger *rathas* was yoked to four horses. Unlike the Persian charioteers who fought with spears and swords, the *rathas* carried archers. Bigger chariots were mainly used for transporting the infantry over long distances. Thus, the chariots somewhat raised the mobility and reach of the armies. In Egypt as well as in Mesopotamia, armies till 1200 BC were characterized by an infantry, equipped with javelins, whose soldiers clustered around chariots and clashed with similarly equipped enemy forces. The smooth river valleys of India, Persia and Egypt allowed chariots a free run. However, the mountainous terrain of Greece obstructed the mobility of chariots, which is why the Greeks rejected them.

Besides the *paiks* and *rathas*, *asvas* or horses made up the third component of the *Chaturanga Sena*. The use of cavalry became common around 1000 BC. The hot and humid fertile agricultural river valleys of India with their extensive paddy cultivation were not suitable for breeding good quality war horses. Strong and fast horses could only be bred in the semi-arid steppe zones, so Indian rulers acquired horses from West Asia and Central Asia. Second grade horses were bred in the Salt Range of West Punjab. Importing horses was not just costly but also uncertain. Occasionally, a hostile foreign power severed the trading links. This dependence on horses from abroad remained a problem for Indian rulers till the eighteenth century.

The fourth component of the *Chaturanga Sena* was the *hastis* or elephants. The induction of elephants into the army was India's contribution to the art of warfare. Even before the entry of the Aryans into India, elephants were used for carrying goods. By about 1100 BC, elephants, procured from the jungles of eastern India, were integrated with Indian military machines. The advantage of an elephant was that unlike the *ratha*, it could be used even in rocky and swampy areas. The *Chaturanga Sena* became an all-weather force. Hindu theoreticians had earlier thought that the best possible campaigning seasons were autumn and winter. Thanks to elephants, warfare became possible even during rainy seasons. The code of *Dharmayuddha* laid down that a foot soldier was to be opposed by another foot soldier and a *ratha* by another *ratha*. All these cultural constraints were swept aside in the combat between the *Chaturanga* armies. The use of poisoned arrowheads became common. At Jhelum, the *Chaturanga Sena* of Paurava collided with the Macedonians.

MAY 326 BC

'An army superior in activity can always anticipate the motions of a less rapid enemy.'

—HENRY LLOYD (1729–83), British military theoretician

'The conqueror should know the comparative strength and weakness of himself and of his enemy; and having ascertained the power, place, the time of marching and of recruiting the army, the consequences, the loss of men and money, and profits and danger, he should march with his full force; otherwise he should keep quiet.'

—KAUTILYA, 300 BC

The Greeks did not possess detailed knowledge of the terrain and inhabitants of Punjab. For guidance about fords across the rivers and passage through the jungles and mountain passes, Alexander depended on his Indian vassals. He was informed by his local Indian spies that Paurava had mobilized an army of 50,000 *paiks* [40,000 infantry; the rest functioned as charioteers—*rathins*—and as *mahouts* (elephant drivers)], 4,000 horses, 1,000 chariots and 200 elephants. Alexander, with about 30,000 men prepared to cross the Jhelum.

From the wood available in the jungle around the river Indus, the Greeks constructed boats to carry men and horses. Paurava had stationed his elephants along the river bank, and the Greek horses feared these gargantuan black beasts. One attempt to cross the river resulted in the horses jumping from the boats into the river. The river was also quite wide where Paurava had set up his camp. Alexander decided to search for a point where the river was not only narrow but also hidden from Paurava, so the Greeks could cross the river unobserved. Alexander launched his plan to confuse his enemy. For disrupting Paurava's intelligence system so that the Indian king would not be able to meet him with his full force while crossing the river, Alexander divided his army into many groups and continuously changed their positions. Try as he might, Paurava failed to get a clear picture of the strength and intentions of Alexander's force, which deliberately moved from place to place along the river bank. Paurava, on the other bank, followed the movement of Alexanders detachments. After a point, Paurava got tired of needless movement, thinking Alexander had lost heart and was waiting for reinforcements. Paurava's soldiers got lax, slipping up in monitoring the movement of Alexander's force. This was exactly what Alexander had intended. Meanwhile, his soldiers discovered a narrow ford across the Jhelum further upstream from their camp. They kept this discovery a secret.

One night when it was raining heavily, Alexander went upstream with most of his soldiers. The river was about a thousand yards wide where the Greek forces crossed it. They started crossing at 3 a.m. and the landing was completed by sunrise. Alexander was able to ferry across only 11,000 soldiers because his boats lacked the carrying capacity for transporting the remaining 19,000 in one single night. But Paurava was unaware of Alexander's nocturnal adventure. As dawn broke, the Indian scouts brought news to their king that the Macedonians had landed. To deceive the Indians, Alexander had left in his camp (which was pitched just opposite Paurava's camp on the other side of the river), servants and 5,000 Indian auxiliaries who were dressed like Greek soldiers. He also deliberately left all the tents spread out in his camp. As a result, Paurava could not be sure whether the force that had crossed the river was merely a scouting party or the Greek main force. He nevertheless, had to make a split-second decision.

Paurava fell for Alexander's hoax that the principal Greek army was waiting in the camp to cross at an opportune moment. He concluded that the Greeks were carrying out a reconnaissance. To check it, he sent a small contingent of 2,000 cavalry and 200 chariots under his own son, Paurava junior. He would soon regret his decision. Paurava's son clashed with the Macedonian cavalry patrolling the beachhead at about 6 a.m. In the encounter, the Greek heavy cavalry killed Paurava's son along with 400 Indian horsemen. All the chariots were lost but 1,600 of the 2,000 horsemen from Paurava's son's contingent returned to Paurava. The reality dawned upon him rather belatedly, that his son had clashed with the main force of the Greeks. It was still early morning and the rain had stopped, when Paurava advanced from his base camp with his main army that numbered 30,000 infantry, 5,000 *mahouts* and *rathins*, 3,600 cavalry, 300 chariots and 85 elephants. The Indian king left behind 10,000 infantry, 5,000 *rathins* and *mahouts*, 500 chariots and 115 elephants to guard his camp, still fearing a Greek landing at his rear.

The Killing Match

Alexander deployed his 6,000 heavy infantry arranged in a *phalanx* in the centre. About 1,000 horse archers were stationed on its left flank. The right flank of the *phalanx* was guarded by 4,000 Companion Cavalry which could be categorized as heavy cavalry. Just opposite the Greek battle order, Paurava deployed his army. The Indian centre was composed of 30,000 *paiks*. In front of them were stationed 300 *rathas*. Behind the infantry were stationed 85 elephants. Each elephant was stationed at a distance of about fifty feet from one another and Paurava's battle line was about five and half miles long. On the right flank of Paurava's line were stationed 1,600 cavalry and on the left flank were 2,000 cavalry.

Alexander opened the battle around ten that morning, by launching his 5,000 strong cavalry against Paurava's chariots. Each chariot was 7.5 ft. in height and about 9 ft. in width. Ajatasatru, the ruler of Magadh (Bihar), had invented chariots fitted with long knives around their wheels to scare away the enemy infantry. These chariots were similar to the scythe chariots which Alexander's army had encountered at the Battle of Arbela (or Gaugemela) against the Persians on 1 October in 331 BC. However, just as the Greek cavalry in Gaugemala had triumphed, here too, it destroyed the Indian chariots. This was possible because both troopers and horses in Alexander's Companion Cavalry were covered with armour plates. The arrows shot by the archers from the chariots fell, impotent. Further, horseback provided a more mobile platform than the lumbering chariots. Central Asian horse archers in the Macedonian Army picked off the *rathins* from a distance. This was possible because the terrain did not favour chariots, whose wheels got bogged down in the muddy banks of the Jhelum. Surrounded by fast moving horsemen, the archers in chariots were, in a manner of speaking, sitting ducks.

After dealing with the chariots, Alexander's Companion Cavalry of 4,000 armoured troopers charged the 2,000 strong Indian cavalry stationed at Porus' left wing. Apart from being half the size of the Greek cavalry, the Indians were also at a technologically disadvantageous position against the Companions. Unlike the Companions, Paurava's horsemen were not equipped with metal greaves, shields and helmets. Alexander's Companions had lances made of tough cornel wood and unlike the Indians, the Greek did not ride bare back. Blankets or cushions were firmly tied over the back of their horses, giving them a better grip on their mounts. They could ride faster and more accurately, increasing the thrusting power of their lances.

In addition, the Companions had the advantage of superior tactics and discipline. Alexander's cavalry, organized in successive lines, was trained to close with the enemy in a gallop. They carried out repeated attacks on the Indian horsemen who lacked any unit level organization. In a short time Paurava's cavalry on his left flank started retreating with the Companions in pursuit.

Simultaneously, the 1,000 Scythian mounted archers attacked the 1,600 Indian cavalry on Paurava's right. The Scythians did not have a numerical edge over the Indian cavalry. However, Paurava's cavalry failed to hold even this part of the front. Horse archery was a novelty for both, the Greeks and the Indians. While campaigning in Bactria and Sogdiana, the two northernmost *satrapies* of the Persian Empire around the river Oxus (Amu Darya) and Jaxartes (Sir Darya), Alexander had been so fascinated with the lethal speed and mounted archery of the steppe nomadic horsemen that he had hired a thousand of them before entering India. The Scythian horse archers wore no armour and were not suited for a frontal charge like the Companion Cavalry. Instead, they fought from a distance with the aid of long-range weapons. To shoot arrows from horseback while the horse was moving at high speed, the nomads used light composite bows made of the horn and sinews of animals. Arrows from such bows could penetrate armour even when shot from a distance of a hundred yards. It took little time for the Scythian mounted archers to destroy the Indian cavalry at Paurava's right flank.

While Alexander's cavalry was annihilating the Indian cavalry, the Greek *phalanx*, which seemed to present a wall bristling with 16 ft. long spears marched in unison towards the Indian infantry. The Indian infantry had a numerical edge of 5 : 1 over the *phalanx*. But the weakest component of the *Chaturanga Sena* was its badly trained infantry. In contrast, the Greeks drilled their infantry with the aid of drums, so that soldiers marched in unison during combat. Drilling raised cohesiveness and corporate identity within the infantry. Drill and discipline enabled the Greek infantry to operate as a concentrated body of massed pikemen capable of pushing and thrusting without stumbling over each other in the chaos of the battlefield. For better control and integration of efforts, the *phalanx* was divided into tactical sub-units. Thus, in close quarter combat, the Greek infantry, with its superior integration of collective effort, fared better than its Indian counterpart. As the *phalanx* collided with the chaotic Indian infantry, discipline proved to be a telling factor in the climactic Battle of Hydaspes.

Besides superior training, the Greek infantry had better weapons. The Indian infantry was armed with broadswords made of iron. But they got no chance to use them on the Greeks. Before the Indians could reach the line of Greek infantrymen, the latter, with their long *sarissas*, created havoc among the Indian rank and file. Paurava's infantry had no metallic body armour and helmets; instead they carried shields made of raw ox hide and wore cotton turbans on their heads. The iron tipped *sarissas* easily pierced these shields and turbans. Standing alongside each other in several rows, the Greeks, with their pikes, stabbed and pushed lethally at the Indian *paiks*.

The only weapon available to Paurava's infantry for destroying the *phalanx* before the *sarissas* came too close, were long bows. The Indian bows, made of wood, were 5 ft. long and heavy. To shoot their 3 ft. long arrows that could penetrate even metallic armour, the bowmen had to press the bows with their left feet. The huge size of these bows proved to be a further hindrance for the Indian infantry. It had rained heavily the day before the battle. And on the slippery banks of the river, the bowmen failed to get a grip on the ground. The bows lost their accuracy. Even normally, these heavy bows could not have been easily manoeuvrable against Alexander's fast-moving cavalry when they attacked the flanks and rear of the *paiks* after driving away Indian cavalry.

Towards late afternoon, Paurava realized that the battle was going badly for him. His cavalry had already vanished from the battlefield and his infantry was being massacred by the indomitable *phalanx*. The Indian king realized that it was time to play his last trump card: the elephants, which constituted his tactical reserve. The Greek cavalry and infantry feared these beasts which Europeans had never seen before. It was Paurava's last chance. He decided to launch a frontal assault with his elephant fleet. Generally, an Indian king was supposed to lead the army from a two-horsed chariot. However, to raise the morale of his elephant corps, Paurava himself mounted an elephant and led the charge.

Though the Indian infantry was being impaled on the pikes of the *phalanx* and the Indian cavalry had left the battlefield for good, the battle was not lost for Paurava. His elephant charge somewhat stabilized the situation, with the great beasts causing havoc among the Greek infantry. The tusks of the elephants were covered with brass plates fitted with sharp iron spikes and many Greek soldiers were impaled on them. A large number of *phalangites* were also elevated from the ground by the elephants' trunks before being trampled to death under the elephants' feet. But then, suddenly, the Indian line was attacked from the rear by Alexander's cavalry. The Greek cavalry, after pursuing the retreating Indian cavalry for some time, had come back to the battlefield in the nick of time. Instead of attempting to loot Paurava's camp, the disciplined Greek cavalry had returned to the battlefield to finish the enemy.

After the disintegration of the Indian infantry, the Macedonian army concentrated on the remnants of the Indian army: the elephants. While the *phalanx* attacked from the front, the Greek cavalry charged from the rear. Continuous coordination between the Greek cavalry and *phalanx* resulted in the elephants being encircled; they were pushed gradually into a smaller and smaller pocket. Inside the tightly packed pocket, they lacked room to manoeuvre. The coup de grâce was delivered by the *phalanx*. The pikes pierced the legs of the elephants which were merely covered with padded and quilted cloth. The elephants screamed in pain and ran amok. The terrified *mahouts* tried to kill their elephants by piercing their skull with the poisoned iron rods which they carried; but the Scythian mounted bowmen now targeted the *mahouts*. The wounded elephants, crying in pain, ran back into the Indian lines, thus, turning Indian defeat into a disaster.

Paurava continued to fight valiantly, throwing darts from elephant-back, and in turn, he received several wounds. The wound on his right shoulder was serious, and he fainted from loss of blood. Meanwhile, the Greek cavalry surrounded the king's elephant, slew the *mahout* and captured Paurava. The battlefield was full of screaming soldiers, neighing horses, trumpeting elephants and the rattle of sabres. Small pockets of Indian soldiers were battling on. But when they saw that their king had been captured, disaster turned into a rout. The soldiers began to flee and the massacre started. As dusk fell, the battle ended. Around 20,000 infantry and 3,000 horsemen of Paurava lay dead on the blood-soaked banks of the Jhelum. The Greeks captured 9,000 men and 80 elephants as spoils. However, the battle was not easy, even for Alexander's veterans. It had lasted for eight hours, and the Macedonians had lost 280 cavalry and 720 infantry, killed mostly by the elephants. About 1,000 killed and several thousands wounded in an army of 11,000 testifies to a tenacious battle.

ALTERNATE HISTORY: ALEXANDER DEFEATED

'There was no opportunity for advice nor command; chance held sway everywhere.'

—SALLUST, 86–35 BC

Luck was with Alexander because it had rained heavily the day before the battle and the slippery ground in turn made the heavy Indian bows useless. But even otherwise, the dice was loaded heavily in favour of

Alexander. A technological and managerial gap existed between Hellenic Greece and ancient India. Indian craftsmen did not mass-produce sophisticated weapons in the absence of a military system supported by state infrastructure. At least one component of the Indian army was technologically obsolete at the time Alexander invaded India—the chariots. Rain or no rain, the archers in the *rathas* were vulnerable to the armoured Greek cavalry and the *phalangites*. Even the scythe chariots of Darius had failed completely on the dry plain of Gaugemela against the Greek *phalanx* and Companion Cavalry.

The secret of Alexander's victory lay in achieving operational surprise as well as in the Greek superiority in tactics and training. The absence of an integrated all-arms approach was largely responsible for the collapse of Paurava's army against the combined arms tactic of mounted archers, heavy cavalry and *phalanx* of the Macedonian army. Under Alexander, the Greek cavalry, like the Indian cavalry fought without stirrups. The Greek cavalry had an edge, however, in tactical training and coordinating its charge with the *phalanx*.

This was possible because Alexander was leading a professional army, with a hierarchical command structure in which specialists were put in charge of the different units. In contrast, Paurava's force was not a standing army. Paurava depended on tribal organizations which brought their own arms and were led by their own chiefs. Punjab was full of mercenary fighters who were under the tribal organization known as *pugas*. This region was densely populated with a thriving agricultural economy. Between the Jhelum and Beas, there were 500 cities and the smallest of them contained at least 5,000 inhabitants. This explains how a relatively minor king like Paurava could raise an army of about half-a-lakh at short notice. Besides clan ethos, Paurava's soldiers were motivated by religious zeal and carried idols of Vishnu and Ganesha into battle. However, neither size nor religious motivation was effective without a proper chain of command and tactical discipline. Against the professional ethos of a permanent bureaucratic force, Paurava's forces were sadly disorganized.

Instead of meeting the Macedonian army in the battlefield of the Jhelum, could Paurava have considered other options? Could he have performed better by entrenching himself in one of the big cities of his kingdom and forcing Alexander to conduct siege warfare?

Greek technical superiority was even more pronounced in siege warfare. The *lithobolos* or stone casters represented the application of Greek mathematical science and engineering knowledge in the construction of military hardware. In the *lithobolos*, springs of animal sinew, rope or human hair were twisted or stretched through a series of winches and levers for massive propulsion power. These machines were used for throwing stones 90 kg. heavy. With such siege engines, it wouldn't have caused Alexander too much trouble to destroy the walls of Indian fortresses and cities.

The best bet for Paurava would have been to eliminate Alexander either through a commando-style operation or by sending *vishakanyas*. Ancient India had a tradition of beautiful damsels functioning as contract killers. They murdered their male clients by offering them poisoned alcohol while making love to them. The Greeks had a tradition of going on drinking orgies at regular intervals. On such occasions, wine flowed freely and even the guards got drunk. Alexander was known to be susceptible to wine and women. Paurava could have made a de jure peace offering by sending some jewels and a female contract killer. If the Greek high command accepted and celebrated their easy victory, there would have been an inevitable orgy. Paurava could then have launched a 'Butcher and Bolt' sort of expedition for eliminating Alexander, or if possible, the entire Greek leadership.

Even when the battle started all may not have been lost for the Indians, but Paurava went on making mistake after mistake. Paurava could have designated a special force for killing Alexander in the battlefield as the battle was in progress. Alexander's elimination would have turned the scales in favour of the Indians because his extraordinary military leadership was the backbone of the Greek army. He was undoubtedly one of history's greatest military leaders, on par with Julius Caesar, Chingiz Khan, Timur and Napoleon Bonaparte.

While the principal requirement for leaders of ritual warfare was individual bravery, the principal skill that military leaders of inter-state warfare needed was managerial capability. This does not mean that personal courage was unnecessary. To motivate the soldiers and to retain their loyalty, the leader had to expose himself to personal danger. At times, Alexander himself was in the forefront of the battle. The sight of their blue-eyed monarch, long hair flowing, mounted on a charger, energized the Macedonian soldiers. Meanwhile, he also coordinated the various components of his army in the battle. Continuous combat among large groups of warriors, which was characteristic of inter-state warfare, gave rise to strategy, tactics and bigger armies. Managerial skill was necessary for feeding the army, organizing their equipment and marching. The sophisticated Macedonian military bureaucracy, under the eagle watch of Alexander, was able to supply 1,000 tons of food, water and forage for the men and animals in the Greek army as it marched forward. While Alexander represented an amalgam of both heroic and managerial genius, Paurava exemplified tribal leadership that was completely out of tune with the requirements for conducting a decisive battle.

Greek historians agree that unlike the cowardly Darius, Paurava did not leave the battlefield but continued to fight till the end. When brought before Alexander, Paurava, though bleeding and a captive, remained defiant. A tall and graceful figure, Paurava retained his dignity. When Alexander asked him how he would like to be treated, Paurava famously replied, 'like a king'. Later, Alexander made him a vassal ruler as the Greeks required collaborators for administering occupied territories. However, individual bravery was hardly enough for this kind of war. Overall, Paurava's generalship was poor. In Henry Lloyd's terminology, Alexander displayed 'superior activity' compared to Paurava. The Indian king merely reacted to Alexander's operational initiatives. For about a month when both Alexander's and Paurava's armies faced each other, Paurava failed to seize the initiative, instead, waiting on the bank of the Jhelum for his ally Abhisares, the king of Kashmir and Himachal Pradesh. Abhisares was playing a waiting game of his own. He was a fence sitter and his objective was to join the winning side. Instead of waiting for such dubious allies, Paurava should have crossed the Jhelum, thus, taking the offensive on the other bank of the river. This may have encouraged the tribes between the Jhelum and Indus to rise against the recently arrived Macedonian invaders. At that time, the Macedonian army was divided into small groups reconnoitring the bank in search of fords and to collect forage for cavalry. So, there existed a golden opportunity for Paurava to defeat and destroy these small, less effective groups of Macedonian soldiers. Such actions would have at least forced Alexander to detach troops for guarding his long line of communications, which would have resulted in greater numerical superiority for the Indians for the main battle.

In fact, the modern term 'strategist' is derived from the Greek word *strategos*. And Alexander proved to be the archetypical strategist. His strategic genius lay in crossing the Jhelum unobserved and Paurava's greatest mistake was thinking that only a minor detachment of the Greeks had landed. Alexander's operational deception was of the same magnitude as that of the Allies during the Normandy landings in June 1944. An attack is not usually expected in a night fraught with natural calamities. But both Alexander and General Dwight D. Eisenhower decided to launch their attacks on stormy, wet nights. Both Paurava's and Hitler's weather experts believed that the enemy would not dare cross in bad weather. Even so, had Porus marched with his main army to meet the Greek detachment which had crossed with Alexander, he could have attacked them while they were coming ashore, unprepared for battle. The phalangites were yet not in battle position. Paurava's elephants would then have crushed the *phalangites*. Even after the destruction of the force under Paurava's son, when it dawned upon Paurava that the main Greek army had indeed landed, he failed to concentrate all his forces. Hitler's actions were similar to that of Paurava. After the German local command informed the *Fuehrer* headquarters that the Anglo-Americans were landing in Normandy, Hitler thought that only a minor Anglo-American detachment had landed. He held back his crack troops, the panzer divisions. Both Paurava and Hitler grossly misjudged enemy strength. After the Normandy landing, Hitler feared more invasions. So, he retained several panzer divisions in the Low Countries. Paurava also left behind a significant chunk of his force in order to meet another probable Greek landing at his rear as he marched upstream to meet Alexander. After Alexander had crossed the Jhelum, Paurava refused to attack him. He waited to see how Alexander would launch his troops against the Indians. Unlike Alexander, Paurava lacked any overall tactical plan to use his infantry, cavalry, chariots and elephants in coordination against the Greeks. He allowed each segment of his army to be separately defeated by the synchronized charge of the Greek heavy cavalry, Scythian mounted archers and heavy infantry. Instead of acting like a general, Porus functioned like a tribal chief in the mould of a heroic warrior, what in modern terminology might be termed platoon leader. He played the role of a non-commissioned officer at the head of a small band of warriors rather than a general.

Despite all these errors, there could still have been a chance of victory. If instead of heavy bows, the Indians had used the lighter bows that were used by Assyrian soldiers, things would have been more difficult for Alexander's troops. And the thought of making a tactical retreat in order to fight another day, once his elephant charge had failed, never took birth in Paurava's infertile brain.

LEGACY OF THE BATTLE OF JHELUM

'Are we afraid of not being able to learn from others?'

—PUBLIUS RENATUS FLAVIUS VEGETIUS,
Roman military theoretician, AD 400

Hydaspes resulted in a paradigm shift in Indian military theory and practice. Around 300 BC, Kautilya, the greatest military theoretician of ancient India, put forward the lessons of the Battle of Jhelum for the Mauryas. Kautilya emphasized the importance of training before battle. Training involved wrestling and healthy diets that were supposed to make the troops more efficient for close quarter combat. In accordance with Kautilya's instructions, Indian kings encouraged tiger hunts which not only kept the soldiers physically fit but also encouraged bravery among the recruits. Nevertheless, the *Arthashastra* failed to take notice of the tactical superiority of the Greek heavy infantry, the *phalanx*. In close quarter combat, Mauryan infantry was no match against the *phalanx*. The Indian infantry was armed without any uniformity and lacked the kind of training which taught collective manoeuvring before the enemy force.

The Battle of Hydaspes taught the Indians that only a regular army composed of professionals supported by a permanent bureaucracy could stop an aggressive invader. Chandragupta Maurya, the founder of the Mauryan Empire, who ascended the throne in 321 BC, maintained a standing army. An aspect of military professionalization is the practice of using special troops for different theatres. This trend also seeped into the Mauryan military machine. For instance for combat in the jungle, the Mauryas used the *atavika bala*, composed of soldiers recruited from forest tribes. Further, the Indians realized that elephants had been useful against the Greek infantry but they needed support from cavalry. Besides maintaining 9,000 elephants, Chandragupta had about 60,000 horses in his cavalry branch.

The post-Jhelum Indian military organization met its litmus test when it fought against the contemporary superpowers—the Greek Empire of Seleucus and the Indo-Greeks of Bactria. When

Seleucus invaded Mauryan India in 303 BCE, he was defeated. This was because the veteran Greek *phalanx* had mostly been destroyed in internecine warfare among Alexander's generals. Seleucus tried to fill the ranks of the *phalanx* with Persians who, however, had no tradition of soldiering as heavy infantry. They were not as effective as the Macedonian *phalangites*. Additionally, unlike Paurava, Chandragupta deployed not only a larger number of elephants but also more cavalry.

After his defeat, Seleucus signed a peace treaty with Chandragupta exchanging the provinces of Kabul, Sind and Herat for 500 Indian elephants. Seleucus used these elephants against the other generals of Alexander who challenged him in West Asia. The military use of elephants in extra-Indian territories had a 'domino effect'. In response to Seleucus' use of these living Indian tanks, Ptolemy, another general of Alexander, deployed African elephants in his battles against Seleucus. But the African beasts were no match against Seleucus' Indian elephants. Not only were the Indian elephants much bigger, they could also be tamed more easily compared to the African ones. Like modern amphibious combat vehicles, Indian elephants were able to swim across big rivers. With their practice of deploying a large number of elephants and horses, the Sungas, the successors of the Mauryas, were able to defeat Demetrius the Greek King of Bactria in a battle that was fought on the bank of the Indus.

That the *rathas* were useless for warfare became a lesson accepted by Indian kings. The chariot corps was abolished. However, Indian rulers faced a problem because the horse archers who first came into India with the Macedonians started crossing the Indus in larger numbers from AD 150 onwards. No agrarian civilization could come up with an effective military response to mounted archers. The archers from the steppe lands threatened India and Persia as well as the Roman Empire. The Indians tried to cover the 'missile gap' resulting from their lack of horse archers by using infantry slingers who threw stones with the help of slings to hit enemy soldiers from a distance. But the slingers could never aspire to the deadly reach that the mounted archers gained from their range of composite bows. Further, being immobile, the slingers could hardly transfer their missile power to the crucial arenas of the battlefield as swiftly as horse-mounted archers.

CONCLUSION

Dharmayuddha in India and Hoplite warfare in Greece emphasized a code of conduct that was somewhat akin to the modern Hague Convention. The cultural blockage that reduced the carnage of war resulted partly from ethnic affiliations. The Aryan tribes spoke the same language and were of the same ethnic stock. Linguistic and cultural affinity of this kind existed among the citizens of the polis. This may have given rise to a certain empathy which in turn resulted in the genesis of cultural constraints. However the shift in social structures, the consequent changes in the political economy and advances in technology gave rise to 'real warfare' in India. The Greek interlude accelerated the shift towards 'real war' in the subcontinent. The Macedonian army on one hand and the *Chaturanga Sena* on the other, represented the instruments of 'real warfare' in the Occident and the Orient. The interaction between the two armies accelerated the shift towards more intense warfare, as exemplified in the rise of the post-Jhelum Indian military machines. In the aftermath of Hydaspes, as 'real warfare' became more intense, the impact of combat on society continued to increase. During the Kalinga campaign of Asoka (262 BCE), the last great Mauryan Emperor, about 1,00,000 people were butchered and 1,50,000 men from Kalinga were carried away as slaves. This became the trend for the future. Herein lies the decisive importance of Hydaspes.

2

Crescent Over Hindustan

The Second Battle of Tarain, AD 1192

WITH SHOUTS OF '*Allahu Akbar*', the horsemen charged forward. Seeing the advance of the Islamic cavalry, the Rajput king seated on the *howdah* of an elephant blew his conch. The Rajput warriors, heavily dosed with opium, rode forward to check the invaders they called the Turuskhas. As the opposing forces met, blood gushed out from the wounds caused by the spears and arrows.

This was the Second Battle of Tarain. The Turuskhas were the soldiers of Mahmud Ghori who was also known as Mahmud bin Sam. The Rajput chiefs fought under the leadership of Prithviraj Chauhan whom Ghori's chroniclers called Rai Pithaura. Mahmud Ghori, originally a petty chieftain of Ghor, captured Ghazni in AD 1174. Having overthrown the Ghaznavid Empire and established his power over Afghanistan, Ghori decided to add Hind to his expanding empire. This brought him in conflict with the Rajputs. The Rajputs were the product of inter-marriages between the local populace and the Parthians and Scythians who settled in India around AD 200. After the breakup of the Rashtrakuta Empire at the end of the tenth century, the Rajput chiefs spread out from Rajasthan to north India. In the last decade of the twelfth century, the Rajputs, under the leadership of Prithviraj, were considering establishing an empire in north India, when Mahmud Ghori turned his attention towards India.

THE RAJPUTS AGAINST THE *JEHADIS*

'When you meet those who are infidels, strike their neck until you have overwhelmed them, tighten their bonds, and then release them, either freely or for ransom, when war lays down its burdens. Thus it is, and if

God wished, He would crush them Himself, but He tests you against one another. Those who are killed in the path of God, He does not let their good deeds go for nothing.'

—*The Koran* on *Jehad*, seventh century

The clash between the Rajputs and the Muslims represented a confrontation between opposing military cultures: the Turks' 'real warfare' opposing the *Dharmayuddha* or 'ritual warfare' of the Rajputs. *Dharmayuddha* does not denote warfare for religion. *Dharma* stood not for religion but for a way of life. *Dharmayuddha*, as discussed in the first chapter, represented certain cultural constraints which limited the lethality of combat. It was the opposite of *Kutayuddha* which encouraged deception and lethal combat. *Kutayuddha* in India reached its zenith under the Mauryas, but in the post-Gupta age, the pendulum of war swung again towards ritual combat, finding its apogee under the Rajputs. Rajput chivalrous warfare was somewhat akin to the ritualistic *Dharmayuddha* of the early Vedic era. In contrast, the blending of religious warfare with steppe nomadic warfare among the Turks resulted in a radicalization of 'real warfare' or an Islamic *Kutayuddha*.

Climate, terrain, social structure and the nature of enemies shape military culture. The Turks of Central Asia, also known as Tatars or Turkomans, fought the Iranians and the Mongols who fielded large cavalries. The Turks responded by deploying cavalry armies of steppe nomads with no tradition of infantry. The Eurasian steppe, which extended from Chinese Turkestan till south Russia, was the breeding ground for the best horses in Eurasia. The nomads depended on horses for hunting as well as for transportation. Horsemeat was considered a delicacy among the nomads. Wells were few and far in between the Eurasian steppe and in times of need, the nomads would drink blood from their mounts to quench their thirst. Being so dependent on horses, the nomads had to breed them to sustain themselves even in times of peace. Central Asian armies, which had to cover long distances over semi-arid plains, found that only a cavalry force was suited to their needs. The symbiotic relationship between nomad and horse was central to the nomadic socio-economic structure.

Islamic civilization came to Central Asia when the Arab armies entered Khorasan in the eighth century. The result was an amalgamation of steppe nomadic warfare with the elements of *jehad*. Under the Umayid Caliphate, the core of the Caliph's cavalry force was composed of Syrian Arabs. In about AD 750, the Umayid Caliphate was replaced by the Abbasid Caliphate which recruited mounted Turkish nomadic bowmen of the Central Asian steppe who had accepted Islam. They stopped recruiting Arabs, who were supporters of the Umayids. Turkish mounted archers were more effective than Arab cavalrymen who were armed with lances. Turkish nomads were trained in archery from their childhood. For food, they used their bows to shoot at birds and animals.

Both the Caliphate and its successors used the Mamluk institution to induct Turks into the army. From the ninth century onwards, the Mamluks or the Turkish mounted archers constituted the core of the Islamic armies from the Indus in the east to Egypt in the west. 'Mamluk' meant slave, but the connotations of the term were different from those in the western world. Generally, poor Turkish boys were sold by their parents to merchants, who in turn sold these boys to the powerful Amirs. They became the Amirs' retainers and received military training as well as education. Occasionally these slave-soldiers enjoyed more power and prestige than the Amirs' natural sons. Under the Amirs, the Mamluks reached top positions in the army and frequently after the death of their patrons even succeeded to their offices, and in some cases even to thrones. A merchant bought Kutub-ud-din Aibak in Turkestan, and he was given training in archery at Nishapur. When he attained adolescence, he was sold to Mahmud Ghori. He accompanied Ghori to India as an officer. His loyal and efficient service was rewarded with the governorship of Ghori's Indian provinces. After Ghori's death, Aibak established the Delhi Sultanate.

Turkish warlords mobilized their Muslim retainers by pointing out that war against the enemies of faith was necessary and obligatory by decree of Islamic law. Al-Muttaqi' Al-Hindi (1477–1567), an Islamic theorist, described the spirit of Holy War waged by Muslims from the eleventh century onwards in the following words: '*Jehad* is incumbent upon you with every *Amir* . . . Paradise is under the shadow of swords.' Taj-ud-din Hasan Nizami, who lived in the thirteenth century, has written about the Islamic military experience in South Asia thus: 'The dark-skinned Hindus . . . appeared as if they were demons who had besmeared their faces with ink and soot, or that they were sentinels of hell with their visages blackened with tar and pitch.' Racial and religious difference resulted in increasing barbarization of warfare.

Besides being motivated by religious zeal the prospect of capturing wealth, women and slaves were the usual added incentives. Mahmud Ghori's campaign in India enabled the Turks to capture 50,000 male and female slaves from India. Capturing slaves had not been a goal for Alexander. Therefore, like Asoka's invasion of Kalinga, Ghori's invasion had more impact on Indian society than the Greek invasion did.

The Turks initially settled in western Asia as Mamluk soldiers of the Caliphate and established their autonomous dominions. They clashed with the Byzantine Empire and its West European allies from the eleventh century onwards. The West European knight's chief battlefield tactic, somewhat akin to that of the Rajput cavalry, was to launch a frontal charge by heavy cavalry against the enemy. The arrows of the Turkish bowmen were ineffectual against the thick plate armour of the knights. The Turks had to strategize afresh. They were forced to develop heavy armoured cavalry to supplement their light unarmoured mounted archers. The horsemen also realized the necessity of group cohesion to effectively oppose the synchronized charges by the European knights. West European knights trained their cavaliers in jousts and tournaments to encourage solidarity among soldiers. The Western Turks developed similar equestrian games, known as *furusiya* exercise that were held in stadia and witnessed by large numbers of people. These games not only introduced an element of competitiveness among the participants but also functioned as a training ground for raw recruits. Not for nothing is competitive sport likened to battle. The traditions of group training and armoured cavalry seeped into the Eastern Turks, settled in Afghanistan and Khorasan, who later invaded India.

Back in early medieval India, military organization of the Hindus was in the throes of decline. The soldiers of ancient India were known as *Balas*. There were various types of *Balas*. The regular professional soldiers who constituted the core of the Mauryan army were known as the *Maula Balas*. Recruited and maintained by the state, they were the most loyal to it. However, the practice of recruiting the sons of dead soldiers in place of their fathers reduced the efficiency of the *Maula Balas*. In post-Mauryan India, kings had to depend on the *Bhrta Balas*, who were mercenaries led by their chiefs. During emergencies, they were hired either on a daily wage or for a fixed sum for a particular time period. In addition to the *Bhrta Balas*, the kings depended on the *Sreni Balas*. These were soldiers maintained by financially powerful autonomous trade guilds for their own security. In the post-Gupta period, in Mandasore, the trade guild of silk merchants maintained a corps of archers. In times of need, the kings hired soldiers from these guilds. The *Sreni Balas* and *Bhrta Balas* were more loyal to their guilds and to their chiefs than to the kings. The state gradually lost its monopoly over agents of violence. This accelerated centrifugal forces that eventually resulted in the disintegration of Hindu polities in the post-Harsha period.

After the death of Harsha Vardhan in AD 647, Hindu chiefs began fighting amongst themselves. The principal power to emerge after Harsha was the Rashtrakuta Empire, whose base was central India. The forested rocky and hilly terrain of this region was not suited for large-scale cavalry manoeuvres. All the Hindu armies accordingly deployed a large number of elephants, which were used as battering rams. Unlike in Central Asia and Iran, enough water and foliage were available across India for maintaining large numbers of elephants. The elephant corps was supported by indisciplined *paiks*.

After the Rashtrakutas, it was the Rajputs who were supreme and their military machine focused on cavalry along with elephants. Culture and ecology shaped the combat effectiveness of the Rajput army. Because the climate of India did not favour the breeding of horses, the quality of horses fielded by the Rajputs was inferior to the mounts of the Turks. Hindu rulers tried to redress the situation by importing horses. Since Khorasan and Afghanistan were under the control of the Caliphate's successors like the Ghaznavids and the Ghorids who were eager to invade India, Hindu rulers were not successful in their attempts to import Central Asian horses. Indian kings imported horses from Arabia, and horses constituted the largest item of import into India from West Asia. Around AD 600, the port of Cambay alone handled 10,000 horses every year. However, in terms of speed and stamina, Arabian horses were no match for Central Asian steppe horses. Sadly for the Indian buyers, the leg muscles of the much awaited Arabian horses got damaged by the long-distance overseas voyage. The Hindus also fumbled in the feeding of the horses, knowledge of whose diet they were unable to acquire. The end result was that most of the horses became lame. Rajput chiefs suffered both from strategic and tactical disadvantages because of the horse factor. They could neither conduct rapid raids like Mahmud Ghazni nor counter them. Given the famed mobility of the Central Asian mounts in the battlefield the Turks could mount attacks at whatever point they wanted, easily and effectively. Speed enabled the Turks to surprise their opponents. Speed and surprise in combination produced a lethal multiplier effect leaving the Hindus fatally paralysed both in mind and body.

Rajput military conduct was similar to that of medieval west European knights. Bards and musicians who accompanied the Rajput forces were the keepers of Rajput chivalry as they wrote poems eulogizing the deeds of famous Rajput chiefs. The code emphasized that an unarmoured enemy was not to be attacked by armoured soldiers. Enemy soldiers were not to be attacked while they were eating or drinking. While the Turkish invaders derived their 'will to victory' from group cohesion strengthened by religious enthusiasm, the Rajput chiefs disdained collective effort. As in 'ritual warfare' of the early Vedic Age, the Rajput chiefs were eager to exhibit individual valour and personal honour in the battlefield. *Vira charitas*, or brave hearts, in the battlefield were the pride of Rajput warfare. It was a sin for Rajputs to indulge in deceptive tactics and false manoeuvres to fool the enemy. If they fought straight, they believed they would achieve immortality after death. Like medieval West European knights, Rajputs could only conceive of a head-on attack. Unlike the Turks, they had no concept of maintaining an advance guard to harass the enemy before throwing the main body of the army into the principal engagement.

Between Paurava and Prithviraj, the *Chaturanga Sena*, from a four-limbed army, regressed into a two-limbed force. Neither *rathas* nor *paiks* found place in the Rajput battle order. The abolition of *rathas* was a rational decision in view of their performance at Gaugemela and Jhelum. But the *paiks* were abolished to satisfy the Rajput chiefs' concept of elitist warfare. In such a paradigm, common infantry soldiers had no role to play.

The increasing effectiveness of horse archery after the spread of the stirrup around the sixth century made even the disciplined infantry of west European armies feel helpless. Stirrups enabled riders to exercise a better and firmer grip on their mounts. Hence, they were better able to loosen volleys of arrows accurately even when the horses were moving at high speed. The Roman legion, the lineal descendants of the Greek *phalanx*, was the best disciplined heavy infantry that the ancient world had ever seen. Even they had failed between AD 100 and AD 350 against the Parthians and Huns who employed horse archers without wooden saddles. The Roman legions would collapse ignobly against mounted archers using iron saddles which became common from *c.* AD 800 onwards. The period around AD 800 could be aptly termed the 'age of steppe horsemen'. The Rajputs were devastatingly outclassed, with their anachronistic methods of combat in an era of brutality.

TARAIN: THE EQUESTRIAN ENGAGEMENT

'The exertion of two self-controlled parties who harbour enmity against each other with projectile weapons and other arms for the accomplishment of their own benefit, is called war.'

—*Sukraniti,* ancient Sanskrit text

Mahmud Ghori, the Sultan of Afghanistan, fought two battles in two years at the same place with the same enemy. Both battles were purely cavalry encounters. In AD 1191, Ghori fought the Rajput confederacy of one lakh cavalry led by Prithviraj at a place named Tarain or Tararoi, about eighty miles from Delhi. Tarain was a small village 14 mi. from Thaneshwar. The Muslim army was divided into three bodies: right, left and centre. Mahmud Ghori himself commanded the centre. The Rajputs opened the battle by making a frontal cavalry charge. Due to their numerical superiority, the Rajputs were able to cut off Ghori's centre from the right and left wings of his army. The cavaliers at Ghori's centre were afraid that they might be cut off from the rest of their army and destroyed piecemeal. In order to raise the flagging morale of his horsemen, Ghori set an example of personal bravery. He charged toward Govind Rai, ruler of Delhi, and the brother of Prithviraj. Abdullah Sirhindi's *Tarikh-I-Mubarakshahi* comments that as Ghori neared the elephant of Govind Rai, he threw a lance which broke Rai's teeth. Undaunted, Govind Rai flung a spear towards the Sultan. Mahmud slipped from his horse, seriously wounded. It was touch and go. Ghori's soldiers, believing that their Sultan had died, were on the point of breaking. But one Khalji soldier carried Mahmud to safety.

Seeing Ghori was wounded but not dead, his soldiers at the centre gained heart. They broke through the surrounding Rajput cavalry, and rejoined the right and left wings of Ghori's army. Since Ghori was seriously wounded, saving him became the first priority for his army. The Islamic army carried out a fighting withdrawal from the battle zone.

As the army retreated to Ghazni through Multan and Uch, a garrison of 2,000 men was left at the fort of Tabarindh under Zia-ud-din Tulaki to delay the Rajput field army. The Rajput cavalry-oriented force was not acquainted with the art of storming fortifications. Cavalry was not suited for laying siege to forts and the Rajputs lacked both the siege machines and infantry to storm and destroy fortress walls. Tulaki was able to keep Prithviraj at bay for thirteen months. Within this time, Mahmud Ghori had raised 1,20,000 cavalry. However, Ghori had to keep an eye on the Khwarizm Shah of Central Asia. To prevent the Shah from invading his northern dominion, the bulk of Ghori's army had to remain in Afghanistan. He could only detach 40,000 cavalry to invade India again in AD 1192. In response, the Rajput confederacy mobilized 2,00,000 cavalry and 3,000 elephants. The figures represent the force that could be theoretically mobilized. The real strength of the field army was much less. Nevertheless, the Rajputs enjoyed substantial numerical superiority over their Turkish opponent.

Mahmud Ghori was apprehensive about the outcome of the ensuing confrontation remembering his earlier defeat. This time he did not travel with his family. He advanced alone to meet the Rajputs. The stage was set for another climactic confrontation that would decide which ruler would dominate Hind.

The Muslims and the Rajputs were camped opposite each other. Mahmud Ghori was eager to avoid facing the elephants of the Rajputs. Ghori's army raided the rear of Prithviraj's camp. Prithviraj had to hasten back only with 80,000 cavalry, as elephants would have slowed his rate of march. As the Rajputs neared Mahmud Ghori's new position, Ghori launched a night attack with specially trained soldiers, who in modern terminology, could be categorized as commandos. Since the Rajput warrior's code of conduct was against night attacks, Prithviraj's soldiers were entirely unprepared. Despite being numerically inferior, Ghori's commandos were able to return unscathed having caused much loss among the enemy.

The *corps de elite* of Mahmud Ghori's army was the mounted Turkish bowmen. They were seasoned soldiers who were Mamluks or slaves of the imperial household. Besides constituting the officer corps, they also formed an elite contingent. They were supplemented by Afghan cavaliers who fought principally with lances. Mahmud Ghori divided his force into five divisions. The first four divisions of light cavalry were composed of 7,000 horse archers each. About 12,000 heavy cavalry constituted the fifth division. The Turkish cavalry was of two types: skirmishing cavalry and shock troops. The former, which could be termed light cavalry, was similar to the Scythian cavalry which fought during the Battle of Jhelum on Alexander's side. Each such cavalryman carried a composite bow and iron arrows. They avoided head-on assaults and instead shot arrows from a distance aiming to disorganize the enemy. The bowmen took aim to hit the head of the enemy-general, and his eyes in particular. Such arrows could even pierce cuirasses. Since Turkish mounted archers had stirrups, unlike the Scythian mercenaries of Alexander, they were able to hit targets with great accuracy even as their horses galloped at a high speed.

The shock troops were cavalrymen who possessed heavier armour— cuirasses, shields, and heavy weapons. Even their horses were protected with armour. When enemy formations had been disrupted by the continuous shower of arrows from the skirmishing cavalry, the heavy cavalrymen charged in a body with lances. Each heavy cavalryman wore a *khod* (a helmet) with *mighfar* (network of steel) beneath it. Even if the helmet cracked under enemy blows, the *mighfar* protected the head from metal splinters. With this new technology introduced by the Muslim militaries, the helmets of the Turkish horsemen were more sophisticated than the helmets used by Alexander's Companion Cavalry. Ghori's horsemen of the heavy cavalry wore a coat of mail in which small rings held together metallic scales, resembling the scales of a fish. Not only were these armours lighter than the fully metallic Greek body armour, they also provided better protection. Turkish horses were able to run faster and longer than the mounts of Alexander's Companions. With better horses, and more effective but lighter body armour, Turkish cavalry could charge at speeds greater than the Greek cavalry.

Early in the morning, the four divisions of Turkish horse archers numbering 28,000 attacked the Rajput army simultaneously from front, rear, right and left, but did not press home the charges. The aim of the mounted archers was to harass and wear out the enemy through skirmishing tactics. Prithviraj used an elephant as a command vehicle. From his elephant, Prithviraj ordered his men to fight the skirmishers. The Rajputs deployed only heavy cavalry armed with straight swords. They never got an opportunity to use their swords on Ghori's skirmishers. When the Rajput cavalry tried to pursue the mounted archers, the latter retreated. Because of their heavier armour and inferior horses, the Rajput cavaliers were unable to match the speed of the unarmoured Central Asian mounts. When the heavy Rajput cavalry stopped pursuing the horse archers, the archers returned to attack again. Such a hide and seek game tired the Rajputs and their mounts. The blazing sun not only exhausted the Rajput warriors in their cumbersome armours, it made them thirsty. Towards late afternoon, the continuous rain of arrows by the horse-mounted archers perplexed the frustrated Rajputs, resulting in a stampede among them. At that critical juncture, Mahmud Ghori launched his division of 12,000 heavy cavalry. They smashed through the Rajput ranks. As the sun was setting, Prithviraj realized that the battle was lost. While Govind Rai died in the battlefield, Prithviraj attempted to escape from the combat zone. When the Rajput soldiers saw that the *howdah* of Prithviraj's elephant was empty, they lost heart and gave up the fight only to be killed by the Ghorid horsemen.

Besides the superiority of the Central Asian mounts and arms, victory went to the Ghorid army because of its superior C3—command, control and communications—and the utter inability of the Rajputs to learn from past experiences. Mahmud Ghori's integration of 'missile power' (use of horse archers as missile men) with shock action by heavy cavalry had historical precedence in the clash between Subuktagin, the ruler of Ghazni, and Jaipal, the ruler of Kabul, which had occurred about two centuries before the battle at Tarain. Jaipal's numerical superiority, like Prithviraj's, was enormous. Subuktagin had divided his horse archers into units of 500 men and they harassed the Rajput cavalry throughout the day. When the Rajputs got tired, Subuktagin used his reserve heavy cavalry to batter them.

The command apparatus of the Turkish forces was superior to that of their Rajput opponents. While Turkish militaries had a hierarchical command system, unprofessional, divided command was always a problem for the Hindus. The Muslim army was commanded by the

Sultan who was himself a warlord. In Islamic polities, persons with military abilities became Sultans. The *Sipah Salar* (general officer) and the *Muqaddam* (officer in charge of the advance guard of the army) assisted the Sultan. On the other hand, several Rajput kings who were not professional military leaders led the Rajput forces. The only professional leader of a Hindu army was the *Senapati*. However, civilian Rajput kings were afraid of delegating full authority to the *Senapatis*. To prevent military coups, each *Senapati* was allowed to command only one-fourth of the army. To monitor the *Senapati's* actions, a civilian minister was also appointed. The nature of the Rajput confederacy too prevented the emergence of a centralized hierarchical command apparatus. The confederacy was an assortment of various chiefs and Prithviraj was only one among equals. He had no authority to give orders to the other chiefs. Prithviraj, as a consequence, was not in a position to force the implementation of any coherent battle plan. The Rajput army was a headless Goliath.

Mahmud Ghori was able to exercise effective command and control over the army in the battlefield. Orders for attack, retreat and counterattack were given through various types of drums and trumpets. One kind of drum used was the *kos*, a large brass kettledrum. Along with it, smaller Arabian drums known as *jalajils*, made of deerskin, were also used. Abdullah Sirhindi, a historian who lived in the medieval age, writes that signalling was also done with the aid of the tambourin, which was a sort of mandolin with chords of brass wires. Formations were moved quickly and effectively amidst the chaos of battle with the aid of *payats* with distinct *akhtars* inscribed on them. *Payats* were the precursor of regimental flags. Different units had *payats* with distinct *akhtars*. Besides functioning as rallying points in the battlefield, such flags also served as visible symbols of the unit personnel's esprit de corps.

In contrast, the Rajput army had no such command techniques for redeployment of their formations once the battle started. The Rajput chief had no mechanism either to exercise overall control over military formations or to coordinate the disparate formations to respond to quickly changing battle scenarios. The Rajputs had to stick to a rigid pre-battle war plan which became useless once the battle begun. The Rajput practice of getting intoxicated with *bhang* before battle might have given them Dutch courage for a frontal charge but it did not sharpen their intellect for tactical manoeuvres in the battlefield.

On a personal plane, Prithviraj's leadership was worse than that of Paurava. When the spectre of Greek invasion haunted Paurava, he at least focused on matters military rather than being amorous or alcoholic. After the First Battle of Tarain, instead of honing his forces for another inevitable Muslim invasion, Prithviraj luxuriated in music and the companionship of his beautiful queen, Sanjukta. Unlike Mahmud Ghori, Prithviraj had neither a tactical plan nor any tactical reserve while fighting the Second Battle of Tarain. He could only think of the age-old frontal charge by massed Rajput cavalry. In contrast, Mahmud Ghori developed his tactical plan after the first encounter with Prithviraj's forces. While in the First Battle of Tarain, Mahmud, like Alexander at the Battle of Jhelum, had divided his force into three divisions, in the second confrontation, Ghori came up with an innovation by dividing his army into skirmishing cavalry and shock cavalry. Finally, Prithviraj, despite his imposing bulk, was not even personally courageous like Paurava. When the Second Battle of Tarain was going badly, Prithviraj, the false hero, did not think of either making a last ditch stand like Paurava or of conducting a tactical retreat deep into north India. Observing the carnage of the killing zone, Prithviraj, as ingloriously as Darius, stepped down from the *howdah* of his elephant and mounted a fast horse to escape. In the event, death overtook him as he was captured by Ghori's cavalry at Sarsuti and then executed.

COUNTERFACTUAL HISTORY:

RAJPUT *BLITZKRIEG* WEST OF INDUS?

'Victory in war does not depend entirely upon numbers or mere courage; only skill and discipline will ensure it.'

—PUBIUS FLAVIUS VEGETIUS RENATUS

If instead of the decadent leadership exemplified by Prithviraj, the Rajput confederacy was led by a commander of the stature of Skandagupta, would it have been possible for it to check the onrush of the Islamic armies, and conduct offensive campaigns to the west of Indus? Skandagupta, the last great Gupta emperor (r. AD 457–67), had been able to repulse the Huns who had overrun Persia and the Roman Empire. A commander had to establish himself in the good opinion of his men. To do this, he had to be a model for them, setting an example in the endurance of hardship and being affectionate and accessible to the men under his command. Rajput chiefs were prevented by preoccupations of caste from being accessible to ordinary troopers. Skandagupta, while campaigning, lived like an ordinary soldier. He used to sleep on the ground, not in a luxurious royal tent like Prithviraj did. This sort of 'leadership by example' earned him the loyalty of the common troops who did not perceive the battle as an elite game but were motivated to fight and die for their ruler. Is it possible to argue that if the Rajputs had Skandagupta for a leader, then the course of the two battles of Tarain would have been different? Personal leadership is important in battles but it is mediated by certain other structural constraints. A good leader would become a failure with a bad army. Alexander displayed extraordinary generalship but he also had the professional army constructed by Philip. Alexander would not have been able to achieve much with the Persian rabble that Darius possessed. Skandagupta's success over the Hun menace was possible because in addition to his personal qualities, the Gupta monarch possessed an army of a kind denied to Prithviraj. After the Parthian invasion of India, the Indian monarchs realized the military necessity of maintaining horse archers. The Guptas maintained heavy horse archers wearing chain mail up to their knees and they were able to check the light Hun cavalry. The signalling system evolved by the Guptas was superior to that of the Rajputs. The Gupta cavalry carried pennants of many colours, to act as rallying points, and to represent orders for attack, retreat and counter-attack by the reserves. Before the Guptas, pennants were carried by the chariots. This shift under the Guptas reflected the importance of cavalry in the Gupta battle order. The Gupta cavalry was trained under the demanding eyes of the central government. In ancient India, there were centres of military training known as *asramas*. Boys of sound physique were enrolled in them at the age of eleven. Students stayed at the boarding houses where they were provided with food and education. The convocation ceremony was known as *curikabandhanam* when a dagger was ceremoniously tied to the dress of the successful pupil as a token of his military education. Important dignitaries of the state were invited to such ceremonies.

However, such military seminaries disintegrated with the rise of feudal chiefs. Towards the end of the Gupta period, the practice of issuing land grants to feudal chiefs for maintaining military contingents resulted in the emergence of semi-autonomous warlords. As the central government withered away after AD 500, feudal lords emerged supreme. The petty kings depended on the cavalry supplied by these feudal chiefs. This sort of cavalry was neither disciplined nor trained to function as a collective unit. Prithviraj's force was composed of such an indisciplined cavalry. With such cavalry, tactical manoeuvre in the combat zone was out of question.

After the First Battle of Tarain, Prithviraj's conduct could be blamed because he failed to pursue Mahmud Ghori's retreating cavalry and annihilate it. The faulty C3 of the Rajput military system was also responsible for such indecisiveness. With their divided command, the Rajput army gave up the chase after pursuing the retreating Ghorid army for only 40 mi.

If Prithviraj had been able to launch an elephant charge instead of a cavalry charge, would the course of the Second Battle of Tarain have been different? Again, the answer is negative. In fact, in the post-Tarain period, many Rajput chiefs, witnessing the impotence of Rajput cavalry charges against horse archers, attempted to crush the Muslim cavalry with a frontal charge by the elephant corps. The superiority of the mobile horse archers against semi-immobile elephant-centric armies was proven when in AD 1194 at Chandawar, Raja Jai Chand with Kanauj's army of 300 elephants was decimated by Mahmud Ghori's 50,000 horsemen.

Turkish cavaliers were not affected by elephants as Alexander's men had been. The impact of elephants on the Turkish cavalry was far from spectacular because of familiarity. Turkish horsemen had been continuously engaging with Hindu armies along the Indus region for two centuries before Tarain. Both Turkish horses and men were conditioned in fighting the elephants. They had developed some tactics in response. The Arabs before the Turks had used naphtha fire to frighten the elephants of Dahir's army in Sind. The Turks also used naphtha fireworks effectively when they faced the elephant-centric Hindu armies. Finally, the Turks had many more horse archers than Alexander did.

It was not possible for the Rajputs to turn the tide even by practising horse archery. When faced with a new sort of weapon system, the configuration of a military organization cannot be changed suddenly. It takes decades to build up and develop fighting skill based on a new martial tradition and to perpetuate the organizational culture required for absorbing the new hardware. Only after experimenting for a hundred years were the Guptas able to field mounted archers. The Guptas had also been lucky; the Huns, unlike the Turks, never seriously thought of conquering India. Unlike the Guptas, the Rajputs did not experiment with horse archery for two reasons. One, their cultural conservatism and second, their decentralized political structure. For military innovations to occur, one needs a centralized political machinery with a stable revenue base. This was something which the Gupta monarchy possessed at least till the time of Skandagupta. However, the decentralized Rajput confederacy was unable to conceive and implement any programme for adoption of new military techniques. Further, the elitist Rajput worldview shaped through the cultural lens of *Dharmayuddha* blocked any attempt to adopt the combat techniques of the 'unclean' *mlechhas*.

It is a region's socio-economic fabric that spawns the military culture. Unlike the Turks, the Hindus of the Hindu Shahi dynasty were settled agriculturists rather than steppe nomads. Hence, even though the Hindu Shahi kingdom of eastern Afghanistan lay very close to the breeding ground of Central Asian horses, they failed to make proper use of the tactics of mounted archery. This explains the collapse of Shahi power in the tenth century against the onslaught of Mahmud Ghazni. Mahmud Ghazni had found that his Central Asian foes were able to field large numbers of superior mounted steppe archers against him. Ghazni's Central Asian foes fielded excellent cavalry, but were unfamiliar with elephants, having had no access to them. In a brilliant tactical move, Mahmud Ghazni used elephants in conjunction with cavalry against his steppe enemies. Since the Turks of Ghazni had no tradition of fighting on elephants, the Ghaznavids for manning their elephant corps recruited a large number of Hindu auxiliaries from India.

What if Prithviraj had entrenched himself within the city of Delhi instead of meeting Ghori's cavalry in the field of Tarain? Would he have escaped death and disaster? In siege warfare, too, the Islamic armies had a definite edge over the Hindus. And Rajput fort construction did not exhibit any advancement over the previous period. Muslim armies employed *manjaniqs* that were somewhat similar to the *lithobolos* of the Macedonian army. These were catapults used to hurl stones for breaking the walls of the fortresses and cities. Muhammad bin Qasim during his invasion of Sind in 710–12 CE introduced *manjaniqs* in South Asia. Smaller catapults threw darts against the defenders guarding the fort wall. When the walls disintegrated, scaling ladders were used to cross over and overwhelm the invaders inside the forts. For storming the forts, the Ghaznavids and later the Ghorids developed a specially trained infantry force. The *Tabakat-i-Nasiri,* written around the thirteenth century, comments that the shields of such an infantry were made of raw hide and cotton. These shields were so thick that neither spears nor swords were able to pierce them.

In fact, in the post-Tarain era, unable to match Turkish mobility, the Rajput chieftains reverted to 'positional warfare'. Instead of attempting to meet the nimble but lethal Turkish mounted archers in the battlefield, the rajas tried to avoid battles. They focused on fortifications for the protection of their agricultural enclaves. This defensive strategy, fortifying and awaiting invasion, gave rise to what in twentieth century terminology is termed 'Maginot mentality'. But the static, defensive posture of the Hindu rulers was also unsuccessful in checking the Islamic tide. The massive Hindu fortifications were characterized by 50 ft. thick mud brick walls with square towers at regular intervals. The watchmen in the towers alerted the defenders in case of a raid. Such fortifications provided some protection to the Hindus against Turkish cavalry raids but failed utterly when the Islamic forces conducted siege warfare to capture cities. Spears and rocks thrown by the defenders from the towers did little damage to the enemy. On the contrary, Turkish rock hurling catapults completely destroyed the fortifications.

The Rajputs could have earned themselves a chance by avoiding a decisive engagement with Ghori and conducting a protracted attritional campaign, instead. The Rajputs should have retreated deep inside India, burning all the grain and hay and poisoning all the wells on the way. This would have demoralized Mahmud's soldiers. All his cavaliers, accustomed to the cold climate of Afghanistan and Turkestan, complained about the heat of Hindustan. A summer campaign in north India was the last thing they would have tolerated. The *Taj-ul-Ma'athir* says, 'Due to the intense heat of the sun, the armours on the bodies of the warriors were blazing. The bodies of the combatants seemed to be burning under their armour and cuirasses.' If Mahmud had forced his soldiers to conduct a summer campaign, there could have been a mutiny similar to the one that had rocked Alexander's army at the Beas more than a thousand years before Tarain.

Mahmud Ghori also faced constant threats from the Turks of Central Asia. He was not in a position to maintain a large number of cavalry in India indefinitely. After Tarain, he was forced to transfer most of his officers to meet the Turkish threat from Khorasan. Hypothetically, if the Rajputs had refused to meet Ghori at a battlefield, and by ravaging the countryside severed the supply lines of the Ghorid army, then after a few months of useless campaigning, Ghori would have been forced to retreat to Ghor.

In the thirteenth century, when a Muslim army under Bakhtiar Khalji entered Assam, the ruler of Kamrupa (Assam) was able to destroy the invading force by following the scorched earth policy. Rajput politico-military culture stood in the way of conducting guerrilla war. The Rajput concept of warfare was against causing misery to poor and innocent people as is inevitable in scorched earth strategies. Rajput valour also demanded that the enemy should be met in a designated battlefield (as in Hoplite warfare) for a final showdown. Strategic retreat was unacceptable to the Rajputs since their sense of honour was against the concept of fleeing the battlefield. If Prithviraj attempted to follow such a policy, which in Rajput eyes was 'dishonourable', then he might have been assassinated by his peers or replaced by his brother Govind Rai. Rajput culture demanded that the Rajputs met the Turks in a decisive battle in which tactics, arms and organization made a Turkish victory almost inevitable. There is no space for contemplating alternate scenarios in the clash between the nomadic military culture seeped in a particular religious ethos, and Rajput chivalry.

THE SECOND BATTLE OF TARAIN: NET EFFECT

'The decision by arms is for all major and minor operations in war what cash payment is in commerce.'

—CARL VON CLAUSEWITZ

The defeat of the Hindus in the hands of Islamic invaders was nothing new. For three centuries before Tarain, the Arabs and Ghaznavids had defeated the Hindus repeatedly. But the pre-Tarain Islamic victories were not as decisive as the Second Tarain. The Arabs conquered Sind from the Hindu ruler Dahir but could not penetrate into Punjab and Gujarat, held by the Rajput chiefs. In contrast, Mahmud Ghazni defeated the Rajput rulers seventeen times. One reason was that the Arabs lacked horse archers like Ghazni's. Nevertheless, Mahmud Ghazni's impact on India was less than that of Mahmud Ghori. Mahmud Ghazni was interested only in conducting raids to capture Hindu slaves and loot wealth. However, Ghori wanted to establish his dominion in Hindustan by permanently annexing territories. The outcome of Ghori's policy was the two battles of Tarain.

The second battle of Tarain was lethal for the Rajput confederacy and opened the floodgates to Islamic invaders resulting in a *blitzkrieg* in north India. After the Second Tarain, individual Rajput rulers offered ineffective resistance to Ghori and region after region fell to the Islamic cavaliers as a result. One of the principal tactics of the Ghorid army was to designate some marksmen among the mounted archers to target the Rajput ruler because the loss of their chief resulted in utter disintegration of the Rajput army. When Mahmud Ghori's lieutenant Qutub-ud-din Aibak encountered the force of Chait Chandra, the Raja of Benaras, special marksmen were ordered to kill the leader. A bowman put an arrow into the eye of Chandra and Aibak was saved from a slugging match with the war elephants of Chandra.

Tarain had a dialectical effect on the force structure of the combatants of both sides. This battle not only sounded the death knell for the bipolar Hindu forces (i.e. elephants and horses) but was also responsible for the restructuring of victorious Islamic armies. The elephants continued to inspire awe among Turkish historians, as was the case with the Greek historians who chronicled Alexander's exploits in India. Regarding the elephants faced by Mahmud Ghori and his lieutenants, Hasan Nizami has written:

In the open space of the battlefield, the elephants, fitted with litters and covered with armours stood in a row like a mountain of steel. The huge elephants, each one as big as a patch of cloud, ran across the battlefield like wind and fire, and with their crystal like tusks caused the molten cornelian of blood of the warriors to flow on the ground. With this blood their emerald like trunks were dyed red like ruby and coral. Every now and then the lasso like trunk would show from the beneath the armour to demonstrate anger and bitterness. Sometimes the trunk would bend like a polo stick as if it would carry away the ball of heavenly sphere, at other times it would curl up like a dragon threatening to swallow the loop of heaven.

The military efficiency of the elephants is clear from the above account. Even the mounted bowmen found an armoured elephant a somewhat difficult target. While one arrow was adequate to down a horse or a warrior, an elephant, struck by a multitude of arrows, looking like a gigantic porcupine, would continue to resist.

Hindu chiefs, who became vassals after being defeated by the Sultans, were ordered to surrender their elephants. For instance, Raja Sulakshan Pal, the ruler of Gwalior, after being defeated, surrendered ten elephants to Mahmud Ghori's officers. This reduced the military potential of the Hindu chiefs, simultaneously raising the military effectiveness of the army of Islam in India.

The policy of integrating elephants with mounted archers can be traced back to Mahmud Ghazni. Because of the Mongols in Central Asia during the thirteenth century, the overland trade route for importing horses and bowmen from the Central Asian steppes to the Turkish dominion in India snapped. The Turks in India were forced to depend on the less powerful Arabian horses and on cavalrymen armed with spears. In the long run, this resulted in diminishing the power of their cavalry in relation to invaders from the Central Asian steppes. The large number of elephants in the armies of the Turks in India was an attempt by the Sultans to fill the 'cavalry gap'.

Besides integrating elephants into their war machine, the Turks began using Hindu converts as infantry armed with swords. Initially, the Turks in India depended on Central Asian Turks and Afghans to fill their military ranks. However, the Mongol conquest of Central Asia and Afghanistan stopped the inflow of Turkish and Afghan military labourers into India. Hindus who accepted Islam were inducted both, into the officer cadre as well as the rank and the file. Besides the military necessity, such a policy had political advantages as it resulted in the cooption of the hitherto hostile Hindus into the fold of Turkish rule.

While on the one hand, the Turks accommodated Indian military manpower and techniques of warfare like elephants into their army, the Hindu rulers also attempted to raise the military effectiveness of their cavalry by imitating Turkish military practices. To develop horsemanship, the Muslim cavaliers played *chagan* (polo). The players were divided into two teams. The teams tried to score goals by driving a ball through the opponent team's goal post. The balls were made of wood covered with leather and they were pushed with the help of cane sticks that were curved at the lower end. The Hindu rajas introduced this game to improve the horsemanship of their cavalry recruits. This somewhat explains the sporadic resistance by scattered Hindu chiefs for three centuries in the aftermath of Tarain.

CONCLUSION

Tarain, like Hydaspes, drove home the message that the size of the military forces engaged in combat need not be crucial. Rather the culture of combat, which in turn shapes the techniques of warfare and the nature of technology, is the determining factor.

No agrarian society was able to stop nomadic mounted archers. Tarain, in a way, was a repetition of Manzikert. At the Battle of Manzikert fought in AD 1071 in Turkey, the Western Turkish horse archers were able through skirmishing tactics to destroy the Byzantine Empire's heavy cavalry, which, like the Rajput cavalry, was armed with lances and swords. Both Tarain and Manzikert were decisive battles. The victory of the Western Turks at Manzikert reduced the Byzantine Empire into a minor power just as the victory of the Eastern Turks at Tarain was a death blow for the Rajputs.

3

The Men on Horseback

The First Battle of Panipat
21 April 1526

'He who hath entered the assembly of life, Drinketh at last of the cup of death. He who hath come to the inn of life, Passeth at last from Earth's house of woe. . . .'

—ZAHIR-UD-DIN MUHAMMAD BABUR

AN INNOCUOUS LOOKING flat field in Panipat, northern India, was to be the site of one of the bloodiest battles in India's history. It was summer, 1526. Even the soldiers accustomed to battle were fearful of the blood and gore they were expecting. Zahir-ud-din Muhammad Babur, just before joining the battle, noted in his autobiography the feelings of his soldiers in the following words: 'Some in the army were very anxious and full of fear.' Babur, besides being a general, composed Turki verse. His favourite, which he used to read to his retainers before the onset of a great battle, was the one quoted in the epigraph above. A veteran of a hundred fights, Babur was not afraid but hopeful that if by any means he could defeat his enemy, his days of wandering would end. As a matter of fact, the ensuing battle was to enable Babur to establish the Mughal Empire which, in terms of territorial extent and grandeur, could be compared with the Roman Empire.

FROM RAGS TO RICHES

Babur was a warlord from Central Asia. He belonged to the Chaghthai branch of the Turko-Mongol tribe. When they settled in Hindustan, they came to be known as the Mughals. Babur used to boast to his followers that he had the blood of both Chingiz Khan and Timur flowing in his veins. His father was the ruler of Farghana, a small principality between the kingdom of Khiva and the Takla Makan desert. Farghana Valley spreads across eastern Uzbekistan, southern Kyrgyzstan and northern Tajikistan. In 1494, on the death of his father, Babur ascended the throne. His scheming uncles and cousins made sure Babur soon lost that throne. He became a wanderer, collecting a band of marauders. Shaibani Khan, the great Uzbek ruler, was raising a storm in Central Asia. It was a time of troubles. Opportunities were open for aggressive military adventures. In 1505, Babur was able to capture Kabul. He acquired some firearms that gave him technical superiority over the Afghans armed with scimitars and bows. For several years, he tried to reconquer his hereditary domain but failed. Only at the age of thirty-six did a frustrated Babur turn towards Hind.

The deficit economy of the bleak mountainous plateau of Afghanistan forced Babur's attention towards India. The story of the riches of India and the plunder picked up by his distant predecessor Timur inflamed Babur's passion. Moreover, Babur required money and glory to keep the Afghans and the Hazara soldiers under his control. Otherwise, they would desert the Mughal standard and join the rebellious chieftains who, from their hilly strongholds, were threatening Babur's shaky rule. By the 1520s, the once powerful Delhi Sultanate, established by the generals of Mahmud Ghori, was in shambles. Bahlul Lodhi, an Afghan general, had grabbed control after a palace revolution. His son, Sikander Lodhi, managed to retain power. However, things started falling apart with the accession of Sikander's son Ibrahim Lodhi. India seemed a tempting fruit ready for picking to the hardy warriors of Babur. News had reached Kabul of the continuous rebellions by Lodhi nobles against Sultan Ibrahim of Delhi.

Some among Babur's entourage discouraged him from embarking upon a rash adventure in Hindustan. The hot climate and dusty plains of north India were anathema to the Central Asian followers of Babur. Ibrahim's rule was tottering, but he still commanded vast demographic and economic resources. Numbers, the Mughals knew, could turn the scales in any encounter.

Babur decided to test the quality of Ibrahim's military responses by conducting frontier raids. In 1519, Babur took the fort of Bajaur, plundered Bhira and then returned to Kabul. In 1520, Babur led a plundering expedition to Sialkot. He continued such raids till 1524. The inaction of Ibrahim's Delhi government encouraged Babur to stake everything towards a decisive throw of dice. Babur crossed the Rubicon when he launched his main invasion in the winter of 1525. His force crossed the Indus near Attock. While soldiers and their mounts huddled together on rafts, Babur and the senior Mughal commanders had boats at their disposal.

Initially, the Delhi court thought that Babur was leading yet another plundering expedition. But when the Mughals conquered Punjab, Ibrahim realized the gravity of the situation and set his military machine, a rusty one no doubt, in motion. Ibrahim himself accompanied his army, which was under his general Bahadur Khan. Lethargy, indiscipline and indecisiveness dogged the Lodhi army. Instead of acting fast and moving as quickly as possible to prevent deeper inroads by Babur, Ibrahim's force marched only 2–4 mi. everyday. Even this rate of march was not maintained continuously. After one day's march, the Lodhi force halted for two or four days. It was as if Ibrahim did not know whether to advance or retreat.

Ibrahim had more than a 1,00,000 men and 1,000 elephants. However, it is improbable that he brought his whole force to fight the Mughal invaders. It was impossible to move 1,000 elephants simultaneously because each such animal required huge amounts of water and fodder daily. Moreover, while the Rajput ruler Rana Sanga threatened the southern boundary of Ibrahim's domain, recalcitrant Afghan chiefs created problems in the eastern part. To guard against these two threats, Ibrahim had to detach a substantial number of troops and elephants. Nevertheless, Ibrahim's force at Panipat outnumbered the Mughal army.

One of Ibrahim's commanders Daud Khan Lodhi advanced 7 mi. from the main army with a contingent of 6,000 men, to test the Mughal army's strength. Several skirmishes occurred between the Afghan and Mughal advance guards before the main battle was fought. In such encounters, Babur's mobile cavalry took many Afghan prisoners.

Babur was a complex, multifaceted man. He could revel in poetry and compose verses. He had a naturalist's eye for fruits and flowers. But when fighting a war, he was a ruthless and pragmatic politician. Thanks to his long experience of fighting in Central Asia, Babur was adept at using violence to terrorize his opponent. His strategy was to weaken the enemy psychologically by projecting a ruthlessness that would make the enemy feel helpless. On 5 March 1526, Babur deliberately killed all his Afghan prisoners and made a pyramid with their skulls in the style of Timur. Beside the date 5 March 1526, Babur jotted down in his memoirs: 'Ustad Ali Quli and the matchlock men were ordered to shoot all the prisoners, by way of example. . . . Most of the prisoners, by way of warning, were made to reach their death doom.' On 12 April 1526, the two opposing forces finally met at Panipat.

Babur needed a quick victory because he was far away from his base Kabul and threatening clouds were hovering along the perilous northern frontier of his kingdom. The Uzbeks were threatening to invade his domain. To provoke Ibrahim into hasty action, Babur, as advised by deserters from the Lodhi side, decided on a night attack. The sally on the night of 19 April was made under the command of Mahdi Khwaja. The nocturnal raid created confusion and disorder in the Lodhi camp; it heightened pressure on Ibrahim and clouded his judgement.

21 APRIL 1526: CARNAGE

21 April was a Friday, a holy day for Muslims. Ibrahim decided to try his luck. It was early morning when news reached the Mughal camp that the enemy was advancing. The camp was transformed into a scene of hustle and bustle. Men began putting on their armours. Babur realized that since Ibrahim was commanding a bigger force, he might attempt to attack the Mughal flanks. So, Babur deployed his army with its right side protected by the suburb of the town named Panipat. To protect the left side of his army, Babur ordered his soldiers to dig a ditch. At some places, the ditch was covered with mud in order to allow counter-attack by small groups of about 200 cavalry each. They constituted crack units and were known as the 'braves'.

Babur anticipated the mad onrush by Ibrahim's foot soldiers and mighty elephants. He realized that if somehow he was able to check the frontal assault of Ibrahim's soldiery, then due to lack of discipline and training they would run out of steam. Babur insisted on constructing field fortifications. His men collected 700 *arabas* (carts). These carts carried guns as well as the troops' baggage. The guns placed on the carriages discharged balls weighing 5.25 pounds each. Some of the guns were bigger which threw heavier shots, each weighing 52 pounds. Ustad Ali was ordered to join up these carts with ropes of raw hide. Babur admits in his memoirs that this was a typical Ottoman tactic for stopping an enemy cavalry charge. Ustad Ali had witnessed the Battle of Chaldiran fought on 22 August 1514, near Tabriz, between the Ottomans and the Safavid ruler of Persia Shah Ismail. In this encounter, the Ottomans chained their carts together to stop the Persian cavalry charge. The tactic of chaining carts to form a laager was also common among the Magyar tribe of Hungary. Between every two carts in Babur's line, six wooden tripods were set up. For support the matchlock men placed their handguns on these tripods while firing. The matchlock men under Ustad Quli supplemented by the cannons in the carts under Mustafa were in charge of securing the centre of Mughal army.

Humayun commanded the right wing of the Mughal line. At that time, he was a youth of eighteen. He had begun shaving just days before the Battle of Panipat. The Mughal left was under Muhammad Mirza. The advance guard was under Khusrau Kukuldas. Abdul Aziz was in charge of the reserve. The Mughal centre was divided into two parts. The right hand of the Mughal centre was under Chin Timur and Khalifa Khwaja commanded the left part of it. The most crucial component of the Mughal force was the *tulghama* contingents. They were the flanking parties: their aim being to charge at the enemy's sides and thereby to turn their flanks. After this, the two *tulghama* contingents were to join hands at the rear of the enemy thus completely surrounding him. Babur had learned the *tulghama* tactics the hard way. The Uzbek tribes of Central Asia were adept at implementing this tactic. In May 1501, the *tulghama* contingents of the Uzbek Shaibani Khan attacked Babur's left and right wings and drove them to his centre. As Babur's centre was jam packed, Shaibani's flanking parties joined hands at Babur's rear. Babur's army was thus encircled, enveloped, and then eliminated. Babur himself escaped alive, though with difficulty. Some twenty-five years after this catastrophe, Babur decided to use this technique against the inexperienced Lodhis. The *tulghama* parties deployed at the extreme end of the Mughal right and left were under Malik Qasim and Qara Khazi.

Babur's plan was to allow Ibrahim to attack first and then check it through prudent use of field fortifications, cannons and matchlocks. If this succeeded, the Afghan attack would come to a halt; Babur, then, planned to throw his fresh *tulghama* parties against Ibrahim's exhausted troops to encircle and eliminate them.

When the order to advance was given, Ibrahim's troops moved forward in a disjointed manner and the detachment on Ibrahim's left were able to reach the Mughal right. It was accident, not part of a well thought-out battle plan. The Lodhis had no plan. The reserve under Abdul Aziz strengthened the Mughal right. Simultaneously, Babur ordered the 'braves' (crack troops) to counter-attack and Ibrahim's left wing came to a halt. Moments later, the Lodhi right wing, with some elephants, clashed with the Mughal left. There was close quarter hand-to-hand combat with Ibrahim's infantry, armed with swords. After facing a lethal attack from crossbows during the siege of Samarkhand in 1501, Babur had added to his infantry branch archers armed with crossbows. A combination of arrows loosened by the crossbow-men and shots of the matchlock-men and cannon, stopped the elephants. Given the lack of a coherent plan, the Lodhi troops were confused. They were undecided whether to attempt an advance again or retreat. Babur realized that the decisive moment had arrived. He ordered his centre to stand firm and the right and left wings to advance and attack the Lodhis.

To add confusion and horror, Babur simultaneously launched his trump card: the *tulghama* contingents. They seized the moment of confusion and rushed forward shouting '*Hai, Hai*'. The turning parties, galloping forward at high speed, discharged arrows towards the flanks of the enemy. At this moment, Babur's force looked like two horns of a crescent attempting to swallow the Lodhi army. Troops on the left and right of Ibrahim felt the pressure of the *tulghama* parties and started retreating towards their centre. Most of the men were now crowded in the centre. Pressed on from all sides, they lacked the space to move freely or use their arms properly. The rain of arrows loosed on Ibrahim's massed troops by the mounted archers resulted in a massive slaughter. The Lodhi army became a panic-stricken mob. In the ensuing stampede, many soldiers were trampled down by men of their own side. It was high noon. In Babur's words, by midday, the battle was over. The Lodhi soldiers tried to flee the battlefield but were slaughtered. Ibrahim, like Paurava, possessed personal courage and he fought and died in the battlefield. Even his arch enemy, Babur paid respect to his dead body, touching it and crying out over it, 'Honour to your courage'. Though Babur's casualties were minimal, statistics offer us a glimpse of the deadly nature of the battle. Over 70 per cent of Ibrahim's forces suffered casualties. About 35,000 soldiers on the Lodhi side were wounded and 15,000 dead soldiers from the Lodhi force lay scattered on the battlefield. The battle lasted for six hours. On an average more than 40 Lodhi soldiers had died every minute. The medieval battlefield could be a mass slaughterhouse.

FATAL FRIDAY FOR IBRAHIM: ACCIDENT OR A HISTORICAL INEVITABILITY?

'Is there one cruel turn of Fortune's wheel unseen of me? Is there a pang, a grief my wounded heart has missed?'

—BABUR

On the evening of 21 April, as Babur sat down for his evening prayer amidst the dead bodies strewn across the field of Panipat, an advance guard under Humayun's command was sent to occupy Delhi. The victory made Babur the *Padshah* of Hindustan. Babur, ruler of poverty-stricken Afghanistan with merely 12,000 soldiers, had defeated Ibrahim who had at his disposal a bigger army and a treasury filled with money. Actually, the result of Panipat was not the product of a random roll of dice. Technological and managerial superiority gave Babur a decided advantage both in siege warfare as well as in set-piece battles.

The geological frontier of the subcontinent ran along the Indus. The best possible chance to stop an enemy was along the bank of the river as it descended from the hill passes of Afghanistan. Once the enemy crossed the Indus, everything became easier for it. The hostile party after entering the fertile plain of Punjab could maintain an army easily, while the level ground also offered a mobile enemy the possibilities of conducting wide manoeuvres. In such manoeuvre war, the advantage lay with the side with the better cavalry. The five rivers of Punjab were easily fordable and there was no natural obstacle in the flat plains of Punjab. Babur, unlike Alexander, was lucky because he did not have to cross the Indus against an enemy waiting on the riverbank. Ibrahim was in no position to contest Babur's crossing of the Indus. In the 1520s, the battered realm of the Lodhi Afghans was merely a shadow of the erstwhile Delhi Sultanate. Ibrahim's authority was confined to the Ganga-Jamuna doab. The governors of the outlying provinces were practically independent. In fact, the Lodhi governor of Punjab actually encouraged Babur to invade India. He thought that Babur, after defeating Ibrahim, would merely plunder the rich cities of north India and go back to Kabul. This, assumed the Lodhi governor of Punjab would further weaken Ibrahim's authority and would allow him to assert independence from Delhi government. By the time the governor found out that Babur was not merely a plunderer but an empire builder, it was too late. He found himself in chains.

Besides following a superior strategy, Babur unlike Ibrahim had an excellent killing machine at his disposal. An army had to be fed, clothed and armed continuously to be maintained in a state of high efficiency. One trait of good leadership was that the commander had to concern himself with these aspects. Babur fulfilled all these tasks. He divided the responsibilities among his *amirs* and *maliks*. Abdul Malik was in charge of the armours for the soldiers and the horses. Abdul Aziz was appointed Master of the Horses, and his job was to maintain the cavalry. The Mughal military intelligence operated with high efficiency. Babur employed many news writers to acquire real time intelligence about the enemy. Even before the day the battle of Panipat was fought, the news writers in Mughal pay were passing on to Babur the detailed information about deliberations in Ibrahim's camp.

Unlike Ibrahim, Babur was able to maintain his control over the various contingents of his army in course of the battle. Once the battle was joined, Ibrahim lost all control over his disparate forces. He himself continued to fight valiantly till the end. However, Babur did not rush into the fight like a grub-street subaltern. Rather, Babur moved up and down and encouraged his troops. Then, in accordance with the demands of the battle, he ordered the *tulghama* parties and the reserve to engage the enemy as if he was moving formations on a chessboard. Babur was able to convey his wishes to the various contingents' commanders at different times with the aid of ox tail standards. This was a Mongol practice. The Mongols understood that in the din and bustle of fighting, even if the general shouted with all the power in his lungs, his orders would be inaudible to the different contingents' commanders scattered over a wide area. In order to overcome the limitations of voice control, the Mongols came up with signals operated with the aid of ox tail standards. The ox tail standards were inscribed with different messages: advance, retreat, counter-attack and so on. According to the demands of the battle, the general raised the required standards before the different commanders leading the various contingents. In addition, the standards also functioned as visible rallying points for demoralized soldiers in the bloody battlefield. Besides these standards, Babur also employed selected horsemen called *tawachi* to convey orders to formation commanders leading the various contingents. In Western military parlance, such officers were known as staff officers or aides-de-camp of the Commander-in-Chief.

Command orders could also be implemented in the Mughal army because of the presence of a clear cut, hierarchical chain of command. The smallest unit in Babur's army consisted of a ten-soldier unit under a commander. The commander at the next level commanded five such units. Babur also realized that in the heat of battle, communication between lower-level commanders and higher-level commanders might suffer. Accordingly, he instructed lower level commanders to think and act on their own without waiting for detailed orders from those higher up. This sort of decentralized command set up in which commanders of subordinate formations are encouraged to use their own initiative within the format of a general plan laid down by the Commander-in-Chief is termed *Auftragstaktik* by nineteenth-century German military theorists.

Ultimately, the successful conduct of battle depends on the performance of the rank and file. Babur's soldiers fought to die for him. This was because of Babur's 'heroic command'. He shared all hardships with the troops during his long sojourn in Central Asia. While campaigning, like Alexander, Babur lived in soldier's tents and consumed the food that the ordinary troopers ate. This endeared Babur to his soldiers and generated staunch comradeship. In contrast, Ibrahim was haughty and his soldiers hardly knew him. Ibrahim's soldiers were gathered from the *bazaars* of Delhi when news of Babur's invasion filtered to the Lodhi court. Babur was a stickler for discipline, knowing an indisciplined army is a liability in the battlefield. Babur maintained discipline by regularly paying his soldiers and providing their food. Soldiers were paid through the pay master, Muhammad Jani Beg. Mustafa was in charge of collecting supplies for feeding the army. Babur also used violence to discipline his men. Soldiers molesting civilians and looting their property were flogged to death.

Ibrahim had an enormous hoard of treasure which was amassed

by his father Bahul Lodhi. Yet, at the time of the battle, the soldiers had not been paid for many months. Instead of distributing his treasure to eliminate the arrears of his soldiers, Ibrahim hoarded his wealth. Distribution of largesse may have provided Ibrahim a chance of survival. As things stood, his soldiers were unenthusiastic about risking their lives for an ungrateful master. In the end, his short-sighted policy lost Ibrahim his life as well as his treasure.

Babur was justified in saying that 'the Indians know how to die but not how to fight'. The Afghans had no chance against the Mughals in a set-piece battle. But was guerilla warfare a possibility for Ibrahim Lodhi? Babur's base in Afghanistan was always threatened by the ruler of Balkh, and it would have been impossible for Babur to station a large field army permanently in India had Ibrahim decided on a prolonged attritional campaign. However, for a regime to wage guerrilla war there were certain preconditions. Most crucial was social cohesion between the rulers and the ruled. In addition, the guerrilla leader had to be a charismatic personality who could convince the people that he was fighting for a just and noble cause. Some 150 years after the First Battle of Panipat, Shivaji was able to get the message of 'just national war of liberation against Muslim tyranny' across his social base. Shivaji succeeded in conveying a message convincingly: he was fighting the unjust rule of the Muslim Aurangzeb in order to re-establish the golden age of the Hindus. In contrast, the Lodhi Sultanate was the rule of an alien minority over a Hindu majority. The Afghans occupied all the top civilian and military positions. The Hindu ryots had no incentive to support Lodhi rule. In addition, Ibrahim was highly unpopular. He was regarded as an oppressor and people longed to be free from his rule. Ibrahim's diabolical personality had alienated most of his nobles. They feared that their lives were dependent on the whims of a young tyrant. Many Lodhi nobles either joined Babur openly or at least sat on the fence when the titanic clash between the Afghans and the Mughals occurred at Panipat. One Lodhi chieftain, Alam Khan, ran away to Kabul prior to Panipat. He made a pact with Babur that he would join the Mughals if Babur decided to invade India. In return, Babur promised him a principality after the destruction of the Lodhi Sultanate. In a nutshell, while Babur was not in a position to conduct a lengthy counter-guerrilla war, Ibrahim too was not in a position to implement a guerrilla strategy.

One could hypothesise about what would have happened if instead of confronting Babur at Panipat, Ibrahim had taken refuge with his army and treasure at the fort of Delhi. Still, Ibrahim would not have been able to escape defeat and death. Babur was not only an experienced battle commander but also an expert in siege warfare. His heavy cannons could breach fortifications in Afghanistan and India quite easily. In addition to his cannons, Babur had large stone throwing machines known as mangonels, which were similar to the *lithobolos* of Alexander's army. Before Panipat, on 6 January 1519, Babur had captured the fort of Bajaur quite easily. First, cannons and mangonels breached the wall of the fort. Additional breaching points were made when Dost Beg, with his sappers and miners, undermined the wall of the fort with mines. In the next phase, the Mughal infantry, with huge shields for protection, advanced to the points where the fort wall had been blasted open. In the third phase, they climbed to the fort with scaling ladders. Then, soldiers armed with falconets (handguns) and crossbows destroyed the defenders inside the fort with ease. The Afghan garrison, which had never seen hand-held firearms, found that the shots discharged by Ustad Quli Khan's musketeers penetrated their armour. Babur could have implemented such fort-destroying techniques had Ibrahim decided to take refuge in Delhi.

Babur had brought the guns from Kabul. Even if Babur's communication with Kabul had been cut, he would have been able to maintain his firepower. Some of the commanders in his army were capable of casting cannons. They had learnt the art of casting cannons from the Ottomans, who, in turn, had learned it from the Europeans. In Babur's army, firearms of all sorts were known as *feranghi* shots. In his memoir, Babur provides an account of gun casting in August 1526:

Ustad Ali Quli had been ordered to cast a large mortar for use against Biana and other forts which had not yet submitted. When all the furnaces and materials were ready, he sent a person to me and, on Monday, the 15th of the month, we went to see the mortar cast. Round the mortar mould, he had had eight furnaces made in which were the molten materials. From below each furnace, a channel went direct to the mould. When he opened the furnace holes on our arrival, the molten metal poured like water through all these channels into the mould. . . . The mould was left a day or two to cool; when it was opened, Ustad Ali Quli with great delight sent to say, 'The stone chamber is without defect'.

CONCLUSION

Babur was not an innovator of battle techniques like Alexander. However, he was not a mere imitator of other peoples' tactics either. He synthesized firepower-oriented Ottoman battlecraft with Uzbek cavalry techniques. This complex compound was able to generate a devastating military strategy to which neither the Lodhis nor the Rajputs had any answer. Babur's cannons were quite primitive. It was not unusual for them to explode after firing the first shot. The best cannons could fire at most up to sixteen times in a day. The cannons and muskets did not provide Babur with crushing firepower superiority. Nevertheless, the frightening sound made by the guns created psychological terror among Babur's opponents. They thought that Babur was resorting to black magic. Babur's victory was more due to judicious use of his men on horseback, the *tulghama* parties. Armed with composite bows, a mounted archer could fire six times faster than a matchlock man. In the sixteenth century, an arrow shot by a composite bow had more range and accuracy than a shot fired by a musket. While a matchlock man offered a static target to the enemy, the mounted archer was highly mobile. Babur had created an unbeatable combination for himself.

4

Chance in History

The Second Battle of Panipat
5 November 1556

Two armies so collided
That they struck fire out of water;
You'd say the air was all crimsoned daggers,
Their steel had all become solid rubies.

—ABUL FAZL on the clash of the Mughals and Hemu

AN ARROW SHOT by a common trooper, whose name is lost in the mist of anonymity, missed its original target and landed in the eye of a general who was winning the battle. The course of history was changed by that arrow. The victorious army lost the battle and subsequently, the empire. On its ruin emerged a new empire that dominated Hindustan for 300 long years.

When Babur died in 1530, his eldest son Humayun ascended the throne. But it was an uneasy throne. The Afghans, especially in east India, were rallying under a horse dealer turned warlord named Sher Shah. It would have required a military genius in the mould of Babur to subdue them. Humayun was anything but a military leader. In 1539, Sher Shah drubbed the Mughals at the Battle of Chausa. Humayun escaped to fight another day but was finally defeated at Bilgram the next year. Humayun took refuge in Persia. And in India, Sher Shah established the Sur or Suri dynasty. In 1554, Humayun invaded India with 15,000 cavalry. In 1555, he occupied Lahore. On 22 June 1555, at Sirhind, Humayun defeated Sikander Suri, the ruler of Delhi, despite Suri's 80,000 horses strong cavalry. Humayun owed his victory to the superior mobility of his Persian horses. But Humayun met an untimely death on 24 January 1556. And momentous events were unfolding further east.

ENTER GENERAL HEMU

Hem Chandra was born in a Gaur Brahmin family of Alwar in Rajasthan. The hereditary profession of his family was agriculture. However, some members of his family were traders of saltpetre, one of the chief components of gunpowder. This probably explains Hemu's familiarity with firearms from a young age. Constant war among Sher Shah's family members led to decline in agriculture. This, along with the opportunities available for rapid upward mobility in the world of murky power-politics, encouraged Hemu to leave farming for armed service. Recruitment of Hindus was an established practice among the Afghans. Since Afghanistan was under the Mughals, Indian Afghans could no longer recruit soldiers from there. The manpower shortage which the Suri dynasty faced, especially when the Mughals attempted a comeback after the death of Sher Shah, forced them to open the gates of the Afghan army to ambitious Hindus like Hemu. Sher Shah recruited Rajput zamindars from Mungher and Bhojpur. Hemu had no formal training in warfare. His initial entry was, therefore, in the non-combatant branch of the Afghan force. During campaigns, Hindu businessmen known as Modis supplied the Afghan troops. Hemu took employment under one such Modi who used to work for Islam Shah, son of Sher Shah. Hemu proved to be an 'organization man'. Islam Shah promoted him to the post of Superintendent of Market. His job was to ensure supplies to the entire Afghan army. Impressed by his organizational abilities, Islam Shah appointed him as the minister responsible for food and civil supplies. The rapid rise of Hemu under Islam Shah owed something to Islam's fear of Afghan nobility. Islam Shah tried to check the Afghans by promoting Hindus to higher positions. When Islam Shah campaigned against the Niazi chieftains, Hemu was given the additional post of Chief of Intelligence. Islam Shah wanted Hemu to spy on rebellious Afghan nobles. Appointing a Hindu to such a high post had a precedent: even under Sher Shah, a Rajput zamindar from Bihar named Brahmajit Gaur held the same post.

In 1553, Islam Shah was succeeded by Mubariz Khan. Adil Shah, a nephew of Sher Shah, opposed him. Hemu offered his service to the easy-going Adil Shah. In return, Adil Shah appointed Hemu as his Prime Minister. Subsequently, Hemu also became the Commander-in-Chief of the Afghan army. He defeated Sultan Muhammad, the ruler of Bengal, and then Ibrahim Suri, who attempted to ascend the Sur throne. Even Hemu's arch-enemy, Abul Fazl, noted that prior to the Second Panipat, Hemu had fought and won twenty-two battles. By the time Hemu challenged the Mughals under Akbar, he was a veteran of military affairs.

After the death of Humayun, while the Mughals were busy re-establishing their authority in Punjab, Hemu was establishing a base in eastern India. By this time, Hemu was the real power behind the throne of the debauched Adil Shah. Hemu increased his power further by recruiting his own clansmen. For instance, Hemu's nephews Mahipal and Ramaya became generals in the Afghan force. His brother Jujhar Rai became the Governor of Ajmer.

Hemu understood that without an ample supply of cash, soldiers could not be fed and horses and elephants could not be maintained. Elephants were especially costly engines of war. Each elephant required three servants, and cost Rs.33 or so each month for maintenance. In uncertain times, it was dangerous to depend on any *killadar* for a steady supply of cash. While campaigning in the field, Hemu loaded the available treasure on elephants and horses. His logistical system was sophisticated and much in advance of his times. He stopped pillage and plundering by his soldiers to prevent alienating the civil population of rearward areas. Such alienation could lead to security concerns and the necessity of garrisoning. Foraging destroyed the discipline of the soldiers, and the dispersal of the soldiers who had left to search for food, made it impossible for the commander to find them when required. Hemu, therefore, ordered his soldiers to buy provisions with cash. Hemu had captured the famous fort of Chunar in Bihar, and the treasure of this fort along with Hemu's managerial capacity in providing food and money to the soldiers regularly resulted in the Rajputs and the Afghans flocking to his banner.

As the Mughals and Afghans readied for battle, the gods seemed to be angry. The rains failed and the devastation produced by continuous warfare resulted in a famine in the Delhi region during 1556–7. We might speculate that this calamity was partly man-made but became more devastating due to the deleterious effects of the Little Ice Age.

Malnutrition made the populace susceptible to plague. We have Abul Fazl's testimony:

At this time, there was great scarcity in the cities and villages of India, and there was a terrible famine. Though they were finding signs of gold, they could see no trace of corn. Men took to eating one another; some would join together and carry off a solitary man and make him their food.

It is an interesting parallel that during the German siege of Leningrad (1942–3), stories abounded that in desperation, the Russians had become cannibals. With his skill in the management of the grain market, Hemu was still able to feed his war elephants, even at a time when the people of Delhi and Agra were suffering from a shortage of food. The success of Hemu's logistics can be gleaned from the fact that while encamped at Bayana, 50 mi. south-west of starving Agra, he was able to feed his 500 war elephants with rice, sugar and butter. And these elephants were the source of victory in his first encounter with the Mughals. In 1556, the Mughals advanced towards Agra. In response, Hemu moved from Chunar. The stage was set for a climactic confrontation which would decide who would rule Hindustan: the Mughals or the hybrid Afghan-Hindu regime of Hemu.

DARKNESS AT NOON FOR THE MUGHALS

'They advance at a gentle pace, but when they encounter, the strong are as powdered antimony under their feet.'

—ABUL FAZL on Hemu's battle elephants

After Humayun's death, it seemed that a Mughal *Gotterdammerung* was in the offing. The Mughal army was theoretically under the thirteen-year-old Akbar. Akbar the Great was still a young boy. The emperor who was to become the greatest patron of scholars among Mughal kings was not at all interested in reading and writing. Humayun used to reprimand him often. At that time, Akbar's interests were *shikar*, wine and young girls. Bairam Khan, a wily noble, was the de facto ruler of the Mughals. The firepower advantage which Babur enjoyed against the Afghans had vanished by this time: even the Afghans now had firearms. In the non-European world, the Ottoman Turks were the most famed for manufacturing artillery. Both the Afghans and the Mughals copied Ottoman artillery. Hemu's army and the Mughal army were at the same technical level. Hemu advanced with 50,000 cavalry, 1,000 elephants, 51 cannons and 50 falconets. The Afghan force was not only numerically superior but also under veteran Hemu. His army was mostly composed of Afghans, Rajputs and Brahmins from Bihar and Uttar Pradesh. With Hemu's continuous success, the morale of his soldiers had soared.

The Mughal cause seemed hopeless. While Hemu threatened them from the east, Sikander Suri from the Siwalik Hills was causing concern in the west. Sikander was in a position to severe Mughal communication with Kabul. Bairam Khan was forced to divide the much smaller Mughal army into three battle groups. The first battle group was left in Delhi under Tardi Beg Khan to meet Hemu, while Bairam Khan and Akbar with the second battle group went to Punjab to deal with Sikander Suri. Worse was to follow. Muhammad Sulaiman, Akbar's cousin and Governor of Kabul, declared himself independent. Munim Khan, a loyal Mughal *amir* of Akbar was sent with the third battle group to chastise Sulaiman. On 14 February 1556, when Akbar was proclaimed *Padshah* at Kalanaur, ironically, he had no empire to speak of.

Hemu advanced through Gwalior and Agra and reached the outskirts of Delhi. On 7 October 1556, he clashed with the 5,000-strong Mughal detachment under Tardi Beg Khan. The encounter, known as the Battle of Delhi, took place 5 mi. east of the Qutub Minar. The Mughal army was divided into four wings: the vanguard, the centre under Afzal Khan, the right wing under Qasim Makhlis and the left wing under Abdullah Uzbeg. The Mughal vanguard started the action by attacking Hemu's right wing. Rai Husain, the commander of Hemu's right wing was killed, along with 3,000 men. This encouraged the Mughal left wing to advance further. Tardi Beg remained with the centre. The right and left wings of the Mughals attempted the classic Mughals tactic of outflanking and encircling the enemy by attacking and destroying the enemy's wings.

Hemu's tactical novelty was to launch an attack towards the enemy's centre with a select corps of his special troops. They were a sort of suicide corps. It was under his direct command. This body, thrown into battle when the moment seemed opportune to Hemu, was somewhat similar to the Persian Emperor Xerxes' Immortals and Napoleon's Imperial Guards. Meanwhile, Hemu's left and right wings deliberately started retreating in order to entice the Mughal right and left wings to pursue them. At that juncture, when the Mughal centre was separated from their two advancing wings, Hemu launched his select corps consisting of 3,000 horses and 300 elephants against Tardi Beg and drove him out from the battlefield. When the Mughal right and left wings returned to the battlefield, they saw that their centre had been smashed by the charge of Hemu's select corps. The Mughals started retreating from the field of battle. However, Hemu did not pursue the defeated enemy to annihilate them because he thought that the Mughals were deliberately conducting a tactical retreat before launching a counter-attack with their mounted archers. The steppe nomads usually did follow the technique of retreating to encourage the enemy to advance before surrounding him. In reality, the defeated Mughal army at that time was in no position to counter-attack Hemu. Still, the victorious army of Hemu was able to capture 1,000 Arab horses from the retreating Mughals. While Tardi Beg and his forlorn soldiers retreated to Sirhind, Hemu occupied Delhi and started striking coins in his name. At last, he decided to do away with Adil Shah's authority. Hemu crowned himself as Raja Bikramaditya.

When news of this disaster floated back to the Mughal camp in Punjab, most of the Mughals were for going back to Kabul in order to recuperate and reorganize before meeting Hemu. However, Bairam Khan exhibited the will to victory. He took a hard line and executed Tardi Beg for his incompetence. Full of fury, Bairam Khan made an inspiring speech to the army commanders arguing that they must either conquer or perish. His brave words along with the slaying of the defeated commander had an effect on the Mughal soldiery. Bairam Khan gathered all possible soldiers and advanced towards Delhi with an army of 20,000 men. It was to be the final, decisive attack. The Mughals marched down from Jalandhar to Karnal. Almost twenty-nine days after the Battle of Delhi, the Mughals and Hemu clashed again at the historic field of Panipat, 53 mi. from Delhi.

Hemu advanced in three columns. The right wing was under the Afghan Shadi Khan. Hemu's sister's son, Ramaya, a fat Brahmin, commanded the left wing. The centre was under the Rajput, Bhagwan Das (not to be confused with Raja Bhagwan Das, a *Mansabdar* of Akbar). Besides 30,000 Rajput and Afghan cavalry, Hemu possessed 500 war elephants, all heavily armoured with iron cuirasses weighing about 8 *maunds* each. Musketeers and crossbow men were placed on elephant-back. Field Marshal Bernard Montgomery in *The Path to Leadership* writes 'the beginning of leadership is a battle for the hearts and minds of men'. Hemu understood this principle well. Just before joining battle, Hemu distributed treasure and land grants among his soldiers in order to win their affection and to motivate them to fight. In addition, the victory at Delhi had raised the morale of Hemu's soldiers. A confident Hemu started marching from Delhi to meet his foes.

5 NOVEMBER 1556:

ENTER GODDESS FORTUNA

'In warfare slight events can often turn the scales and produce serious reversals.'

—JULIUS CAESAR

Disquieting news reached Hemu's camp just before the battle. Hemu had sent his artillery in advance of the body of his army because the heavy artillery considerably slowed down the marching rate. Moreover, given the lack of good roads and the widespread famine, it was difficult to march with all the soldiers and animals in the army. The carriage elephants that carted artillery were especially voracious eaters. Each such animal consumed about 21.5 *mans* of grain every day.

Fatally, Hemu assigned only a small guard to escort his artillery. After the disaster at Delhi, the Mughals reorganized the *harawal-i-manqula*, which operated as their long-distance advance guard. The best soldiers were put in it and it was sent for deep strikes inside enemy territory. This practice was first instituted by Timur. The Mughal advance guard captured Hemu's artillery. The sudden and rapid advancement by the Mughal advance guard under the leadership of Lal Khan of Badakshan proved to be a decisive tactical move.

However, all was not lost for Hemu. He still had three times the Mughals' cavalry of only 10,000. Sher Shah, a matchless cavalry leader, had defeated the Mughal army twice under Humayun, without any artillery. Hemu himself relied on his war elephants for launching the decisive attack.

The Mughal army had evolved with the passage of time. The Mughal commanders had learned from their past mistakes and strategized keeping in mind Hemu's probable tactics. The Mughal deployment at the Second Battle of Panipat was more complex than Tardi Beg's deployment during the Battle of Delhi. The Mughal contingent of *Altmash* appeared for the first time in their order of battle. It was stationed between the vanguard and the centre in order to prevent isolation of the centre from the advancing vanguard. To put further pressure on the enemy's wings, the right and left wings were strengthened with *uqci* (flank archers). To counter the possibility of an enemy charge against the Mughal centre, the rear guard and the reserve were deployed at a distance at the rear in order to provide support.

The Mughal vanguard along with the right and left wings under Muhammad Qasim (same name as the Arab general who conquered Sind in 710–12 CE), Iskander Khan and Abdulla Khan, respectively, charged Hemu's left and right wings. The Mughals tried to implement their classic *tulghama* tactic of destroying the enemy's flanks and then going into the rear of the army to surround and finally trap the enemy force. Mughal troopers armed with swords were not too eager to charge the big black elephants. Both to the horses and their riders, the enormous beast of Hindustan appeared frightening indeed. Abul Fazl provides a portrait of the emotions of the Mughal soldiery:

The mountain-like and dragon-mouthed elephants, which had been collected by so many Indian rulers. . . . Among them were 500 palmary (sira) elephants, each of them a paragon for swiftness and dexterity. In might and courage they were exemplars. . . . Though the racehorse of Iraq be swift, they could not outstrip those elephants. In truth each one of these famous elephants was capable of disordering a large force. They were especially calculated to confuse the onset of cavalry, as the horses had never seen such terrific forms. How can the attributes of those rushing mountains be strung on the slender thread of words. They ruined lofty buildings by shaking them, and sportively uprooted strong trees. In the hour of battle and contest they lifted up man and horse and flung them into the air.

Muhammad Qasim's horse archers, with their accurate long-distance archery, were able to pick out the fighters seated in the *howdahs*; they also shot continually at the legs of elephants. The Central Asian nomads had used such enveloping tactics in order to trap and capture wild herds of animals in the desolate steppe land. However, the elephants, like the battle tanks of the twentieth century, were able to take a lot of punishment. The arrows from the mounted bowmen made the legs of the elephants look like wasps' nests. Still, the elephants retained their place in the field of battle.

Hemu's tactics at Panipat were similar to his victorious tactics in the Battle of Delhi. His right and left wings conducted a tactical retreat to entice the Mughal left and right wings away from the battlefield. When the Mughal centre under Shah Ali Quli Khan was isolated from the advancing wings of the Mughal army, Hemu launched his select corps against a particular point at the enemy centre with the objective of smashing it. But the Mughals had learned something from the Battle of Delhi. Anticipating Hemu's charge, the Mughals had dug a ditch to protect their centre. However, Hemu's elephants belonging to his select corps were able to cross the ditch. Hemu and his subordinate commanders used big elephants as command vehicles. Each such command elephant had a name to distinguish it from the others. Hemu, not comfortable on horseback, was riding a big black elephant named Hawai. His soldiers drew strength from seeing him high on elephant back. Besides being visible to the ordinary soldiers, in order to keep an eye over the rapidly changing battlefield, an elephant offered an excellent command platform. Though his physique was small, Hemu had a commanding voice and his soldiers were inspired when they heard the orders he barked. From his *howdah*, he shouted and encouraged his select corps to advance. The scene was reminiscent of Paurava riding an elephant and exhorting his men to fight at the battlefield of Hydaspes. The charge of the select corps created panic in the Mughal camp. The Mughal centre was on the verge of collapse. Abul Fazl comments:

Hemu . . . rode proudly on an elephant . . . which was one of his best, and glanced from side to side at the brave swordsmen. . . . Gathering together a band of fierce elephants he showed every stratagem which his powerful capacity could conceive, and every daring deed which lurked in his . . . soul. He made powerful onsets and performed many valorous acts, and dislodged many strenuous soldiers of the sublime army.

Suddenly, an arrow shot by an unknown mounted archer pierced Hemu's right eye. He sank back to the *howdah* in extreme agony. Due to continuous loss of blood, Hemu lost consciousness. The elephant driver tried to take the elephant away from the battlefield. When Shah Ali Quli surrounded this isolated elephant with his contingent, the elephant driver pleaded for his life. In his nervousness, the *mahout* told his captors that it was Hemu in the *howdah*. The Mughal commander could scarcely believe his luck. Hemu was tied up and taken back to the Mughal headquarters in rear of the battlefield.

The absence of Hemu from his towering elephant was noticed some time later by his men. Though victorious, they lost heart. No clear-cut chain of command existed to provide unified leadership after the fall of the Commander-in-Chief Hemu. His soldiers started to flee. Sikander Khan Uzbeg, Commander of the Mughal reserve contingent pursued them till Delhi. The Prussian military theorist Carl von Clausewitz observed in the nineteenth century that real carnage in battle happens only during disorganized retreats. This is what happened now. Bhagwan Das (not to be confused with the Mughal mansabdar Raja Bhagwan Das), Shadi Khan, Ramaya, Mahipal and Hemu's seven brothers as well as his cousins, all died during the confused retreat after Hemu vanished from the field. The field of Panipat was drenched with the blood of 5,000 soldiers. In accordance with the practice of Timur, the Mughals made a pyramid with the skulls of slain enemy soldiers. The Mughals also captured 120 of Hemu's war elephants which provided excellent service when some years later Akbar invaded Gondwana and Bengal.

EXIT, HEMU

Hemu's hands were tied when he was brought before Akbar and Bairam Khan for questioning. On being questioned, he made no reply probably from intense pain as well as shame. Hemu was bound to die due to his fatal wound but on Bairam Khan's orders he was beheaded. His headless trunk was sent to Delhi where it was made to hang from a wooden palisade. This gory sight was a warning to others trying to rebel against the *Padshah*.

In the second encounter at Panipat, unlike the first battle, gunpowder weapons played no significant role. The core of the Mughal army remained horse archers, as in Babur's time. Like Ibrahim Lodhi, Hemu depended on elephants. But rather than Ibrahim's disorganized mob, Hemu had a disciplined army of veterans who had fought several battles under him. According to Akbar's historian Abul Fazl, Hemu's soldiers marched 'in excellent order'. Like Alexander, he was a tactical innovator. He realized that Mughal superiority rested on artillery and horse archery. He copied Mughal artillery and achieved parity at the technological level. However, mounted bowmen of Central Asia were one commodity he could not acquire, since the horse markets of Kabul remained under the loose supervision of the Mughals. Hemu attempted to synthesize the ancient subcontinental tradition of using elephants with the gunpowder technology introduced in the subcontinent by the Mughals. His policy of deliberately enticing the enemy flanks away from their centre by ordering a controlled retreat of his own flanks exhibited not only the troops' discipline, but also high qualities of generalship on his part. The tactic of attacking a particular point of the enemy's centre with a select corps when the enemy's flanks had been separated, was similar to Napoleon's technique of launching the Imperial Guards against an isolated enemy centre at Austerlitz on 2 December 1805. Hemu's generalship was similar to Napoleon's in another way as well. Napoleon used to say that an army marches on its stomach. Attention to the details of feeding soldiers enabled the Corsican military adventurer to traverse Europe at will with his army. Similarly, Hemu's attention to, what in modern terminology is known as Quarter Master General's department, allowed him to criss-cross the subcontinent from Bihar to Punjab swiftly even during a drought and famine.

The Mughal rapid deployment force which moved ahead of the main body of the army and struck deep inside enemy territory deployed a strategy similar to deep penetration by armoured columns, worked out by European military theorists only in the third decade of the twentieth century. This tactic apart, Mughal strategy at the Second Battle of Panipat was not exceptional. Bairam Khan did not appoint an overall Mughal commander for the battle in the fear that even if Hemu was defeated, a powerful Mughal commander might attempt to seize power. Bairam Khan himself did not make any contribution in the battlefield. He was more of a political operator than a *feldherren*.

It was Hitler's belief that since Fortuna was a fickle goddess, a bold man must extract the maximum benefit out of her before she deserted him. At a crucial moment, when the Mughals were losing the battle, luck suddenly deserted Hemu. Both Akbar and Bairam Khan were absent from the battlefield, leaving the fighting to the Mughal *begs*. Yet, Hemu's accidental death caused by the random arrow resulted in an unlikely Mughal victory. Occasionally, history does seem to be the product of a random roll of dice. The accident of 5 November 1556, with the chance it gave Akbar, marked the beginning of the Mughal era.

5

———

Abdali's Organ Pipes

The Third Battle of Panipat,
14 January 1761

IT WAS THE FIRST decade of the eighteenth century. The Mughal Empire was in decline and the Marathas, who had entered the topsy-turvy world of Indian politics under Shivaji in the 1670s, looked as if they were going to succeed the Mughals in founding a pan-Indian empire. But Ahmad Shah Abdali proved to be their nemesis. Ahmad Shah, an Afghan warlord of the Durrani clan, was one of Nadir Shah's greatest generals. Nadir Shah, the ruler of Persia, held that there was no other general of equal capability like Ahmad Shah in Hind, Sindh or Persia. When Nadir Shah died, Ahmad Shah Abdali inherited the eastern part of his dominions. Along with the kingdom, he also inherited Nadir Shah's dream of conquering the Mughals. In 1752, Ahmad Shah conquered Punjab. However, he soon had to leave to meet a threat from the Shah of Persia. Ahmad Shah left his son Taimur Sultan and a general named Jahan Khan with 25,000 troops to guard Punjab.

THE MARATHAS IN THE INDUS

We have already brought Lahore, Multan, Kashmir and other subahs on this side of Attock under our rule for the most part, and places which have not come under our rule we shall soon bring under us. Ahmad Khan Abdali's son Taimur Sultan and Jahan Khan have been pursued by our troops and their troops completely looted. Both of them have now reached Peshawar with a few broken troops. . . . We have decided to establish our rule up to Kandhar.

—RAGHOBA's letter dated 4 May 1758 to the *Peshwa*

The *Peshwa* Balaji Baji Rao, who was the leader of the Maratha confederacy from 1740 onwards thought of himself as the potential dictator of the subcontinent. In his dreary palace at Poona, with his Chitpawan Brahmin advisors, the *Peshwa* made grandiose plans of conquering all of India. In 1753, he ordered his lieutenants to collect two taxes named *chauth* and *sardesmukhi*, from the Mughal provinces of north-west India. At that time, the Marathas dominated many fronts. The Nizam had been humbled. Mysore, Bengal and Orissa were subjected to repeated raids. The Rajput states in western India and the Mughal successor states of Awadh and Rohilkhand lived in fear of Maratha incursions daily.

The *Peshwa* directed his brother Raghunath Rao alias Raghoba to lead the expedition to the Indus. In 1757, Raghoba crossed the Chambal with an army of 50,000 soldiers. By April 1758, Taimur and Jahan Khan had retreated to the west of the Indus. At this critical juncture, the *Peshwa* called Raghoba and most of his troops down to south India to crush the Nizam. Only 15,000 Maratha troops were left in Punjab. The impatient *Peshwa*, not finishing one job completely before initiating another, had miscalculated. Raghoba's recall gave breathing space to Ahmed Shah Abdali. While Abdali was preparing an army to invade India again, he received diplomatic support from the Rohilla leader Najib-ud-Daulah and the Nawab of Awadh, Shuja-ud-Daulah. In Najib and Shuja's reckoning, Abdali was bound to return to Afghanistan after a temporary stay in India. And in the meantime, if Abdali could crush the Marathas, then Najib and Shuja would be saved from paying *chauth* and *sardesmukhi* to them. Abdali advanced and crushed the Maratha forces in Punjab. The ominous news finally travelled deep south.

After defeating the Nizam at Udgir on 3 February 1760, Balaji Baji Rao appointed his cousin Sadashiv Rao Bhau in place of Raghoba to lead an expedition to north India to destroy the Afghan menace once and for all. Raghoba, charged with financial mismanagement during the earlier north Indian expedition, was superseded. His north Indian expedition had resulted in a deficit of Rs.88 lakh for the Maratha exchequer. The Bhau, unlike Raghoba, had no experience of fighting but he started out with a big force from the Deccan.

NEMESIS: PRELUDE TO PANIPAT

'Without supplies neither a general nor a private is good for anything.'

—XENOPHON, Greek military theorist
and commander, 401 BC

There is a saying that when God wants to destroy someone, he first drives that person insane. Sadashiv Rao Bhau, on the eve of his destruction, was not actually mad but had become overwhelmingly arrogant. Before Panipat, the Jat king Suraj Mal advised Bhau:

In the first place, the families of the chiefs and soldiers, the large train of baggage, and the heavy artillery, will be great impediments to carrying on the kind of war which you have now in hand. . . . The Durranis are still more expeditious than you. It is therefore advisable to take the field against them quite unencumbered, and to leave the superfluous baggage and followers on the other side of Chambal, under the protection of Jhansi or Gwalior, which places are under your authority-----In this arrangement, you will have the advantage of a free communication with a friendly country behind you, and need be under no apprehensions respecting supplies to your army; and there is reason to believe that the enemy will not be able to advance so far, but will by this plan of operations be obliged to disperse without effecting anything.

Bhau dismissed Suraj Mal's sage advice as mere the chattering of a Jat zamindar. The Maratha chiefs differed among themselves regarding the combat technique to be adopted against Abdali. While Malhar Rao Holkar wanted to harass Abdali with guerrilla warfare, Bhau was for a pitched battle. Bhau was an admirer of European warfare with its emphasis on disciplined infantry supported by light artillery. The French commander Bussy had trained Ibrahim Khan Gardi (Gardi comes from the French word *Garde)*, a soldier of fortune from south India. Ibrahim had raised an infantry corps armed, equipped and disciplined in the French style for his master, the Nizam. After he left the Nizam and joined the Marathas, Ibrahim's troops played an important role in defeating the Nizam at Udgir (February 1760). This convinced Bhau that Ibrahim's corps could deliver a similar deathblow to Abdali's force. Bhau rushed in towards the north where even an able general like Baji Rao (*Peshwa* from 1720–40) would have feared treading.

After taking Delhi, which was a prestige victory but useless from the strategic point of view, Bhau moved further up to Kunjpura in order to cut Abdali's line of communications with Afghanistan. However, the superiority of Afghan horses ensured that Abdali severed Bhau's line of communications with Delhi instead and hemmed him in from all sides. In desperation, Bhau entrenched himself in the historic field of Panipat. The situation facing the Marathas becomes clear from a letter Sadashiv Rao Bhau wrote to Poona on 16 September 1760. Bhau stated:

The main difficulty is about food. We cannot obtain loans owing to disturbed conditions outside and the presence of the enemy; all banking operations are in abeyance. . . . There is terrible scarcity of provisions in our camp. Relief from outside has become impossible. . . . Abdali is in better condition.

Abdali obtained provisions from Rohilkhand, which was under his ally Najib. Moreover, Abdali had an officer who was solely responsible for distributing provisions among the soldiers.

Towards the end of December 1760, it became clear to Bhau that he needed more troops to meet the Afghan tornado. In the winter of 1760, like Hitler during the December of 1942, the *Peshwa* falsely told his theatre commander Bhau that he was preparing a relief army. Like Field-Marshal Friedrich Paulas in Stalingrad, Bhau too, looked in vain for the arrival of the relief army. It never came. Like Paulas, Bhau was forced into battle under the most adverse circumstances. On the night of 13 January 1761, the Maratha sardars desperate from the lack of provisions for their men and forage for the horses forced Bhau into battle the next day.

A LONG DAY: 14 JANUARY 1761

'Artillery is the God of War.'

—JOSEF STALIN

On the morning of the battle, Abdali was a picture of perfect calm, inspiring confidence among his subordinates. In the dim winter dawn, the forward deployed Afghan horsemen noticed that there was great commotion in the Maratha camp. When the reconnaissance agents brought news that the Marathas were coming forward, Abdali was smoking his hookah. Abdali's personal tent was red in colour and pitched about 2.5 mi. behind the Afghan front line. Shuja came in agitated and told Abdali his informer had reported that the Marathas were preparing for battle. Abdali used a telescope to view the din and bustle in the Maratha camp and then replied in a tone of great tranquility: 'Your servant's news is very true, I see.' Abdali handed his hookah to his aide and then ordered his officers to report to him. He told his officers to fall in line with their respective contingents.

The Afghan army had 41,800 horses and 32,000 Rohilla infantry. Of the cavalry, 28,000 were regulars with proper training and armour. They also had regular pay. The rest of the cavalry was irregular. Once the regulars had broken through the enemy line, the irregulars were supposed to follow the collapsing enemy, fan out and complete the rout. Like Babur, Abdali arranged his line in the shape of a crescent. While his right and left flanks constituted the two horns of the crescent, his centre, drawn inward, formed the curve. The Rohillas under Hafiz Rahmat Khan, Dundi Khan and Banghas Khan formed the extreme right of the Afghan line. They were clan leaders from Rohilkhand who had joined forces with Abdali for the Panipat campaign. In the centre of Abdali's line was the Afghan Wazir Shah Wali Khan. Najib and Shuja's contingents were deployed on the left of the Wazir. In order to keep an eye on Shuja (who had a fence-sitting attitude), Afghan troops under Shah Pasand Khan were placed next to him. Shah Pasand along with Najib and Shuja constituted the Afghan left wing. The *shutarnals*, Abdali's camel-drawn cannons, were placed in front of the line. Like Wellington at Waterloo, Abdali, mounted on his charger, rode along the front and examined all the units. Satisfied, he ordered his troops to attack. Behind the Afghan first line was placed the Afghan reserve corps which was to be used only on a direct order from Abdali.

Bhau's line, following classical Hindu military practice, was a linear formation with three divisions; right, left and centre. The Marathas had 55,000 horses. Of the cavalry, only 11,000 were regulars belonging to the *Peshwa's huzurat*. The *huzurat* derived regular pay from the *Peshwa*. Apart from the *Peshwa's huzurat*, the rest of the Maratha cavalry was made up of irregulars raised, trained and maintained by semi-autonomous chiefs. The contingents of the various commanders are outlined in Table 5.1.

At the extreme left of the Maratha line was placed Ibrahim Khan Gardi's corps of 9,000 sepoys armed with firelocks with 40 cannons. Behind him were placed Damaji Gaekward, Bithal and Jaswant Pawar's 8,000 cavalry. The *Peshwa's huzurat* cavalry was in the centre under Bhau. Malhar Rao Holkar's cavalry was placed in the extreme right. Between Bhau and Holkar was placed Sindia's 10,000 cavalry. All the Maratha troops were placed in the first line. Bhau had no tactical reserve to fall back upon. The 6,000-strong Pindari cavalry was placed at the rear to guard the Maratha camp because they were good only for looting a defeated enemy.

The battle started at 9 a.m. when the Maratha cavalry from the left wing advanced towards the Rohilla infantry opposite them.

TABLE 5.1: Contingents of the Various Maratha Commanders
at Panipat

Chiefs	Cavalry
Huzurat under Bhau	6,000
Huzurat under Bhiswas Rao, (Balaji Baji Rao's seventeen-year-old son and nominal Commander-in-Chief of the Maratha Army)	5,000
Jankoji Sindia	10,000
Balbant Rao (Bhau's advisor and brother-in-law)	7,000
Malhar Rao Holkar	5,000
Damaji Gaekwad	3,000
Samsher Bahadur (Illegitimate son of Baji Rao I)	3,000
Balaji Jadav	3,000
Bithal Shivdeo	3,000
Jaswant Rao Pawar	2,000
Antaji Mankeshwar	2,000
Hul Sewar and Charcory (Pindari Chiefs)	6,000

Before the battle, Bhau and Ibrahim Khan had emphasized that the Maratha cavalry in the left flank of the Maratha line should cooperate with the Gardi infantry. However, Damaji, Bithal and Pawar, the cavalry commanders, were loath to cooperate with the Western-style infantry. In the absence of a coherent and disciplined force under a unified commander, Bhau's control over the various Maratha cavalry commanders was at best, weak. The Maratha commanders disobeyed Bhau's orders and attacked the Rohillas without waiting for the Gardi infantry to come up. But they were not able to achieve much because the Maratha horses were not armoured and were suffering from the lack of provisions. Further, they had been confined in the camp at Panipat for a month. This seemed to have sapped their vitality. Besides, a charge by light cavalry was bound to break against disciplined infantry armed with matchlocks and muskets with supporting firepower generated by the mobile *shutarnals*. The Maratha cavalry was armed with swords and 12ft.-long lances. The ill-disciplined charge was easily broken by the firepower generated from the Rohilla infantry and the *shutarnals*.

After the left wing of the Maratha cavalry retreated, the Gardi infantry advanced. A firefight started between the Rohillas and the Gardi infantry. The French pattern muskets that the Gardi infantry carried were lighter compared to the muskets carried by the Rohillas, who had a long tradition of making muskets. Thanks to the longer range and heavier ammunition of the Rohilla infantry, they were able to inflict greater losses on the Gardi corps. European arms were obviously yet to achieve a definite technological edge over Indian ones. In fact, the superiority of European armies lay in their discipline, tactical doctrine, bureaucratic, logistical apparatus and hierarchical, unified command. Since the Rohillas outnumbered the Gardi infantry, the latter were soon surrounded. It was nearing noon. Ibrahim Khan requested that the Maratha cavalry placed at the left of the Maratha line intervene by charging against the Rohillas. But the Maratha cavalry commanders remembered the morning's defeat and refused to charge. There was a total communication blackout between Bhau and the Maratha left wing.

While things were getting grimmer for the Marathas on their left flank, Bhau decided to launch a charge of his own. Following the tradition of Hindu military leaders from Paurava to Hemu, Bhau commanded from the back of an elephant. He ordered the best of the Maratha cavalry, the *huzurat* corps to charge against the Durrani Wazir. Bhau watched from the back of his elephant which stood under the shade of a mango tree. The battlefield was a scene of deadly confusion. The Maratha cavalry shouting '*Har, Har Mahadev!*' clashed with the Afghan cavalry which came forward with cries of *Din! Din!* The horsemen of both sides moved forward and backward, right and left, as if they were performing a dance with death. Many combatants had fallen from their chargers and were rolling in the dust, locked in a deadly embrace. Nana Phadnis, who was present at Panipat, wrote in his autobiography that the stench from the wounded men and horses was terrible.

Bhau's charge seemed to be succeeding. The Afghans under Wali Khan gave way. Abdali's centre was disintegrating. Abdali's Wazir dressed in full armour dismounted from his horse and tried to stop his retreating soldiers. In an attempt to rally them, he shouted, 'Our country is far off, my friends; whither do you fly?' But it had no effect. A dismayed Wali Khan sat down on the ground and threw dust in his mouth as an act of desperation. He had never liked the campaign in Hindustan and had always advised Abdali against it. Victory seemed within reach of the Marathas. It was now up to Abdali to save the situation.

Clausewitz writes that a great military commander should be able to see clearly through the fog of war. Abdali displayed this capability.

Abdali knew that defeat was only a step away. If the Maratha charge against his centre succeeded, his field army would be defeated. The Rohillas might give up the struggle and Shuja might turn against him. He was about one thousand kilometres away from his home. He had to act quickly. If the Marathas broke through Wali Khan's rapidly disintegrating centre then Abdali's camp would be in serious danger. Abdali ordered the women of his household to get on horseback ready for escape.

Once the battle started, Bhau lost all control over the various subdivisions of his army. If Bhau had coordinated his charge against Wali Khan with the advance of the Gardi infantry in the morning, then the situation would have been much nastier for Abdali. To be fair to Bhau, the Maratha confederacy at the stage was like the Rajput confederacy. Bhau like Prithviraj Chauhan could not exercise strict control over the semi-autonomous chiefs not the different contingents of the sardars had trained collectively. In contrast to Bhau, Abdali kept tight control over his various units scattered throughout the length and depth of the battle zone. The Durrani units were scattered along a distance of seven miles. Abdali kept himself informed about the situation in all the units through *hircarrahs*. He used post-camels to send orders to his various commanders. Abdali's post-camels were equivalent to the Duke of Wellington's staff officers' mounted on horses moved to and fro throughout the battlefield carrying the Iron Duke's orders amidst the firefight at Waterloo.

Instead of panicking, Abdali ordered his 2,000 *nasaqchis* to the front. About 500 of them were sent to reinforce the Rohillas fighting the Gardi infantry. The remaining 1,500 were sent to Wali Khan's sector. The *nasaqchis* were equivalent to the Red Army's police battalions during World War II who executed stragglers openly and in cold blood. The *nasaqchis'* execution of some of the fleeing Afghan soldiers forced Wali Khan's retreating soldiers back into line. It was 1 p.m., and Abdali had stabilized the situation. The sun had already crossed its high water mark. Bhau's charge had been partially successful but failed to destroy the Afghan centre. Bhau had no more fresh troops to rely upon but Abdali still had fresh troops at his disposal. The turning point of the battle had been reached and Abdali decided to exploit it fully.

The Afghan centre went into the offensive. Wali Khan received a reinforcement of 8,000 troops from Abdali to begin a fresh attack on Bhau. Meanwhile, Najib's infantry moved forward in a north easterly direction and started a flanking attack against the Maratha centre. Faced with a frontal and flank attack, the Maratha centre imploded.

Among the many errors the Marathas made, an important one was their heavy guns, modelled after Mughal guns. The Mughals heavy guns were each dragged by more than fifty bullocks. Such guns were of some use in siege warfare in blasting the walls of a fort but were almost useless in battle. Their mobility in the fluid scenario of a battle was minimal. These guns could fire only once. Such guns were so heavy that when the enemy advanced, they could not be pulled back, and as a consequence, they overshot. Abdali rejected such guns, relying instead on *shutarnals* which were first used in India by Nadir Shah during the Battle of Karnal against the Mughals in 1737. The Durrani army had 200 such camel swivel guns. Also known as *zamburaks*, these guns were later adopted by Ranjit Singh. Each was carried on the back of a Bactrian camel. The gunner sat on the camel alongside the driver. The driver was also armed with a musket, and when not driving, the drivers also took pot shots at the enemy. The Bactrian camels to which Abdali had access had legendary endurance and stamina, and of course, a camel could travel faster and longer than a bullock. So, the *shutarnals* were mobile and in the heat of the battle, Abdali sent them to create gaps at certain points along the Maratha line. Fresh cavalry was inserted through the gaps. These guns slaughtered the Marathas who were getting confined within a smaller and smaller area. At around 2 p.m., Vishwas Rao was struck dead by a cannon ball. This further lowered Maratha morale. Bhau decided to make a last-ditch stand. Though not a great tactician, like Paurava, he was brave.

Holkar, an opportunist who seemed to have been struck by cold feet throughout the battle, decided to leave the field at around 3 p.m. Seeing Holkar leaving, the Maratha cavalry behind the Gardi corps also retreated. The Rohillas in the right wing of the Afghan line had already surrounded the Gardi units and now they got their chance to destroy them. By 3.30 p.m., the Rohillas, having finished the Gardis, attacked the left flank of Bhau. At the same time, Wali Khan pressed from the front into the Maratha centre even as Najib attacked Bhau's right flank. The rout was complete when Shah Pasand Khan advanced through the gap created by Holkar's retreat and attacked the Maratha centre from the rear. Thus developed a battle which in the nineteenth-century German General Staff's military terminology is categorized as

Kesselschlacht (cauldron/pocket battle). Bhau's centre was surrounded from all sides just as the Roman centre was surrounded from all sides by Hannibal at the Battle of Cannae in 216 BC. Abdali completed the Maratha defeat by sending in a corps of 4,000 mounted archers. Just before 4 p.m., when Bhau still had a band of 200 Maratha horsemen around him, an Afghan trooper cut off his head. All Maratha resistance ceased. Two more hours of daylight and a bright moonlit night allowed the Afghans to kill whatever Maratha stragglers remained.

PARALLEL HISTORY: ATTRITIONAL WARFARE
BY THE MARATHAS

In a set piece battle, the Maratha army was no match against the Afghan force. If Holkar had remained in the battlefield, the Maratha defeat would have been delayed but not averted. Abdali's army was more firepower-heavy compared to the Marathas. The *shutarnals*, which were shaped like organ pipes, were the biggest killers in the battlefield. Both in artillery and hand-held firearms, the Afghans had an edge. In the close quarter combat which raged between 9 a.m. and 4 p.m., the Marathas were at a disadvantage. In contrast to the semi-feudal, ill-disciplined and ill-equipped Maratha cavalry, Abdali's cavalry not only exercised regularly, but was much more disciplined and well organised. Like Alexander's Companion Cavalry, the Durrani regular cavalry was organized into well-defined units. Abdali deployed twenty-four *dastas* which were equivalent to regiments. Each *dasta* contained 1,200 horsemen. Of these *dastas*, 6, known as *koleran*, were made of elite slave soldiers. They wore full armour and constituted Abdali's shock troops.

It is as if the Marathas had learned nothing from the history of warfare. Like Paurava and Prithvi Raj Chauhan, Bhau had no tactical reserve. But Abdali, like Babur, kept a reserve force of select horsemen. He launched them at strategic moments. For example, launching his tactical reserve against the Maratha centre at Panipat at an opportune moment generated immense psychological gains for Abdali.

Ahmad Shah's superiority in pitched battle could have been negated if the Marathas had conducted their traditional *ganimi kava*, or guerrilla warfare, in Punjab and in north India. Abdali was in no position to maintain his field army in India indefinitely. The Shah of Persia posed a threat to Abdali's western frontier. Some local clan leaders who received the support of the Shah of Persia challenged Abdali's rule in Afghanistan. The Sikhs were harassing the Afghans in Punjab by continually severing their lines of communication. The Marathas could have established a strategic alliance with the Sikhs to cut Abdali's lines of communication which stretched from Kandhar to Kurukshetra.

But it was difficult for Bhau to implement such a strategy. According to an eyewitness report about Bhau's army, 'Lofty and spacious tents, lined with silks and broadcloths . . . vast numbers of elephants, flags of all descriptions, the finest horses, magnificently caparisoned . . . cloth of gold was the dress of the officers, and all seemed to vie in that profuse and gorgeous display.'

The ominous contrast with Shivaji's slim and trim army is evident. To conduct a gruelling guerrilla war, Bhau needed to have trimmed his army. On no account should Bhau have taken along 2 lakh non-combatants with his field army. At Panipat, when the Marathas faced a severe scarcity of provisions, the presence of huge number of camp followers merely added to their woes. If Bhau had left the non-combatants at the fort of Gwalior, far away from the theatre of war, he would have been better able to feed his army and move quickly from place to place.

One could argue that Maratha guerrilla warfare which had succeeded against the lumbering Mughal army of Aurangzeb among the hilly fastness of the Deccan may not have succeeded against the Afghans in the plains of north India. The Afghans riding on Turki horses could outride and outmanoeuvre the Maratha ponies. After all, before Panipat, Saha Pasand Khan rode a hundred miles in twenty-four hours, and surprised Holkar's force. Attai Khan had performed an equally daring feat in December 1760 against Govind Ballabh Pant who, with 12,000 Maratha horsemen, was trying to ravage the Gangetic doab from where Abdali's army, situated at Panipat, was drawing its supply.

At Panipat, the Marathas faced one of the best generals of eighteenth-century Asia while their *Peshwa*, Balaji Baji Rao, was among the most inept they had ever had. His father, *Peshwa* Baji Rao I, had been a great cavalry leader. Baji Rao I understood that in a battle, the small Maratha ponies were no match against hardier and bigger horses bred in Afghanistan. When Nadir Shah invaded the Mughal Empire, despite the Mughal *Padshah* Muhammad Shah's plea to Baji Rao I, he refused to cross sword with the Persian army at the Battle of Karnal in 1737.

Baji Rao I followed the policy of 'wait and watch' by deploying his army along the river Chambal. After defeating the Mughals, Nadir Shah returned and Baji Rao I entered north India and established Maratha rule in that region.

It was all the more important for Balaji Baji Rao to follow his father's wait and watch policy because by 1750, the Marathas were suffering from strategic overextension. The East India Company was becoming powerful in southern and eastern India. The Nizam was still a force to reckon with in central India. Instead of husbanding his forces and concentrating them for a final clash with the Company, Balaji Baji Rao gambled his field army to fight a threat which was not even permanent. Balaji Baji Rao was neither a military leader like his father Baji Rao I, nor a diplomatic genius like the first *Peshwa*, Balaji Viswanath (1713–20). Balaji Baji Rao could not win over Abdali's Indian allies. Nor could he launch long-range cavalry raids like Baji Rao I. He was a man of ease and pleasure, who even at an advanced age, was more taken up with affairs of the heart rather than those of the state. Even as his army battled enormous odds in Panipat, the *Peshwa* was otherwise occupied. Agents travelled throughout the Deccan in search of a suitable bride for him. In the cold of December 1760, as his soldiers were starving and freezing in Panipat, the *Peshwa* consummated his second marriage with much fanfare at Paithan.

CONSEQUENCES

About 15,000 Rohillas and 5,000 Afghans were killed and wounded at Panipat. Among the Marathas, 30,000 died in the battlefield. Another 10,000 died while retreating. About 10,000 were reported missing. And about 50,000 hapless Maratha camp followers, both men and women, were slaughtered in cold blood or sold to slavery. Of the *Peshwa's* grand army only 11,000 fear-stricken troops were able to take refuge at the fort of Gwalior. In a span of seven hours, the Marathas had lost everything they had gained in seventy years. After being defeated by Abdali, they retreated behind the Chambal.

The only positive effect of the battle was that the Maratha confederacy was able to get rid of the inefficient and incompetent Balaji Baji Rao. He died either of a cerebral haemorrage or a heart attack. In fact, Balaji Baji Rao could be categorized as the last victim of Panipat. In the long run, the real beneficiaries of this battle were the British. They silently absorbed Arcot and Bengal. It was left to the ill-fated Shuja-ud-Daulah to check them. The Third Battle of Panipat was important in other respects also. This battle was decided neither by the charge of elephants nor by horse archers. Rather, artillery and gunpowder infantry significantly altered the texture of the combat. These were the two arms that would dominate the global military landscape at least till the First World War. The Third Battle of Panipat, therefore, marked a definite break from medievalism and the beginning of modern warfare in South Asia.

6

Red Phoenix Rising

Buxar, 23 October 1764

FROM A MARGINAL trading power, the East India Company became a powerful political force in the eighteenth century. One battle that transformed the 'nation of traders' occupying coastal enclaves in Bengal and the Deccan to an ever-expanding imperial power in South Asia, was Buxar. Racial superiority, as claimed by the imperial historian G.B. Malleson, did not win the British this battle. It was the technological and managerial superiority of the Company that destroyed its opponents.

THE EUROPEAN MIRACLE

'The invention of gunpowder and the constant improvement of firearms are enough in themselves to show that the advance of civilisation has done nothing practical to alter or deflect the impulse to destroy the enemy, which is central to the very idea of war.'

—CARL VON CLAUSEWITZ

Till 1500, Europe compared badly with Asia in terms of demographic, economic and military resources. Through the Middle Ages, Norse, Magyar and Arab hordes assailed the West. However, after 1500, Europe was not only able to push the invaders back, it also started expanding. This, in turn, generated a surplus military cum economic power that sustained the momentum of expansion. By 1800, Europe had taken over about 35 per cent of the world's landmass. This success can be attributed to a radical transformation in all spheres: political, economic and military. Historians still debate whether the military transformation of the West was revolution or evolution. However, none can deny the decisive impact of the European military activities on the non-Western world.

The military transformation of European countries had many aspects. First, after 1700, as the Ottoman navy declined, the Portuguese, Dutch, French and British navies entered the fray. Europe was able to construct ocean-going ships with stronger rigging and caulking. These warships carrying iron guns were easily able to destroy the Arab dhows and Chinese junks in the Indian Ocean. The Mughals had no navy worth mentioning. Aurangzeb's Abyssinian Admiral, Siddi Janjira, could not cope even with the coastal navy of the Marathas under their Admiral Kanhoji Angre. By the first decade of the eighteenth century, the Maratha navy too was in shambles. In a daring amphibious operation, the Company's *paltans* from the Bombay Presidency captured the bases of the Maratha navy in the hilly regions of the Konkan coast. Having conquered the sea, the Europeans were able to efficiently transport their manpower to critical points and use the firepower of heavy naval guns against their enemies. Before the advent of the internal combustion engine in the early twentieth century, water transport was the cheapest and quickest way of transporting military stores.

To guard their enclaves at Bengal, Bombay, and Madras, the Company raised the Bengal, Bombay and Madras armies. Just before fighting the Nawab of Awadh, who threatened the British force under Major John Carnac in Bihar in 1764, the British were able to bring in reinforcements through judicious use of sea power. In March 1764, the British agents at Fort William informed their superiors in London, 'We have thought it necessary to request Commodore Tinker to remain with us in the Medway . . . we are sending to the army by the assistance of Bombay Detachment and the marines of his Majesty's ships, Medway and Argo.'

Even the European technique of combat on land underwent a metamorphosis. Lance-wielding cavalry was replaced by firearms-equipped infantry. Instead of aristocrats mounted on their chargers, the common mass armed with muskets dominated the battlefield. This resulted in the 'proleterianization of warfare'. The induction of the general populace resulted in an expansion of the size of armies, and the ever-expanding armies needed to be fed, clothed and armed. Gustavus Adolphus, the King of Sweden in the 1630s, increased the effectiveness of his infantry by adding light field guns. Large armies, firearms and artillery were all costly. The increasingly bureaucratic, centralized states had to intervene more and more in the economic sphere. The result was a symbiosis between capitalism and the new militaries which in turn gave rise to military-fiscal polities.

Further, competition between the various European polities resulted in the production of newer forms of weapon systems. By contrast, arms production in Mughal India was concentrated in the government *karkhanas*, which were subsidized and had no incentive to update their products. In the West, the demand-supply factor and the operation of a free market economy gave rise to innovative new products. Thus, while the Occident could come up with yet more ingenious killing machines at short notice, the Orient, after the lapse of a certain period, were only able to produce crude imitations of European products. This is a tradition that largely continues even today.

The use of newer arms required better fire control which made continuous training and discipline necessary. In the 1590s, Maurice of Nassau, a Dutch prince, organized the European infantry into battalions which were further subdivided into companies. Given their more lethal firearms, the infantry was thinned out over a wider space. This resulted in lengthening the battlefield. It was now necessary to delegate command to men whose life's vocation was war. They were trained in special military academies and undertook the theoretical study of warfare. The emergence of the professional officer cadre completed the transformation of ground war in the West. And when the Western maritime powers brought these revolutionary techniques of war-making into the extra-European world, the result was catastrophic for non-Western peoples.

THE BEAST IN THE EAST

By the 1740s, the beast of modern warfare had been unleashed in India. However, the Company lacked adequate British military manpower. It competed with the British army in procuring recruits from Britain. Even when they found recruits, the hard-won white males, when deployed in the subcontinent, died in large numbers from disease and the effect of the sun. The Company hit upon the idea of raising 'black' or 'native' infantry for service in India. Such troops were called sepoys. The Company recruited Indian Christians, Rajputs and Bhumihars as soldiers. Most of the recruits came from Bihar and the Coromandel Coast. The troops were armed with muskets and were taught Western drill and discipline. Being paid regularly in cash, they remained loyal to their white masters.

An army marches on its stomach and on its boots. In the winter of 1941, at Leningrad, for example, many German soldiers in leather boots fell to frostbite because the German high command had not provided enough straw-filled boots. The Company's military bureaucrats did not forget such mundane but militarily essential items. In one letter, the Company's bureaucrats in London stated: 'In regard to the 5000 pair of shoes desired for the military, as they appear to us very essential for the preservation of our soldiers' health, we have ordered 3000 pairs being as many as could be conveniently sent in ships.' Dressed in their red coats like British soldiers, the *lal paltans* of the Company became the most dreaded representatives of the British Lion in the East, well-equipped, well-trained, well-disciplined and well-armed.

While the Marathas were tying themselves in knots in a shadow duel with the Afghans and the Rohillas, the British steadily expanded their dominion in east India. After the death of the octogenarian Aurangzeb, the last great Mughal ruler, the three provinces of Bengal, Bihar and Orissa became autonomous under a Subadar who took the title of Nawab. The British were interested in these provinces for saltpetre, a crucial ingredient in manufacturing gunpowder. The saltpetre acquired from Bihar not only supplied the Company in Bombay and Madras but also London. In September 1764, Fort William assured the Company directors in London:

Notwithstanding the troubles in Bihar, we have the pleasure to acquaint you that our investment of saltpetre will fall very little deficient. As therefore with the remains of last year and, what we receive from Purneah, we shall have on hand a large stock of that article, we have determined to supply Fort St. George with ten thousand and Bombay with thirty thousand *maunds*, and we have begun to freight the supply for Bombay round on country ships that it may arrive with them early in the season.

Rulers in India woke up to the advent of firepower weapons soon enough. The Nawab of Bengal, Siraj-ud-Daulah, employed 200 Portuguese gunners before advancing against the Company. Imitating British military organization, the Nawabs of Bengal and Awadh also employed infantry armed with matchlocks and muskets. However, the technique of volley firing—firing simultaneously for greater impact—was yet to be mastered by Nawabi armies. Professional non-commissioned officers who were essential for implementing small unit tactics was crucial for maintaining volley fire and then launching an infantry charge with bayonets against the enemy force. One structural weakness of the Nawabi armies was that they lacked adequate number of professional non-commissioned offciers. In February 1760, during the Battle of Patna, Major Caillaud's infantry was able to stop a cavalry charge by the wandering Mughal *Padshah* Shah Alam II at 40 yards range, by volley firing. A bayonet charge by the infantry completed the demolition of the Mughal troops. Despite the repeated failure of cavalry charges against infantry armed with muskets and supported by artillery, Indian military leaders and their political masters continued to overemphasize the role of cavalry. This was due partly to historical tradition and partly to the interests of certain powerful social groups.

Historically, most of the battles in India before the advent of the Europeans were decided by cavalry encounters. Most cavalry commanders were members of the nobility. Their great political power and lavish lifestyles were founded on the cavalry contingents they maintained. They lacked the aptitude to learn new musketry skills and acquire technological know-how concerning artillery. Foreign military experts were available, but they proved to be disloyal as well as expensive. Indian princes, nevertheless, appointed several such foreign military experts—who soon emerged as alternate sources of power, threatening their princely employers. Further trouble was caused by the rivalry between local nobility and foreign military entrepreneurs for the ruler's scarce resources. This hampered cooperation between the cavalry under traditional aristocrats and contingents under foreign mercenary commanders. For instance, in 1757 at Plassey, the cavalry under Siraj-ud-Daulah's loyal commander Mir Madan did not cooperate with the infantry under the French commander St Frais, with unhappy consequences.

The astonishing success of the Company in Bengal can be attributed not only to Western arms but also to the Company's judicious synthesis of Indian resources with Western techniques. The sections to follow will show how.

FALSE HOPE

'As the surest means of deterring as well Shuja-ud-Daulah as all others from attempting to disturb the peace of the provinces, we keep our whole army on the banks of the Karamanasa and the President has wrote repeatedly to Shuja-ud-Daula that we shall never accede to any treaty of alliance or friendship with him until Mir Qasim is either delivered or brought to justice.'

—FORT WILLIAM to the Court of Directors in London,
20 February 1764

After the Third Battle of Panipat, the defeated Marathas retreated south of the Chambal and the victorious Abdali left India. Shuja-ud-Daulah, the debauched Nawab of Awadh, became by default the most powerful potentate in the Ganga-Jamuna doab. Shuja's courtiers broke into his habitual orgiastic idyll to inform him of the unsettled conditions in Bengal where the East India Company was bringing one puppet Nawab after another to the throne. Inflated with undeserved self-confidence and overweening arrogance, Shuja decided to add the ex-Mughal Bengal Subah to his own dominions. The stateless Mughal prince Shah Alam II alias Ali Gauhar also joined Shuja. That a claimant to the Mughal throne had joined his party inflated Shuja's ego. Shah Alam had been defeated by Company troops at Patna about four years before and he tried warning his new ally about the lethal *lal paltan*, but the confident Shuja paid no attention. He was to regret it.

As Shuja advanced slowly towards Bihar in the traditional style with elephants and a cavalcade he received an unexpected guest, the ex-Nawab of Bengal, Mir Qasim. In the summer of 1763, Qasim, annoyed by continuous British interference in his internal administration, had rebelled and was defeated at the Battle of Undwa Nullah (5 September 1763). After Qasim's defeat, the British made Mir Jafar Nawab of Bengal and Qasim retreated to Awadh looking to Shuja for help in recovering his lost Nawabi. However, Shuja divested Qasim of his wealth and kept him a virtual prisoner. With this ill-gotten wealth, he bought over a German mercenary, Walter Reihardt (nicknamed Samru), who was commanding a Western style infantry brigade in Qasim's force. Shuja now had a mixed army. Besides Rohilla and Afghan cavalry, he deployed 5,000 naked faqirs. They were Nagas and Gosains who constituted a suicide corps. Only a third of Shuja's 44,000 strong army was somewhat trained. The rest was a rabble that moved without any discipline, and men, horses, bullocks, camels and elephants all mixed together without any order. It was a picturesque army fit for an anthropological study but not for deadly combat. Near Patna, Shuja's advance guard confronted the Company's army which was pursuing Qasim from Bardhaman. On 3 May 1764, Shuja's rag-tag force battled the Company's troops. His 44,000 soldiers were soundly defeated by 1,000 Europeans and 6,000 sepoys. The indisciplined charge by the faqirs proved to be useless against the firepower and bayonets of the Company's infantry. Slightly chastened, Shuja retreated to Buxar.

23 OCTOBER 1764: THE TRIUMPH OF MODERNITY

'Infantry formed in line should be in two ranks.'

—NAPOLEON BONAPARTE

Shuja prepared for a final showdown at Buxar. The left flank of his army was positioned on the bank of the Ganga and the right flank at the village of Buxar. At the centre were two brigades: that of Samru and another European military mercenary named Madoc. Seeing the performance of the Afghan cavalry under Abdali during the Third Battle of Panipat, Shuja had hired 5,000 Afghan horse troopers who were on the right wing alongside the Rohillas under Raja Beni Bahadur, the ruler of Benaras. The left wing was composed of cavalry under Ghulam Qadir and Kuli Khan. Behind the frontline, Shuja positioned a reserve cavalry. He himself took position on the right of his line.

The total force of the Company amounted to 857 Europeans and 5,297 sepoys; there were also Mir Jafar's 918 cavalrymen and 28 guns. The Company's troops were organized in two lines. Each line was composed of several infantry battalions and every battalion had three, six and twelve-pounder guns attached to it for integral fire support. An infantry battalion had about 900 soldiers which were further subdivided into companies of 100 men each. At the two extreme ends of the first line, were placed 2 sepoy regiments. British infantry was deployed between the sepoy regiments at the flanks. Major Pemble commanded the second line, composed of 200 men of the Bengal

European Battalion at the centre. Its flanks were guarded by 2 sepoy battalions. Heavier 26-pounder guns required for long-range firing were placed in the second line. The second line's function was to fill any gap which might appear in the first line from enemy pressure. The British camp stood behind the second line. Four sepoy companies and Mir Jafar's cavalry guarded it.

At about 9 a.m., the guns at the centre of Shuja's force started a desultory firing. Since Shuja had been at Panipat, he realized the necessity of artillery in battering the enemy from a long distance. Shuja was following Mughal military practice in which the cannonade was followed by a cavalry charge. He had 47 brass guns and 63 iron guns which were capable of firing cannonballs of about 6 to 8 ounces. But Shuja's artillery was not that effective. Most of his guns were of Mughal style, which, compared to Afghan artillery, had already proved obsolete during the Third Battle of Panipat. Imitating Abdali, Shuja also deployed some *zamburaks*. But in range and precision, they were inferior to the field artillery pieces deployed by the Company.

Shuja's artillery, such as it was, did not fire for long. The Company's infantry, after firing a volley, advanced and captured Shuja's guns along with 120 *maunds* of gunpowder and 752 iron shots. At this point, Shuja's Afghan cavalry threatened the British left flank. In parade ground fashion, the two British infantry lines formed a square, the corners of which were protected by field guns. The Company's order of battle prefigured Wellington's at Waterloo (18 June 1815) when his infantry formed a square against the charge of Napoleon's dragoons. From the infantry square poured forth musketry fire supplemented by grape shots from the field guns. Shuja's reserve cavalry attempted to attack the rear of the British lines but were beaten off by infantry forming squares.

Despite their numerical inferiority, the thin red line held. The staunchness of the *paltans* in both attack and defence was an outcome of their superior command system. When a British officer died or was wounded, the hierarchical command structure ensured that the next officer took over, thus maintaining a seamless line of command in the battlefield. Most of the Company's British officers were trained at the military academy at Woolwich. For small unit leadership, which meant commanding 10–25 men, the Company trained many Indian soldiers as Jemadars and Subedars. They were equivalent to European armies' non-commissioned officers.

In contrast, there was no designated hierarchical command structure in Shuja's force. Kuli Khan, from Shuja's left flank, attacked the Company's infantry stationed at the right wing of the British line. His troopers advanced with shouts of '*maro maro*'. They were received by a volley from the Company's infantry. The first line of Company infantry fired and then knelt to reload their muskets. Meanwhile, the second line of infantry began firing. As they knelt to reload, the first line stood upright and fired again. The firing was thus, relentless and continuous. Quli Khan fell from his horse wounded. There was no designated commander to take his place. Within ten minutes the horsemen, without any directing head, were demoralized and retreated with shouts of '*bhago, bhago*'.

By about 12 p.m., Shuja's much vaunted army was in full flight. The infantry brigades of Madoc and Samru hardly put up a stubborn fight. As mercenaries, they lived up to popular reputation: as soon as they saw Shuja's force was in trouble, they left the battlefield. Soon after the battle, Samru took service with the Maratha chieftain Mahadji Scindia. The victorious *paltans* pursued Shuja's army, but for only 2.5 mi., as the Awadh force was crossing the Tora nullah, Shuja blew up the three hundred yard long bridge. This prevented the complete destruction of Shuja's force. Nevertheless, many of Shuja's men were drowned in the stampede.

The decisive force of firepower triumphed over numbers at Buxar. This is evident from comparing the casualties of the two armies. In the British 96th Infantry Regiment, three were killed and four wounded. In the Company's two European regiments (Bombay Detachment and the Bengal Battalion), only 4 were killed and 26 wounded. Another 5 were killed and 5 wounded in the British cavalry. The artillery suffered 20 killed and 7 wounded. Another 7 British soldiers whose regiments could not be identified were also wounded. In all, 32 British soldiers were killed and 49 wounded. Among the sepoys, there were 677 killed or wounded. Around 69 of Mir Jafar's cavalrymen attached with the Company were casualties. The British and Indian cavalry attached to the Company lost 112 horses. With a loss of 827 men, the Company's army had been able to massacre 2,000 and wound 4,000 men in Shuja's army.

COULD IT BE DIFFERENT?

> 'They [Shuja] crossed the Ganges and marched to Karamanasa with a very numerous army both of horse and foot; but their principal strength consisted in the number and goodness of the cavalry.'
>
> —FORT WILLIAM to the Court of Directors, 27 September 1764

One wonders what would have happened if Shuja, instead of attacking the British in 1764, had waited for a few more years, and brought a bigger army into the field? The Company knew that its superiority rested on the possession of gunpowder and gunpowder weapons. Fort William had emerged as the arsenal of the East. For years before Buxar, the British had been stocking muskets, flints, and many barrels of gunpowder in the event of conflict with 'country powers'. Just after Buxar, to guard against any future trouble, Fort William demanded 6,000 bayonets and 2,00,000 flints from London. The Company's members at the Calcutta Council realized that gunpowder imported from Europe deteriorated from damp on the long sea journey. The decision makers in London wrote to Fort William on 15 February 1765:

We must therefore again recommend the improvement of this manufacture as a point of great importance to us, hoping you will in time bring it to such perfection as to render it unnecessary, if possible, to send any powder from hence, which besides the room taken up in our ships, exposes them to great danger. As we are informed Mr. Walton who now proceeds to you is thoroughly experienced in the manufacture of this article.

By 1766, eighteen-pounder brass guns were being cast at Fort William. With British artillery improving, Shuja was actually running against time and a waiting game would not have helped. While the Company perfected its war machinery, it is unlikely that Shuja would have used that time to hone his. Additionally, while the military effectiveness of the Company's army in India was increasing, the directors of the Company in London were anxious to prevent Indian rulers modernizing their armies. Their Calcutta counterparts were forbidden from selling the lead necessary for making shots to Indian rulers. Given the high profit margins, several Europeans merchants from Calcutta smuggled arms in country boats. The Calcutta members of the Company were ordered to prevent this.

Shuja could have struck in February 1764 when the Company's army deployed on the bank of the Karamanasa was rocked by a mutiny. They demanded more money from the British stooge Mir Jafar. The British position was extremely vulnerable at that time. However, with his ineffective military intelligence, Shuja knew nothing about this mutiny, which was quelled when Jafar and Captain Jennings agreed to pay Rs.20 to each British soldier. By March 1764, Major Carnac had brought the situation under control.

In a straight fight Shuja had no chance of winning. Cavalry was predominant in Shuja's force. He failed to realize that the European military transformation had reduced the effectiveness of cavalry in pitched battles. Shuja should have recruited greater numbers of Rohillas, who had a tradition of fighting on foot with firearms; they should have been organized in brigades with the aid of mercenary European military entrepreneurs. Strategic alliances with Maratha chiefs like Mahadji Sindia and the Raja of Berar could have helped Shuja too.

The *lal paltans* were superior but not omnipotent. In a war with an Awadh-Maratha alliance the Company would have fought Shuja's Rohilla infantry as well as Maratha cavalry. Cavalry remained useful for conducting long-range raids and remained a realistic option for such raids till the advent of aeroplanes and lorries during the First World War. The Maratha cavalry, by conducting deep raids into Bengal and Bihar, would have threatened British supply lines. Even Shuja's cavalry, though useless in a firefight within the confined space of a battlefield, would have been good for conducting raids far behind the British lines. Till the 1770s, the Company lacked an adequate cavalry force to guard their dominions against long-range raids by the Marathas. Destructive cavalry raids in Bengal by the Maratha light cavalry allied with Shuja would have dislocated the principal revenue base of the EIC. Then, the Company would have been hard pressed to maintain its military forces in Bihar. Just after Buxar, the British managers of the Company warned their superiors in London:

We have also found it absolutely necessary from the experience of the last campaign to keep in our service a body of horse sufficient to secure our army against the distresses to which they must otherwise be exposed by the cavalry of the enemy. One or two troops of European cavalry will by no means answer this purpose. . . . Two or three thousand good country horses may be so disposed under the conduct of European officers as effectually to cover our army from being alarmed, and harassed, although the number of the enemy may exceed tenfold.

THE BUXAR EFFECT

The Battle of Buxar lasted three hours but with it, the disintegration of the 300-year-old Mughal Empire acquired great momentum. Bengal, the richest province of Mughal India, was now securely in British hands. It was Bengal, which by sending an annual revenue of a crore of rupees, had financed Aurangzeb's war in the Deccan. After Buxar, the revenues from Bengal financed the Company's expansionist moves throughout the subcontinent. Between 1757 and 1766, the Company extracted 28 million sterling from the Bengal exchequer. The British war with Haidar Ali, their two wars with his son Tipu Sultan, and the war with the Marathas in the 1780s, was financed by the Company's collection of 6 million sterling from Bengal. Besides military expenditure, the revenues from Bengal even financed the Company's trade with China.

Shah Alam became a penniless fugitive, dependent on British generosity and whim as the Company did not sign any substantial treaty with him. Shuja, the Wazir of the Mughal Empire, was thoroughly humbled having lost Kora and Allahabad to the Company. Some in the Company's Calcutta Council urged the annexation of the whole region up to Delhi. Instead, under Clive's leadership, a treaty was signed with Shuja that for all practical purposes made him a roi fainèant. Though Shuja was shown outward decorum the British Resident became the de facto ruler of Awadh. Out of Shuja's revenues, the British government maintained a force commanded by British personnel to guard the Company's western frontier. The Company also started recruiting Brahmins and Rajputs from southern Awadh for the Bengal army. This army propelled the continual expansion of the British-Indian empire. The Company's infantry-artillery combine became the model for India, just as Frederick the Great's Prussian army had become the model for Europe. However, the British were to fight many more battles before achieving subcontinental supremacy. The Marathas were already reviving in the Deccan plateau under their indefatigable leader Mahadji and further south, Haidar Ali was gathering strength.

7

The Tiger Caged

The Siege of Seringapatam, 4 May 1799

'It is better to live for a day as a tiger, than live as a sheep for a life time.'

—TIPU SULTAN

ON THE AFTERNOON of 4 May 1799, the fort of Seringapatam, situated on the bank of river Kaveri, fell to the British. The fort was the focal point of Mysore's military power. Its ruler, Tipu Sultan, who portrayed himself as a tiger fighting the British lion, died in combat inside the fortress. One of the most powerful opponents of British colonialism, Tipu's dead body had four wounds; three in the body and one in the temple, the shot having entered a little above the right ear.

Tipu Sultan was born on 20 December 1750. At that time, his father Haidar Ali (1722–82) was emerging as the strongman of Mysore, which was situated at the periphery of the Mughal Empire's Deccan Subah and was ruled by the decadent Hindu Woodeyar dynasty. Haidar was born in 1722 and joined the Mysore cavalry in 1749. His rise was very rapid. In 1753, he became the faujdar of Dindigul. He then became a general of the Woodeyar Maharajah Chik Krishna Raja and in 1761, ousted the Raja in a military coup. He realized that the survival of the Indian states depended on checking the rising power of the East India Company. Haidar attacked the British in 1767 and thus started the First Anglo-Mysore War. When Haidar Ali died of cancer, his son Tipu became the ruler of Mysore on 29 December 1782. At that time, the Second Anglo-Mysore War (1780–84) was on. Fair-skinned and stocky, Tipu had an aquiline nose, black eyes and a large moustache. He loved riding, hunting and going for long walks. Tipu was also a superstitious man. During his last stand at Seringapatam, he wore a talisman on his right arm: it was a silver case enclosing prayers and verses from the Koran. Despite his superstitions, however, Tipu did not neglect realpolitik.

MODERNIZING THE ECONOMY

Modern warfare required money in ever greater quantities. West European states were able to raise and maintain gunpowder armies only by a thorough reorganization of their political and economic structure. Since capital-intensive gunpowder armies were costly, European polities were forced to raise their revenues. This they did by initiating industrialization and by introducing welfare measures that would encourage cultivators to expand the scope of cultivation. The increasing state intervention moulded an economy which was geared for sustaining arms production. Thus emerged what could be termed as military-fiscalism.

Tipu's interaction with the French made him realize that if he wanted to fight the British then he required a modern army and this in turn necessitated reform in Mysore's military-fiscal infrastructure. The Westernized army had to be paid regularly and directly in cash from the central treasury. *Jagir* grants from the state to the nobles began to be reduced and resources were mobilized through direct taxation. Tipu's objective was not only to raise the state's income by reviving the economic health of Mysore but also to make it self-sufficient. The policy of autarky was followed to reduce Mysore's economic dependence on her neighbours who due to British diplomacy might turn violent.

Kingdoms in south India had always imported horses from Arabia. However, long sea voyages in confined spaces made most of the horses lame. Importing war horses was costly and the supply system was shaky. An enemy maritime power could cut maritime supply lines at its will. Besides, the Royal Navy ruled the waves of the Indian Ocean. Tipu decided to set up stud farms under the supervision of an animal husbandry department he established. The department also bred cattle that produced more meat and milk for the general populace. Encouraged by Tipu's scientific temperament, the department was able to breed a special variety of strong bullock that was used for pulling heavy guns and for public transport. Such bullocks were able to cover one hundred miles in two-and-half days. Mysore maintained

20,000 of these animals. They were so famous, that after Tipu's fall, the Duke of Wellington used them in his campaign against the Marathas in 1803.

Mysore's economy remained rooted in agriculture and Tipu took steps to improve the agrarian structure. Both Tipu and his father tried to reduce the burden on the peasantry by taxing them directly rather than going through intermediaries, i.e. zamindars. Tipu issued farmans to the *amils* for improving cultivation. Each poor farmer was given four gold mohurs for bringing new land under cultivation in a system known as *taccavi*. Tipu ordered, 'The patel should recruit new farmers, give them ploughs and also grant the *taccavi*, so that they can commence food production.' To aid the disbursal of loans, Tipu constructed *mullicul tyal cotties* (banking houses). These banking houses were coordinated by a central bank at Seringapatam. The public treasury guaranteed these institutions. To a great extent, these banks were able to protect poor and illiterate cultivators from the ravages of moneylenders and merchants. Tipu was far ahead of his time in this. Only in 1809 did the British set up the Bank of Bengal, the first bank in the British-Indian empire.

Besides financial assistance, the cultivators also required a regular supply of water. Given the erratic Indian monsoon, Tipu undertook a massive project to construct irrigation dams and tanks. A dam over the Kaveri was constructed in 1797. One embankment about 70 ft. high was constructed to conserve water for irrigation. Another tank was built at Daroji in Bellary district by constructing a dam along the Narihalla River. This dam was 8 km. long and 45 ft. high. Their maintenance became one of the primary tasks of the Mysore government. Old dams were repaired. The Moti Talav tank which was originally constructed by the Hoysalas was repaired during Tipu's reign.

To commercialize Mysore's economy, Tipu encouraged sericulture. He sent agents to Bengal and even to south China for silk worms. Bahauddin and Kasturi Ranga, the two agents, were able to get silkworms from Bengal. Certain *taluqdars* were ordered to raise mulberry trees, and Tipu set up twenty-one factories to produce silk. The proceeds from the sale of silk went directly to the treasury. Tipu's government also encouraged planting sandalwood trees for commercial use. It derived revenue from selling resin, incense and sealing wax. Teak and acacia trees were grown because their wood was used to construct the pedestals of cannons.

EUROPEANIZING THE ARMED FORCES

Like any good corporate firm today, Tipu and Haidar to strengthen their force, stole skilled personnel from other armies. Europeanizing the traditional force structure composed of elephants and feudal cavalry was essential. Such a programme required soldiers and especially officers trained in the art of Western warfare. Haidar and Tipu forcibly inducted all the captured British prisoners of war into the Mysore army. By 1767, Haidar Ali had 210 Europeans, concentrated mostly in the artillery. In 1782, the French Admiral Suffren handed over all his British prisoners to Haidar's officers at Cuddalore. They were circumcised and formed into a unit under Sergeant Dempster, a deserter from the Company's artillery department. Tipu and his father especially wanted deserters who were skilled in casting cannons. Captain White, who cast guns for Mysore, was one such deserter. Besides European deserters, Haidar and his son also recruited Indian soldiers trained under the Company. Sayyid Gafur, a cavalry officer in the Company's army, was captured along with Colonel Braithwaite's detachment on 18 February 1782 at Tanjore. Tipu offered him a commission in the Mysore army and Gafur accepted it. He fought valiantly during the last siege of Seringapatam.

The Western-modelled infantry was organized in units of a thousand soldiers each. Such a unit, known as a battalion in European military parlance, was called a *risalah* in Mysore. The *risalahs'* commanding officers were appointed directly by Haidar and Tipu. Equipped with muskets, the soldiers were trained daily for three hours. During the Karnataka invasion of 1790, Haidar distributed four cannons and two munition wagons to each *risalah* to increase their firepower. The *risalahs* were grouped into *qushuns* which were equivalent to a brigade.

Haidar Ali wanted to synthesize the traditional mobile cavalry tactics of the Mughals with Western-style musket-armed infantry; his son Tipu focused on fortifications and infantry. From father to son, there was a transition in the doctrine of warfare from mobile campaigning to static warfare. In 1780, Haidar had about 20,000 disciplined infantry and the same number of cavalry. But Tipu focused on infantry at the cost of his cavalry. In 1786, Mysore had ten factories geared for manufacturing muskets. According to Cossigny, who was the French Governor of Pondicherry, the quality of the muskets produced in Mysore was equivalent to European ones. Before his fall in 1799, Tipu had been able to amass 99,000 muskets for his infantry. Tipu established foundries to manufacture brass cannons and ammunition for artillery was produced in Bangalore. Sulphur for the manufacture of gunpowder was imported from Muscat. Tipu knew that despite all his efforts, there was a technological gap in relation to European armies, especially in the field of heavy weaponry that he hadn't bridged. Tipu's officials faced problems manufacturing musket flints. In 1783, one of Tipu's officials offered to reward British prisoners if they agreed to aid the Mysore authorities in producing arms they lacked. In 1787, Tipu sent an embassy to France to request master craftsmen and founders for making cannons. Mouriset, who was employed in the French royal foundry, agreed to go to India with two foremen, one carpenter and a turner.

Both Haidar and Tipu understood that maritime supremacy not only allowed the British to rush in reinforcements and provisions to danger spots, it also accounted for their domination of the lucrative maritime trade. For instance, ships operating from Bombay sustained the Company's Bombay army's operations in the Malabar Coast. It also allowed the British to threaten the western flank of Mysore. Before the advent of internal combustion engine, travelling on sea was cheaper and faster than marching over land. Father and son set in motion an ambitious shipbuilding programme. Tipu planned to build 23 masted ships with 85 guns in each vessel, at the three ports of Mysore. In addition, 22 smaller ships each with 30 guns (known as *ghurabs*) were to be constructed for the protection of trade convoys. However, the project remained a fantasy of sorts. Constructing a ship was not only very costly; a floating battleship bristling with cannons and capable of long distance oceanic voyages was also the most sophisticated piece of hardware in the eighteenth century world. Only highly advanced industrial countries with dry docks and an iron industry were capable of launching such ships.

FESTUNG SERINGAPATAM

'The English would be obliged to raise the siege for want of provisions, and that their shot had produced little effect on the walls.'

—TIPU SULTAN

After the British invasion of Mysore in 1791 during the Third Anglo-Mysore War (1790-92), Tipu initiated a strategic shift from conducting mobile war to positional fortress-based warfare. He began a massive reconstruction of his chief fort at his capital Seringapatam. An inner rampart of mud was constructed and a wet ditch surrounded it. The outer wall was reconstructed with brickwork, while the inner wall was made of stone. Before the final British assault in 1799, Tipu placed 21,839 soldiers inside Seringapatam and mounted 287 guns on the fortifications. He planned to demolish the Company's *paltans* if they attempted to attack the fort.

On 5 April 1799, the Madras army under George Harris took up a position on the west face of Seringapatam fort only 3,500 yards away from the fort. It was dangerously close, and it had been possible for the British to come so close only because the cavalry balance had shifted against Mysore. While Tipu had allowed his cavalry to dwindle, the British had raised a light cavalry force that prevented Tipu from carrying out war in the Madras Presidency. The Marathas threatened the northern boundary of Mysore, and to add to Tipu's troubles, reinforcements for the British were on the way. The benevolent attitude of the Marathas towards the Company had freed the Company's Bombay army which could now coordinate action with the Madras army. Tipu's strategy was to hold out till the onset of monsoon. Once the monsoon came, he calculated, the Kaveri would overflow and the British would be forced to raise the siege

General Harris's attack began on 9 April. After eleven days, the Bombay army under General Stuart took position on the north bank of the Kaveri. The siege was underway. In the first phase, the Company's artillery was geared for counter-battery fire, with the objective of silencing the enemy's guns. Under the impact of long distance artillery fire from the Company, by the evening of 24 April, all the guns mounted on the western portion of the fort's wall were silenced. Then, the second phase of the artillery campaign, known as counter-bombardment, started. The intention was to keep Tipu's army busy so it could not react to the construction of breaching batteries near the fort's wall. To prevent the construction of breaching batteries, Tipu had posted his infantry in pockets along the banks of the Kaveri. General Harris ordered his redcoats to engage the enemy more closely. On 20 April, the Company's troops attacked about 1,800 of Mysore's soldiers posted on the south-west bank of the Kaveri. In retaliation, Tipu sent out 6,000 of his select infantry commanded by French officers. On the night of 21 April, they took their positions. While they attacked General Harris's force on 22 April, another body of Mysore's troops under the command of Mir Muhammad Hussain and Muhammad Halim attacked Stuart's force. The battle went on for several hours. Thanks to fire discipline, unit control and the judicious use of tactical reserve, the thin red line held. After losing about 700 soldiers, Tipu's infantry retreated. On 26 April, under support of artillery fire, the Company's infantry advanced and drove away about 1,500 of Mysore's troops from the west bank of the river. Tipu had finally lost the infantry battle outside the fort. The rainy season was yet to begin. The strategy of waiting for 'General Monsoon' had failed.

Seringapatam fort was now in grave danger. Two enfilading batteries were set up on the northern bank of the river about 900 yards away from the fort's wall. Three breaching batteries were established on the southern bank of the river only 400 yards away from the outer wall. Their job was to blast the masonry of the outer wall. On the night of 30 April, Lieutenant Lalor, belonging to the 73rd Regiment, was able to sneak into Tipu's line and study the plans of Seringapatam's fortifications. He passed on the information to the gunners who factored in the details of Seringapatam's construction and its weaknesses while planning. On the night of 1 May, all the batteries were completed and the third phase of the artillery battle began. The aim was to smash the walls of the fort. The morning of 2 May witnessed a devastating coordinated firestorm against the fort. It continued day and night. On the evening of 3 May, a breach was reported, and scaling ladders and fascines were sent to the storming parties inside the trenches. The troops that were to storm the fortress had been kept in the trenches through the night. They numbered 2,494 Europeans and 1,882 sepoys. The assault began at dawn, with the storming party divided into two columns. Lieutenant Lawrence of the 77th Regiment led one column. His two sons Henry and John Lawrence would play a decisive role in consolidating the Raj in Punjab during the 1857 Mutiny. Behind the storming party waited the reserve force under Colonel Arthur Wellesley. His job was to exploit the gap in the enemy's defence once the storming parties entered the fort.

Under cover of artillery fire, the two columns rushed forward and crossed the Kaveri. The Mysore troops inside the fort opened fire with muskets and rockets, wounding several. That sultry day, many grievously wounded soldiers died from want to water.

A brigade of engineers under Captain Caldwell had accompanied the storming party. They were to blow up the inner wall of the fort to enable the infantry to enter the fort. Behind the engineers followed the European pioneers under Lieutenant Farquhar. Farquhar's job was to clear the rubble and make a passageway once the engineers had blown up the wall, for the storming troops to enter the fort. The pioneers were also supposed to fill up the ditch before the fortress so the infantry could walk over it.

It was already 12 p.m. Under intense fire from Tipu's infantry, the Company's assault columns seemed to falter. At that critical juncture, General David Baird decided only 'heroic command' would do. Standing up in the trench, deliberately exposing himself to enemy fire, Baird somewhat theatrically drew out his sword and shouted, 'Come, my brave fellows, follow me, and prove yourselves worthy of the name of British soldiers.' With a cheer the British privates followed him. The last charge had begun.

The sun had already crossed over to the western part of the sky and Tipu's fortunes seemed to be following a similar, declining trajectory. Around 1.30 p.m., despite heavy fire from Tipu's forces, the infantry of the East India Company captured the riverbed. When the Company infantry finally breached the northern part of the fort's ramparts, Sayyid Gafur was in command. He died fighting when a cannon shot struck him. Tipu replaced him with Muhammad Kasim.

The Sultan was at lunch when he heard that the *feranghi* infidels had progressed from the ramparts to the fortress itself. He immediately buckled on his sword, and with a few attendants, rushed out, a striking figure in a light-coloured jacket, with trousers of fine chintz, a sash of red silk and a turban. Tipu tried to rally his troops, but despite his inspiring oratory, the Mysore troops melted away under pressure from the advancing 12th European Light Infantry. The defeated soldiers of Mysore tried to retreat into the inner fort through the bridge which connected the inner fort with the outer fort. The soldiers were now engaged in close quarter combat and Tipu was wounded in the confusion. A British soldier tried to attack the Sultan, who wounded the redcoat in his knee. The soldier then fired the fatal musket shot, getting Tipu in his temple. Seeing Tipu falling dead, the dispirited

Mysore soldiers surrendered. Screams and shouts filled the fortress as the victorious ran amok, looting the palace and assaulting the women. The siege cost the Company 192 British troops killed and 657 wounded. Among the British-trained sepoys the casualties were 108 killed and 385 wounded.

POSSIBLE SCENARIO: TIGER DEFEATS
THE LION

In campaigns between 1767–9 and 1780–4, Haidar Ali and his cavalry dominated the Madras Presidency. The mobility of his cavalry allowed Haidar to repeatedly surprise the foot-slogging Madras army of the Company. On 10 September 1780, Haidar surrounded a detachment under Lieutenant-Colonel William Baillie at Kanjivaram (also known as the Battle of Pollilur/Polilore or the Battle of Perambakam), and on 30 April of the same year, General Matthews surrendered to Haidar Ali at Bednur. Another factor behind continuous British disasters was the close cooperation between France and Mysore at land and sea. During the Second Anglo-Mysore War (1780–4), Marquis de Bussy's land operation kept a considerable number of the Company's troops occupied and thus, aided Haidar's progress in Karnataka. French maritime supremacy also helped Haidar Ali by threatening the Company's sea lines of communications with the metropole. For example, the Americans during the War of American Independence (1775–83), under George Washington, emerged victorious against King George's Redcoats because the French navy tilted the balance in favour of the Americans. With their supremacy in the Atlantic, the French navy prevented reinforcements from Britain reaching the beleaguered British troops scattered over the North American continent. Similarly, Count de Suffren, the French Admiral, by dominating the Indian Ocean and the Bay of Bengal, prevented the British from rushing reinforcements to Madras Presidency from the Bombay and Bengal Presidencies and England. French superiority in naval firepower was exemplified by Suffren's fifty-gun flagship named Hannibal. However, the situation turned in favour of the British with the withdrawal of the French naval squadrons from the Indian Ocean in the early 1790s.

Seringapatam was under threat even before 1799. Charles Cornwallis, after being defeated by George Washington in North America at the Siege of Yorktown (1781), became the Commander-in-Chief and Governor General of British-India in 1786. It was a sort of penal posting. The British Empire tried to recoup its losses in America by expanding in South Asia. Hence, the latter half of the eighteenth century witnessed the British state on a land grabbing spree in the subcontinent. The Third Anglo-Mysore War began in 1790. In 1791, after capturing Bangalore, Cornwallis fought a successful battle on the northern bank of the Kaveri. He was forced to draw back, however, because of failure of supplies. Seringapatam was saved for the moment but Tipu was defeated partly because the Marathas had attacked Mysore in league with the British. Tipu lost half of his dominion to the British and twelve of his sons were made prisoners. Loss of territory meant that Tipu's musket producing factories were reduced to seven.

The shift in force structure from mobile aggressive campaigning to static warfare prevented Tipu from carrying out war in enemy territory, a technique which Haidar Ali had practised. In static warfare too, Tipu was at a disadvantage. He stood no chance against the British in sieges. Heavy siege artillery was one of the principal factors behind British success. Scientific techniques of conducting sieges, using engineers, and sappers gave a further technical edge to the Company.

Mysore's military defeat was accelerated by Tipu's diplomatic failures. He failed to detach the Nizam of Hyderabad and the Marathas from the British sponsored anti-Tipu league. The Maratha light cavalry not only escorted the Company's supply columns, it also reconnoitred for the Company's troops. Tipu's grand strategy, of rallying foreign powers against the British Empire, was also unsuccessful. His attempt to enlist Zaman Shah's support in threatening Britain's Indian Empire from the northwest came to nothing. In 1787, Tipu sent an embassy to Constantinople, but failed to provoke the Ottomans against the British. The Porte was having enough trouble with the Habsburg and the Russians. Constantinople was in no position to open a new front in South Asia. In fact, the presence of Mysore's agents in the courts of Hyderabad, Poona, Persia and Constantinople threatened the British, spurring them to mobilize and end the possible threat from Tipu. Unfortunately for Tipu, France was also going through an internal convulsion which resulted in the tottering away of the *Ancien Règime*. Tipu's defeat was only made inevitable by the French inactivity from 1792 onwards.

CONCLUSION

'As a man could die only once, it was of little consequence when the period of his existence might terminate.'

—TIPU SULTAN

While the Company's 24-pounder cannons and 12-pounder howitzers at Seringapatam did much to destroy the fortress, technology was not the only factor in the Company's victory over Tipu. No matter which hardware soldiers are equipped with, it is the determination to fight that matters. In the heat of carnage, the 'follow me' sort of leadership exercised by British commanders strengthened the resolve of the privates to rush forward into possible death zones.

The collapse of Mysore resulted in British supremacy in south India. However, the British were yet to dominate the subcontinent fully. The Marathas from central and west India were still to be subdued. The fall of Seringapatam was, however, the beginning of the end for the Maratha confederacy. Instead of bolstering Mysore as a breakwater against British expansionism, the Marathas foolishly joined the British in carving up Tipu's domain. Too late the vacillating Maratha sardars at Poona realized that the destruction of Mysore had encouraged the British to intervene in the internal affairs of the *durbar* at Poona.

8

———

Open Fire

The Battle of Assaye
23 September 1803

T HE THIRD BATTLE of Panipat resulted in the defeat but not the complete destruction of Maratha power. The Marathas crossed the Ganges again, but in a different incarnation. Rather than the *Peshwa* at Poona, it was the Sindia family at Gwalior which now called the shots. And instead of *bargirs,* the post-Panipat Maratha army was composed of firearms-equipped infantry, supported by cannons. The infantry was recruited not from Maharashtra but from north India.

MARATHA MILITARY MODERNIZATION

'I tell you, General, as to their cavalry, you may ride over them wherever you meet them; but their infantry and guns will astonish you.'

—COLONEL COLLINS to Wellington on 29 August 1803

The aggressive activities of the British war machine transformed the nature of Indian warfare. The princely armies of India, from being cavalry-oriented, became infantry-artillery centric war machine in which warhorses occupied a subsidiary position. Indian powers which resisted the forces of change were wiped out by the modernizing indigenous powers. In the aftermath of the Third Panipat, Mahadji Sindia made a vigorous attempt to Westernize his army. Mahadji was a short, potbellied man, somewhat similar to Hemu. He had himself fought at the Third Battle of Panipat and had been wounded in the knee, becoming lame. Fighting the British in the 1780s, Mahadji realized the uselessness of the Maratha cavalry's *Ganimi Kava* against the firepower-heavy regular infantry of the East India Company. Mahadji understood that he needed a disciplined infantry armed with firearms and backed by artillery for decisive set-piece battles. In contrast, the Rajputs remained wedded to their time-honoured cavalry. As a result, towards the end of the eighteenth century, Mahadji's Europeanized force annihilated the Rajputs.

For his infantry, Mahadji recruited Telingas from south India and Najibs from western Uttar Pradesh. The Maratha military was mostly geared to fight from horseback; it was considered by the Marathas more honourable to fight from horseback rather than as a foot soldier. Notably, the Madras army of the Company also recruited Telingas. And among the Muslim communities of western Uttar Pradesh who were migrants from Afghanistan, there was a tradition of making muskets. They fought as foot soldiers under various regional warlords from the fourteenth to the eighteenth centuries.

Mahadji appointed European officers to train disciplined infantry soldiers armed with muskets. The officers in Mahadji's payroll organized the infantry in brigades which were known as *campoos*. A *campoo* was composed of several battalions. Each *campoo* had its own standard which aided in identity formation, creating unit spirit. It motivated the personnel of a unit to fight hard for the *izzat* (a fusion of personal and collective honour) of their *campoo* in battle. Most of the officers in Mahadji's camp, like Lestenau and Levassoult, were French. However, De Boigne, a Savoyard, was the most famous of Sindia's European commanders.

The modernizing Indian armies came to put more and more of their faith on firepower. Long-distance cannonade before close combat with handgun equipped infantry became a characteristic feature. Greater firepower meant more casualties for both armies. Governments were forced to take care of wounded soldiers not only to restore morale but also to conserve military manpower. It took time and money to train a raw recruit into a disciplined soldier. European governments spent a lot on military hospitals. The Marathas too introduced *palkis* to remove the dead and wounded from the battlefield. When the *campoos* went to battle, advance parties of *beldars* were sent to construct new roads and to repair the old ones. When necessary, the *beldars* also dug new wells for ensuring water supply to the army.

The command system of the Maratha army was also partially

modernized. Field commanders used telescopes for a clear view of the battlefield. Camel couriers brought reports to the field commander about the movement of various sub units scattered over the battlefield. However, the Marathas were yet to come up with officers who specialized in staff duties. In a European army, a staff officer's duty was to convey information to and fro between the field commander and the various subordinate commanders during the heat of battle. The absence of staff officers proved to be a weakness for the Marathas when they fought the Company in 1803.

Supplying the *campoos* remained a weak point in Sindia's military system. Unlike the Europeans, the Marathas did not set up modern systems of supply during long-distance campaigns. They continued to depend on *banjaras*, who frequently failed them. The *banjaras* being profiteers, usually sold grain at higher prices, which was a problem for common soldiers. During the 1787 Rajasthan campaign, many soldiers deserted from Mahadji's *campoos* because of his failure to feed them adequately. Occasionally, the *banjaras* sold their grain to the enemy if offered a higher price.

The basic problem was lack of money. The Marathas had no administrative infrastructure to extract revenues in an organized manner. Unlike Tipu, Mahadji did not take any steps to develop the economic health of his domain. On the one hand, even as revenues declined, Sindia's military expenditure increased. Sindia's *campoos* proved to be costlier than cavalry contingents maintained by Maratha sardars. The total pay of the infantry came to about Rs.60 lakh per month. Mahadji also failed to maintain law and order in his far-flung domain. When his main army was engaged against the Jodhpur and Jaipur forces in 1787, the zamindars in central and north India rebelled. The Sikhs raided Delhi and Agra and stopped all commercial traffic. The net result was fall in revenue when it was required most.

Since Mahadji was not in a position to pay his soldiers regularly in cash, he was forced to issue *jagirs* to the commanders of the *campoos*. The German mercenary Samru, for example, maintained a *campoo* for Mahadji. When he died, his Begum looked after his affairs. She received a *jagir* worth Rs.7,00,000 annually for her *campoo*. In the long run, the grant of *jagirs* made *campoo* commanders autonomous, creating the conditions for the disintegration of the central command structure of Sindia.

Sindia realized that the core of his military strength remained his *campoos* and he gave first preference to the *campoos* when paying. This alienated the Maratha sardars commanding his Deccani light cavalry. They felt that Mahadji was discriminating against his own countrymen while favouring the *feranghi*-led *campoos* composed of non-Maratha soldiers. The Maratha light cavalry's hostility towards the *campoos* made cooperation between the two parts of the Maratha army impossible during combat.

Despite all these defects, Sindia's infantry and field artillery were formidable. Major General Arthur Wellesley, later known as the Duke of Wellington, after defeating Sindia's infantry at the great battle of Assaye commented to his brother Henry Wellesley:

Sindia's French infantry [infantry trained by the French officers] were far better that Tipu's, his artillery excellent, and his ordnance so good, and so well equipped, that it answers for our service. We never could use Tipu's. Our loss is great, but the action, I believe, was the most severe that ever was fought in this country; and I believe such a quantity of cannon, and such advantages have seldom been gained by any single victory in any part of the world.

Let us revisit the gigantic clash at Assaye.

OPENING GAMBIT

'The Marathas have long boasted that they would carry on a predatory war against us: they will find that mode of warfare not very practicable at the present moment.'

—WELLINGTON, 15 August 1803

The Treaty of Bassein signed by *Peshwa* Baji Rao II and the Company on 31 December 1802 transformed the *Peshwa* into a subsidiary of the British. The Maratha chiefs decided to undo this treaty. The most powerful chief was Daulat Rao Sindia, who after the death of his uncle Mahadji in 1794, succeeded as head of the Sindia clan. However, the fissiparous Maratha political structure generated decentralizing tendencies among the various components of the Maratha confederacy. Various chiefs like Sindia, Gaikwad, Bhonsle and Holkar were engaged more in fighting each other rather than forming a common front against the British. Even within the patrimony of a big chief, lesser chiefs challenged his authority. For instance, the region between river Tungabhadra and Poona belonged to the *Peshwa*. But when, in January 1803, Arthur Wellesley advanced through this region, many lesser chiefs made alliances with the British. The rest shut themselves up in their own forts not joining the Maratha field army which, under the leadership of Daulat Rao and Raghuji Bhonsle (chief of the Bhonsle clan and ruler of Berar and Orissa), was readying on the bank of Narmada to meet the British.

Given its revenue problems, the Maratha army found it difficult procuring provisions. Lack of supplies hampered the mobility and effectiveness of the combined forces at crucial junctures. On 29 June 1803, Colonel Collins from Sindia's camp at Selore reported to Wellington, 'Forage is scarcely procurable in these parts; grain or any description bears a most extravagant price. In short, the distress in Sindia's camp is very great.' Lack of food and pay led to indiscipline among Sindia's soldiers, which in turn resulted in low combat effectiveness. Sindia was thinking of launching his horses upon Hyderabad because the Nizam was providing the British with money and grain. However, a jubilant Colonel Stevenson wrote to Wellington on 18 August 1803, 'The enemy are at the foot of Deol Ghat and intend entering the Nizam's country by that pass but have been delayed on account of some difficulties about arrears of pay.'

In contrast, thanks to its financial finesse, the Company had a regular supply of cash. Wellington bought supplies from the zamindars as he advanced towards Poona. Since Wellington and his associates were well supplied with money, they were also able to hire *banjaras*. These grain merchants used 10,000 bullocks to convey grain from Madras and Bombay for the advancing British detachments. With their good liquidity, the British were also able to hire coolies to supplement the bullock convoys that provided grain to the army.

Despite all their defects, however, on 23 September 1803, the Marathas were able to concentrate a considerable force. The total forces under Daulat Rao Sindia included 15,200 cavalry and 26 sepoy battalions. Each battalion numbered 700 sepoys. Colonel Pohlman, a Hanoverian, commanded a *campoo* of seven battalions and another *campoo* consisting of seven battalions was under Colonel Dudrenec. After the German mercenary Samru's death, his four battalions organized in a brigade was commanded by Colonel Saleur. Ambaji

Inglia, a Maratha chieftain of Sindia also brought a *campoo* consisting of four battalions commanded by Major P. Shepherd. The *campoos* were backed by 161 field guns. Raghuji brought to the field 20,000 cavalry and ten infantry battalions.

END OF THE DAY FOR THE MARATHAS: 23 SEPTEMBER 1806

'The whole country is strewn with the killed and wounded both European and natives, ours as well as the enemy's.'

—An unnamed British cavalry officer in the aftermath of Assaye

The day had already progressed considerably when the British clashed with the Marathas. While the 1st and 2nd Madras Infantry Regiments guarded the baggage, Wellington advanced with two European regiments, four sepoy battalions, four cavalry regiments and four brass 12-pounders. Wellington arranged his troops in two lines. The infantry formed the first line while the cavalry constituted the second line. At 1 p.m. the hundred guns which the Marathas had concentrated at the village of Assaye fired upon Company troops. The village was situated between two rivers named Kaitna and Juah. Colonel Pohlman's *campoo* was deployed beside the village. Till 3 p.m., all attempts by the Company's infantry to advance towards the Maratha gun line failed. The British 74th Infantry Regiment situated at the right of the line lost 300 out of 400 men present in the unit. The British infantry and cavalry reeled back. The Maratha cavalry was still an untouched reserve. A cavalry charge at the demoralized British infantry would have completed the British defeat. The fate of Wellington's army was hanging in the balance. One British cavalry officer jotted down the day after the battle, 'Never was artillery more destructively served or better defended. Had their numerous cavalry supported them as they ought to have done, God knows what would have been the issue.' Wellington, a grim looking man not given to hyperbole, portrays the dangerous scene at the forward edge of the killing field, in a letter written to a Major the day after the battle of Assaye was fought: 'The action was very brisk indeed, the fire from the enemy's cannon the hottest that has been known in this country for some time; and our loss in officers and men has been great. . . . Sindia's infantry behaved remarkably well and stood to their guns to the last.' But the Maratha cavalry did not charge and the Iron Duke formed his line afresh. The initiative was passing from the Marathas. After 3.30 p.m. the British cavalry charged the Maratha light cavalry and drove them out of the field. Maratha ponies were famous for skirmishing and reconnaissance. But they were unsuited to face a headlong charge by disciplined heavy cavalry during a set-piece battle. British cavalrymen were not only mounted on heavier horses, they were also trained better. The Company's infantry advanced behind the victorious British cavalry. Sindia's infantry was driven back by the charge of bayonets. By 4 p.m., the Maratha line was in disarray. Then, the British cavalry under Lieutenant Colonel Maxwell charged again, destroying a lot of enemy stragglers.

After three hours of combat, Maratha losses numbered 1,200 dead and 4,800 wounded in the field of battle. Of the wounded, another 800 died. Licking their wounds, the united armies of Daulat Rao Sindia and the Raja of Berar retreated from the Deccan to central India through the Ajanta Ghat. They left behind 60 pieces of cannons. Sindia's *campoos* had lost their supporting artillery firepower. In fact, the back of the Maratha infantry was broken. On 29 November 1803, at Argaum, after a short but vigorous British cannonade, the Maratha regulars left the field. Lack of adequate artillery support in this battle hampered the Westernized infantry of Sindia and Raghuji.

The principal factor behind Wellington's victory at Assaye was the failure of the Maratha cavalry to coordinate its action with Sindia's Westernized infantry and artillery. The Maratha cavalry and the Westernized portion of the army was divided by jealousy and absence of an overall field commander. The battlefield too, was badly chosen. The narrow region between the two rivers provided too little space for the Maratha cavalry to manoeuvre at the rear and flanks of the Company's army. Finally, Daulat Rao was no war leader in the heroic mould. Unlike Haidar Ali and Tipu Sultan, he did not put himself in the front rank of his army and charge at the enemy. He did not come to the battlefield to take command in person, as Wellington had done. Daulat Rao delegated command to his generals and occupied himself with grand strategy: diplomacy and political negotiations. He failed to appoint a field commander who could coordinate with commanders like Pohlman, Dudrenec and so on. The absence of staff officers also prevented the various *campoo* commanders from being aware of each other's positions during the battle. The *campoo* commanders failed to coordinate their actions towards a coherent response to the paltans. Thus, the Maratha command structure in the battlefield was characterized by disunity.

The staunchness of the *lal paltans* under fire completed the British victory. Despite Sindia's artillery firing at them, the Company's infantry advanced towards the gunners and cut them down, albeit at a great loss to them. Why didn't the *paltans* flee in face of the firestorm? One of the cardinal principles of leadership is that officers should not ask their men to do anything which they are not ready to perform themselves. The history of warfare shows that if an officer braves the dangers and leads a charge exposing himself to enemy fire, then men under the officer follow him at any cost. The British officers were brave—it resulted in huge casualties among the British officer cadre. Wellington's despatch dated 24 September 1803 to Major Merrick Shawe, Secretary of the Governor General notes, 'Your brother in the 74th is wounded; Colonel Maxwell [19th Dragoons who commanded a cavalry brigade] was killed; Colonel Harness, Colonel Wallace, and I, believe every officer of the staff, had horses shot under us.' In addition, Captain Mackay of the 4th Regiment died while leading a charge. Lieutenant Bonomi of the 5th Regiment and Captain Douglas of the 7th Regiment died while leading from the front. In fact, Wellington's own charger was killed while he was witnessing the carnage from the forward edge of the battlefield during the firefight. The eagerness of British officers to expose themselves to the hazards of the battlefield encouraged the soldiers and sepoys to fight and die. The British victory was not cheap. The Company lost 20 officers, 30 officers were wounded and there were 1,000 other casualties.

DIFFERENT STROKES:
DAULAT RAO SINDIA AS VICTOR

'A long defensive war would ruin us and will answer no purpose whatever.'

—WELLINGTON from Ahmadnagar to
Colonel Stevenson on 17 August 1803

Could it have been possible for the Marathas to emerge victorious at Assaye? The answer is both yes and no. Daulat Rao was unlucky.

It was his fate to meet as opponent one of the greatest generals in world history, Arthur Wellesley. In India, he was known as Wellesley Bahadur, while in Europe he was known as the Duke of Wellington. Wellington achieved international fame when he stopped the onslaught of Napoleon's celebrated Imperial Guards in the field of Waterloo. The cry of despair among the French troops, *'La Guardes recule'* at 4.30 p.m. on 18 June 1815, marked the end of Napoleon and immortal glory for Wellington. What is little known to students of European military history is that Wellington learnt the intricacies of generalship in the subcontinent. In the vast theatre of India, Wellington had to march and countermarch over hundreds of miles and had to coordinate his actions with those of other supporting armies. This gave him the confidence and the capacity to manoeuvre large bodies of men at war. Wellington himself repeated many times that compared to Waterloo, Assaye was a much more 'hot affair'.

Napoleon urged his officer corps to read about the campaigns of the great masters. On 24 November 1840, Wellington told a friend, Samuel Rogers:

I had Caesar's Commentaries with me in India, and learnt much from them, fortifying my camp every night as he did. I passed over the rivers as he did, by means of baskets and boats of basket-work; only I think I improved upon him, constructing them into bridges, and always fortifying them, and leaving them guarded, to return to them if necessary.

Wellington made boats by synthesizing Indian materials with Western knowledge. His boats were manufactured with bamboo lath and leather by Indian craftsmen. Wellington improved upon the traditional Indian design by sewing hides with leather in order to provide an extra covering. The gunwale was also covered with leather and it was lashed with the framework within, in order to make the crafts stronger. Such boats were about 10 ft. in diameter and about two feet and three inches high. With these boats, Wellington was able to start the campaign during the rainy season with rivers in spate, when the Marathas were neither expecting an invasion nor capable of repelling it. Nevertheless, Wellington was not omnipotent and Daulat Rao could certainly have steered matters his way. Unlike his uncle Mahadji, Daulat Rao was no diplomatic genius. Through concessions and negotiations, Mahadji had been able to maintain an alliance with Tukoji Holkar and the *Peshwa*. Daulat Rao, on the other hand, created much bad blood within the Maratha confederacy by marrying his youngest aunt. Further, unlike Mahadji, the young Daulat Rao failed to show outward respect to the *Peshwa*. The *Peshwa*, therefore, remained neutral during the war and Gaikwad cooperated with Colonel Murray during the latter's campaign in Gujarat. A rigid, arrogant man, Daulat Rao alienated the Holkar family by holding back concessions for collecting revenues from certain areas in central India and Rajasthan. As a result, Tukoji's successor Jaswant Rao Holkar became hostile to Daulat Rao. When Daulat Rao along with Raghuji Bhonsle fought against the Company, Jaswant Rao Holkar, with his 56,000 cavalry, 15,000 infantry and 157 guns, remained inactive. Worse, Daulat Rao had to dissipate his forces guarding north India and central India fearing the possibility of an incursion by the fiery Holkar. Only when Daulat Rao and Bhonsle were defeated at Assaye and Argaum, did Holkar join the battle against the British. Fighting alone, he destroyed Colonel William Monson's force of 12,000 men with 15 guns in Rajasthan. One wonders what would have happened if the Maratha confederacy was unified in 1803.

A traditional Maratha guerrilla campaign by the confederacy would not have succeeded against the British. Wellington had perfected the anti-guerrilla tactics that Napoleon had failed to do in Spain after 1810. In order to counteract the depredations of the Maratha light cavalry, the British hired Mysore cavalry. Thousands of Mysore bullocks enabled the Company's commanders to supply their widely scattered forces. A favourite Maratha tactic was to cut the supply lines of their enemy. Mobile firepower was available to the Company's convoy guards in the form of three- and six-pounder guns drawn either by bullocks or horses. The Maratha cavalry's tactic of destroying villages deep inside enemy territory also failed because Wellington had fortified the villages which were guarded by soldiers armed with muskets. Maratha horsemen armed with swords and spears failed to achieve anything substantial against earthen ramparts, embankments and bullets.

The fort-based strategy with which the Marathas had succeeded against the Mughals would certainly have failed against the British. Great forts like Ahmadnagar fell to the British because of the devastating fire from heavy siege guns like 5.5 in. howitzers and 12-pounder iron guns. Even from a distance of 400 yards, 12-pounder guns could blast the walls of forts to oblivion. The forts of Burhanpur and Asirgarh fell after a token fight. Scindia's soldiers had not been paid for several months and were most willing to surrender when the British offered them gold. If Daulat Rao decided to hold out in Gwalior Fort, then he would have met the same fate as Tipu in Seringapatam.

The only sensible strategy for a united Maratha confederacy would have been Holkar's light cavalry carrying fire and sword in Awadh and Bengal the two provinces which were providing supplies to the East India Company and a simultaneous advance by Daulat Rao's infantry in south India. A long-drawn-out attritional campaign all over the subcontinent would have harassed the British armies and resulted in heavy expenditure for the Company. The Marathas may have been able to tide over a long war through pillage and plundering of the client states of the British: Awadh and Hyderabad along with Bengal, the province which supplied the largest amount of revenue and military manpower to the EIC. All this could have brought upon the Governor General, the censure of the Directors of the Company. The elder Wellesley brother, the Governor General, in such a scenario, would probably have forced upon his younger brother, Wellington, a negotiated peace with the Maratha confederacy.

CONCLUSION

Assaye finished the Marathas for good. After Assaye, Daulat Rao Sindia was in a sad situation. His *campoos* had not been paid for seven months. His demoralized soldiers were in a state of mutiny. Continuous desertion in the wake of defeat was accompanied by the relentless advance of the Company's *paltans* under General Gerard Lake from north India and Wellington from south India towards Indore and Gwalior. The Maratha chiefs were forced to negotiate for peace. It was, indeed, a victor's peace. Daulat Rao, Raghuji, and Jaswant Rao Holkar were forced to disband their Westernized regular infantry and turn out all their European military advisers. They were allowed to keep only traditional Maratha horsemen because in British eyes the light Maratha cavalry by itself was incompetent. Thus, the clock of military history was turned back for the Marathas. In a further ironic blow, Daulat Rao and the *Peshwa* were supposed to pay for the infantry battalions that the British stationed to guard territories they had taken away from the Marathas. Sindia and Raghuji became client princes of the British Raj.

The British gained Orissa from Raghuji, the Konkan Coast from the *Peshwa*, and Gujarat from Gaikwad. The acquisition of the maritime provinces went toward satisfying British paranoia about France sending reinforcements by sea to the indigenous powers. During 1817–18, Holkar and the *Peshwa* fought the Company with light cavalry. Their defeat was a foregone conclusion. As a result of the victory over the Marathas, the Company's borders extended up to the Sutlej. Behind it, the Sikhs were uniting under a vigorous leader named Ranjit Singh. His *Khalsa* Kingdom remained the last stumbling block in the British expansionist drive.

9

—————

Dal Khalsa's Last Chance

Ferozeshah, 21–2 December 1845

'*Sab lal ho jayega.* [Everything will be painted red.]'

—RANJIT SINGH

WHEN ONE COURTIER of Maharaja Ranjit Singh (b. 13 November 1780–d. 27 June 1839) displayed a map of India to his monarch, the latter asked what the red markings meant. The courtier pointed out that the red line marked the extent of Britain's empire in India. Ranjit Singh commented with a sigh that eventually all of India would become red. Like Akbar, Ranjit Singh could neither read nor write. Not only was he very short, he had also lost one eye in his childhood. However, he had extraordinary managerial abilities. He created the preconditions for founding a Sikh nation state and thoroughly Westernized his army. His *Khalsa* army (*Dal Khalsa*) proved the toughest nut for the British to crack.

THE *KHALSA* TRIUMPHANT

'What had become of the 200,000 spearmen of the Marathas?'

—RANJIT SINGH

After the demise of the Maratha confederacy in 1818, Ranjit Singh realized that the only chance of survival depended on the transformation of the feudal Sikh cavalry-centric army into a Western-style infantry-artillery combine. Ranjit Singh's Westernization programme was aided by a host of European military mercenaries. The mercenaries were mostly French and Italians, like Colonel Mouton, Jean-Francois Allard, Jean-Baptiste Ventura and Paolo Di Avitabile. They had fought in

Napoleon's *Grande Armee.* There was also a Spaniard named Hubron. These European officers taught the Sikh infantry the tactic of volley firing. The infantry was organized into regiments and horse-drawn artillery guns were added to provide firepower. Where small firearms were concerned, both the *Dal Khalsa* and the Company's *paltans* were on the same level. Both the armies used Brown Bess muskets of the type used in Spain during the Napoleonic wars. Ranjit Singh not only trained his military forces in Western techniques but also established the infrastructure for a European military system. He set up mills for manufacturing gunpowder and factories to produce guns. John Martin Honigberger was appointed Superintendent of the gunpowder mill and gun factory of Lahore. To supply gunpowder to detachments scattered over Punjab, supply chains were set up across designated routes. Camels were used to transport the gunpowder. The Western-style contingents were paid in cash and several mints were established to meet the demand for coins.

But the Westernized *Khalsa* army was to be the cause of problems. The Sikh sardar commanding traditional irregular cavalry and the Western military entrepreneurs were soon at loggerheads because under Ranjit Singh, European military commanders started getting high civil posts. For instance, General Avitabile was appointed governor of Wazirabad province and General Ventura got the governorship of Dera Ghazi Khan. After the death of Ranjit Singh in 1839, weak successors followed him. Taking advantage of this power vacuum, the Sikh *durbar* removed most of the European officers from active service. Tej Singh, the Governor of Peshawar, became the Commander-in-Chief in place of Avitabile. The absence of Ranjit Singh's directing hand also resulted in the army becoming a Frankenstein's monster for the *durbar*. Each regiment, imitating the village *panchayati* system, elected panches. The panches, who functioned as representatives of their regiments, jointly pressurized the *durbar* for wage increases. The army also emerged as the king-maker.

Given an aggressive *Khalsa* army and a tottering Sikh state, the East India Company anticipated trouble. It concentrated about 30,000 soldiers at various stations like Ambala, Ludhiana and Ferozepore to guard the banks of the Sutlej. On 11 December 1845, the Sikh army crossed the Sutlej. On 18 December, the Company pushed back an advance guard of the *Khalsa* army at Mudki with a loss of seventeen guns.

The Company's army, under the joint command of the Commander-in-Chief General Hugh Gough and the Governor-General Lord Hardinge, prepared for a showdown with the Sikhs. The Company's *paltans* were organized into four divisions. For additional firepower, the *paltans* possessed two horse artillery brigades and one division of foot artillery. While Tej Singh besieged Major General John Littler's division consisting of one Queen's and five sepoy regiments at Ferozepore, the main Sikh army under Lal Singh prepared for battle at Ferozeshah.

21 DECEMBER 1845: BLACK DAY
FOR THE RED COATS

In traditional Mughal style—which was followed by the Marathas at the Third Panipat—the Sikhs entrenched their army at the village of Ferozeshah. However, unlike Bhau, who had been forced by supply difficulties to move out of his entrenched camp to give battle to Abdali, the Sikhs waited for the British to attack them. The Sikh camp was in the shape of a parallelogram about 1 mi. in length and half a mile in breadth. The camp was defended by 60,000 infantry. The influence of Napoleonic officers ensured that the Sikhs depended on artillery to destroy enemy infantry. The Sikhs had amassed a hundred artillery pieces. Of them, sixty were very heavy guns.

After marching throughout the night, the Company's troops reached the outskirts of the Sikh camp at Ferozeshah on 21 December at 10.30 a.m. Gough was a hard-headed, honest man, but of limited intelligence. Knowing this, Hardinge decided to accompany the field army in order to check any rashness on the part of Gough. A headstrong man, Gough was for attacking immediately. Hardinge restrained him, deciding to wait for Littler who was coming up from Ferozepore. Though the distance between Ferozepore and Ferozeshah was only ten miles, Littler's force started arriving only at 2 p.m. With Hardinge awaiting those troops, the attack only commenced in the late afternoon, at 4 p.m. As in Buxar, the Company's troops were organized in two lines. The three infantry divisions under Major-General Walter Gilbert, Brigadier-General William Wallace and Littler formed the first line. Each division was composed of two brigades and each brigade had two to three regiments. While Gilbert's division was composed of four sepoy regiments and two Queen's regiments, Wallace's division had one

British and three sepoy regiments. The guns were placed at the two flanks of the line as well as between each of the divisions. The second line acting as reserve was composed of Major General Harry Smith's division. The two lines were divided into right and left wings under Gough and Hardinge, respectively. Gough, like the Russian generals Kutuzov and Zhukov, was out of his depth in conducting manouevre warfare. A hundred years later, in May 1945, Zhukov was to launch a massive frontal attack before heavily-defended Berlin, regardless of casualties. Gough, in 1845, also opted for frontal assault against the heavily defended Sikh camp with his infantry.

As the British infantry line formed, the Sikh guns opened up and the British guns started responding. Very soon, it became clear to Gough that the Company was losing the artillery duel due to the comparatively lighter British guns. For the first time, an Indian power had developed artillery which was qualitatively and quantitatively superior to that of the British. Faced with slow destruction, Gough, like Wellington at Assaye, decided to overcome enemy guns by an infantry charge. The three infantry divisions forming the first line were ordered to advance towards the Sikh trenches. In Somme in 1916, the British infantry came in sight of the German machine gunners, only to be wiped out. Gough's frontal plan of attack took the three infantry divisions within direct sight of the Sikh guns. Though the Brown Bess was effective at 300 yards, for greater effect disciplined soldiers used them only when the enemy was 150 yards away. However, Sikh artillery had a range of 800 yards. Well before the Company's infantry got the Sikh gunners within range, they confronted a terrific barrage. One of the Company soldiers wrote that he advanced amidst the whiz of musketry shot. Suddenly, he heard a sound like a piano breaking down. He looked around and saw that a round shot had cracked open the skull of the man next to him. Another British private standing next to his comrade whose head was shattered by an artillery shot found his friend's brain in his mouth and it tasted salty. The artillery had made the battlefield a very dangerous place indeed. John Littler's division took a lot of punishment but still advanced. When the division's regiments were within 150 yards of the Sikh entrenchment, its advance came to a sudden halt. John Littler and Brigadier Reid urged the men on, but they refused to budge. The lanky Hardinge on a horse, deliberately exposing himself to Sikh gunfire shouted, 'Go forward boys', but his 'boys' refused to go forward. For the first time in history, an Indian gun line was able to stop the advance of the *paltans*.

The impossible seemed to be happening; the red line was cracking. In Littler's division, the attack was led by the right brigade under Reid. In the right brigade the 62nd Foot Regiment was supported in front by two sepoy regiments the 12th and 14th. The British regiment in the front held its ground, but the 12th and 14th sepoy regiments at the back retreated, although the Sikhs focused on killing the British. Their logic was that if the white men's attack was hurled back, then the sepoys would retreat. The 62nd Foot Regiment lost 7 officers and 97 soldiers. The tally of wounded was 11 officers and 184 privates. In contrast, in the 12th and 14th Infantry Regiments, 50 were killed and 169 wounded. The combined loss in the two sepoy regiments was less than the casualties suffered by the 62nd Foot Regiment. Still, the 62nd Foot's performance was better than the sepoy regiments'. The British officers of the Company's army tried to explain this by arguing that the *Purbiya* soldiers of the sepoy regiment recruited from Bihar and Awadh were racially inferior compared to the Sikhs, and that the stubbornness of the white regiment sprang from the loyalty and honour inherent in the master race, the British.

Actually, social, cultural and economic factors can partly explain the indifferent performance of the sepoy units. While roast beef and rum strengthened the British troops before the battle, the sepoys had little to eat. Most of the *Purbiya* soldiers, who were Brahmins and Rajputs, were constrained by food and hygiene taboos. The elaborate rituals surrounding their food meant that they often marched fortified by nothing more than laddus. In general, the high caste soldiers prepared their own food in their separate utensils. In the battlefield there was neither time nor opportunity to prepare a hot meal. This was unlikely to make for energetic soldiers.

Second, the combat effectiveness of troops depends on the stake the soldiers have in the battle. The *Purbiyas* were mercenaries, somewhat stiffened by regimental esprit de corps. They were demoralized by the fact that many men from their villages who had joined the *Dal Khalsa* instead of the Company not only got higher pay but were also able to become officers. While the *Purbiyas* were paid Rs.7 per month in the Company army, their brethren in the *Khalsa* army got about Rs.15 per month. In the Company's forces, the highest rank that could be attained by a *Purbiya* at the age of fifty-five was Subedar, which was lower than the post of the youngest white non-commissioned officer freshly arrived from Britain.

Generally, soldiers at the rear of a threatened army always panic first. During the First Battle of Panipat, panic broke out in the rear of Ibrahim Lodhi's army while soldiers at the front ranks faced Mughal cannons and matchlock shots. The German anthropologist Konrad Lorenz's flight or fight behavioural pattern helps us to analyse this phenomenon. Lorenz studied animals and deduced that the survival instincts of animals do not differ much from that of human beings. If one threatens an animal from a distance, the animal has a chance of escaping unhurt. So, the probability of the animal retreating is greater. However, if an animal is threatened up close, it realizes it has no chance of escaping. The hunted attacks the hunter in making a last-ditch effort for survival. Similarly, one could argue that soldiers at the rear of armies retreat because they can escape while soldiers in front perforce have to make a last-ditch stand. The Roman military philosopher Vegetius reminds his readers:

In such situations, where no hopes remain, fear itself will arm an enemy and despair inspires courage. When men find they must inevitably perish, they willingly resolve to die with their comrades and with their arms in their hands. The maxim of Scipio, that a golden bridge should be made for a flying enemy, had much been commended. For when they have free room to escape they think of nothing but how to save themselves by flight, and the confusion becoming general, great numbers are cut to pieces.

As the sepoy regiments melted away, the 62nd Foot started a tactical withdrawal. To provide cover to Littler's withdrawing division, the horse artillery went forward and from a position 300 yards away from the Sikh entrenchment, provided covering fire. Their grapeshots shattered the Khalsa soldiers' limbs and harassed the Sikh gunners, allowing Littler's troops to retreat. Then, Gilbert's division, with two brigades under Brigadier Charles Taylor and Brigadier J. McLaran, went into action. Taylor's brigade advanced with HM's 29th and HM's 80th regiments in the front. The 41st Sepoy Regiment was placed in the second line. The British regiments, covered by a line of skirmishers, advanced slowly but steadily. McLaran's brigade, which was composed of the 1st Bengal European Light Infantry in the first line and the 16th and 45th sepoy regiments in the second line, supported Taylor's attack. The Sikh gunners turned their guns on them. The intensive firing of many guns in such a compact space made the battlefield unbearably smoky. The soldiers had difficulty breathing; they were temporarily blinded by the black acrid smoke bellowing out from the muzzles of the guns. As round shots and shells tore apart the ranks, the men got nervous and started firing wildly. Soldiers interviewed in the twentieth century reveal that nervous soldiers become trigger happy. McLaran ordered his men to hold fire till they came close to the enemy. Following the advance of Gilbert's infantry, the 3rd Light Dragoons were also able to penetrate the Sikh trenches. Sikh gunners, like Maratha artillerymen at Assaye, died at their guns. Behind the gunners stood rows of Sikh infantry. Once the Company's soldiers were inside the Sikh camp, close-quarter hand to hand combat ensued. Muskets could not be used in such fights. While the British soldiers used bayonets to stab their opponents, the Sikhs used their curved swords. The swords and the bayonets caused many ghastly wounds. Besides flesh wounds, the blow of a sword also caused cracks in the bones. As dusk was falling Smith's reserve division, which included two British regiments and four sepoy regiments, went into the offensive. Smith cheered his soldiers, 'Into them my lads; the day is your own', and the men finally occupied the outskirts of the Sikh entrenchment.

When sunlight faded at about 6 p.m., the Company's position looked hopeless. The two hour long battering had resulted in the loss of 215 men while 657 men were wounded. Meanwhile, the Sikhs continued to attack, as a result of which Harry Smith's division was forced to withdraw. When the Sikhs found out that Smith's troops had withdrawn, they occupied the outermost trenches again. Most of the British troops were huddled together at one corner of the Sikh camp. They were assailed by musketry fire and artillery shots both from within and from the outer trenches of the Sikh camp. The experience of this night battle for the Company soldiers was terrifying. Some soldiers were blown to pieces when a magazine exploded. When the thirsty Company soldiers tried to get water from a well inside the camp, Sikh musketeers savaged them. The soldiers of various regiments got mixed up. S.L.A. Marshall, in his classic *Men Against Fire,* points out that in the heat of combat only 16 per cent of soldiers actually make use of their weapons, and often against each other because of the pervading sense of fear. The confusion and panic made the Company's *paltans* fire at each other.

FICKLE *FORTUNA*

'War is composed of nothing but accidents.'

—NAPOLEON BONAPARTE

On the morning of 22 December 1845, Tej Singh with a large Western style infantry force, supported by an artillery park and irregular cavalry, entered the scene. The total force under his command came to about 30,000 men. Tej Singh drove away the Company's cavalry outposts and then started a heavy cannonade. Since the Company's artillery had run out of ammunition they could not fight back. Things were poised for dramatic changes in India's history. If Tej Singh pressed the attack, then the tired and ammunition-less Company army would have been wiped out and the Governor General along with the Commander-in-Chief would have been taken prisoner. This would have resulted in massive political and psychological loss on part of the British. Their prestige, with the 'natives' which was an important fulcrum of imperial power, would have reached rock bottom. Nothing could then have stopped the *Dal Khalsa* from reaching the Ganga-Jamuna doab. It would have been time-consuming and expensive for the Company to raise another field army at Calcutta. By that time, the political geography of India would have been transformed. The fence-sitting Afghans would have crossed the Indus. But this did not happen and history took a different turn. Suddenly Tej Singh withdrew. The Company escaped total defeat by the skin of its teeth.

In war, the difference between victory and defeat mostly depends on timing. If Hitler had started Operation Barbarossa two months earlier in 1941, then the *Wehrmacht* probably would have reached Moscow before the advent of the Russian winter. Similarly, the timing of the Sikh attack against the Company was erroneous. The Sikhs missed several chances. In 1839, the Company invaded Afghanistan, and its field army was wiped out in the outskirts of Kabul by the Afghan irregulars aided by 'General Snow'. Only one man from the army, a Dr Brydon, reached the British camp of Jalalabad. The Company sent a relief army under General Pollock. If the Sikhs had attacked Pollock's army when it was entering the Afghan passes, the British-Indian Empire would have been sent into limbo. Earlier too, in 1843, if the *Dal Khalsa* had descended across the Ganga while the British were busy fighting Sindia's troops at Maharajpur, the Company would have been in a very bad shape. However, the Sikhs failed to exploit such windows of opportunity.

The failure on part of the *Khalsa* to attack at the right time and the right place point to lapses in the *durbar's* strategizing. After Ranjit's death, the *durbar* was engaged in a game of musical chairs. Kings like Nau Nihal Singh and Sher Singh were raised to the throne only to be assassinated. The situation seemed to stabilise with the ascendancy of Rani Jindan. Rani Jindan is a character shrouded in a mist. British accounts as well as contemporary Sikh literature depict her as a vulgar woman. However, the reality is that she was not only young and beautiful but also shrewd and active. Like many monarchs, Ranjit Singh had innumerable wives. Besides women, Ranjit was also fond of opium. He had been paralysed a long time, when, just before his death, his youngest wife Jindan became pregnant. Rumours flew. The Rani was said to be having an affair. After Ranjit's death, Jindan was caught in her bedroom with two young men. Jindan was certainly no prude when it came to making love. She came to power acting as the regent of her son Dalip Singh. To strengthen her power base, Jindan made Lal Singh, a tall and handsome but unintelligent man, the Wazir. Lal Singh's only achievement was to win the Rani's affection.

Though there was no love lost between the Rani and Tej Singh, and both agreed that the *Khalsa* army was becoming unruly. The only option for them was to encourage it to attack the Company. If the *Dal Khalsa* was victorious then the *durbar* would take the credit and if it failed, it would be humbled, and the *durbar* would be able to rein in the soldiery. The *durbar's* position was similar to the Pakistan civil government's position after 1947. It had to encourage aggressive foreign policies through an over-strong army to survive. The Rani, like Nawaz Sharif during the Kargil crisis of 1999, was forced to go along with the military. Most chroniclers being conservative male chauvinists, the Rani has always been viewed as a corrupt failure. But the cause of the breakdown of civil-military relations in the *Khalsa* kingdom could equally be laid at Ranjit Singh's door.

Despite massive progress in Westernizing the army, Ranjit Singh failed to construct a centralized despotic bureaucratic state. And this seriously obstructed the *Dal Khalsa* during the war. Raja Gulab Singh, a feudatory of the Sikh state and ruler of Jammu, joined hands with the British. If it had better anticipated matters, the *Dal Khalsa* could have eliminated Gulab Singh before the war with the British. The added resources of Jammu state would have helped it against the Company. In 1845, the *durbar* had no long-term policy. The mistrust between the *Dal Khalsa* and the troika which included Tej Singh, Lal Singh and Rani Jindan at Lahore made its functioning arbitrary.

Even with all these deficiencies, when the *Dal Khalsa* crossed the Sutlej, the result of the campaign was not obvious or preordained. Tej Singh's conduct was not only inefficient but close to that of an agent acting for the Company. How Littler was able to give him the slip in Ferozepore in broad daylight remains inexplicable. While Littler joined the British field army in front of Ferozeshah on 21 December, Tej Singh came only the day after, probably hoping the *Khalsa* troops had melted away. But when Tej Singh saw that the *Khalsa* rearguard was still entrenched in the camp of Ferozeshah, he started firing on the Company's army. Tej Singh seems to have had no heart for a serious fight. He was probably afraid that the *Dal Khalsa* would punish him for allowing Littler to escape from Ferozepore. Tej Singh hoped on the other hand, that if he could aid the British in defeating the *Dal Khalsa*, then a generous Company would make him the ruler of the land of five rivers. He accordingly, decided to leave the *Dal Khalsa* to its doom and withdrew when the Company was on the brink of defeat. If the panches under Tej Singh had known how close to defeat the Company's army was, they would have forced their Commander-in-Chief to give battle. The position of the Company's *paltans* on the morning of 22 December 1845 in the field of Ferozeshah was similar to the situation facing Wellington's soldiers at Waterloo in the late afternoon. The men, sorely tired, were down to their last cartridge. One more charge by the enemy and they would have cracked. But with relief, Wellington's soldiers saw that Napoleon's Guards, instead of charging, were retreating. Similarly, in the late morning of 22 December, a relieved Hardinge saw that Tej Singh's force was withdrawing.

GOTTERDAMMERUNG OF THE
DAL KHALSA

After Ferozeshah, the British progress to Punjab was inevitable: it could be delayed but not denied. At Ferozeshah, the Sikh army had proved its mastery of defensive tactics. It was also capable of manoeuvres. In the immediate aftermath of Ferozeshah, when Harry Smith's infantry division and Brigadier General Charles Robert Cureton's cavalry advanced from Jugraon to Ludhiana, a Sikh detachment under Ranjur Singh moved parallel to the British and tried to intercept the Company's troops. At times, the Sikh detachment outflanked the British forces and unleashed artillery fire on them. But in the battle at Aliwal (28 January 1846), Harry Smith enjoyed not only numerical but also artillery superiority over Ranjur Singh's force. Smith carried some 8 in. howitzers on carriages which proved especially destructive.

On 10 February 1846, the Sikh army again challenged the British at Sobraon. However, after the loss at Ferozeshah, the Sikhs could muster only 35,000 infantry. The Company deployed 30,000 infantry. The Sikhs were adept at conducting combined arms warfare by integrating musketry, *zamburaks* and cannons. The three successive trench lines inside the Sikh camp proved difficult for the Company's troops, which had 2,900 casualties—close to the 3,000 casualties suffered by the *paltans* at Ferozeshah. But the Company's 100 artillery pieces against 67 Sikh guns won the day for the EIC.

The Sikh infantry was capable of a fighting withdrawal. Unfortunately for them, a faulty tactical disposition had left them fighting with their backs at the river Sutlej. As they retreated, the bridge over the Sutlej broke. Honigberger claims Tej Singh had deliberately destroyed the bridge. Luck, too, favoured the victors. There was a sudden rise of seven inches in the Sutlej thus damaging the bridge and the best of the Sikh infantry drowned in the river. The gateway to Punjab was open. Very shortly, the Company's *paltans* crossed the Sutlej and the *Khalsa* kingdom passed into history.

The Residency system was established in 1846 in Punjab. Immediately after assuming office, the Resident Henry Lawrence began demobilizing the *Khalsa* soldiers. This resulted in an uprising, led by Sher Singh Attariwala. Many *durbar* troops also sided with Sher Singh. This resulted in the Second Anglo-Sikh War (1848–9). However, the Sikhs lacked their regular infantry and artillery, which had been destroyed in 1845. Sher Singh's predominantly *jagirdari* cavalry force was wiped out in a series of battles characterized by heavy cannonading by the Company's guns and then a frontal assault by their *paltans*. The uprising was finally crushed in 1849.

It is difficult to find fault with the tactical moves of the *Dal Khalsa*. Ferozeshah shows that despite tactical brilliance, an army led and betrayed by an indifferent high command stood no chance against the Company's professionals. The military excellence achieved by the *Dal Khalsa* was ruined by the power games of over-ambitious soldiery and political pygmies who moved in the corridors of power at Lahore. After Ferozeshah, the last military threat to the British within the subcontinent was wiped out. The *Khalsa* infantry's excellence at Ferozeshah and Sobraon even against heavy odds made the British recruit Sikhs instead of 'Pandies' in their sepoy regiments. This resulted in a catastrophe for them in the summer of 1857.

10

———

Under Siege

Lucknow, 1857–1858

Ingredients of a Wagnerian drama characterized the year 1857 in India. Blood, death and disaster occurred throughout the subcontinent and the mayhem continued for another two years. Ironically, the very sepoys who had shed their blood to bring the country under the Union Jack, rebelled against their white masters. On a Sunday in the summer of 1857, the East India Company's Bengal army blew up when, out of its 1,20,000 personnel, about 70,000 men turned their muskets against the sahibs. The campaign to destroy the rule of the *feranghis* was on.

THE SEPOYS STRIKE BACK

For some years before 1857, the sepoys' tempers were running high. The indifferent performance of high caste soldiers of the Bengal army in Afghanistan during the First Anglo-Afghan War and in Punjab during the two Anglo-Sikh Wars resulted in a loss of prestige. The young and arrogant officers freshly arrived from Britain abused the sepoys as 'Pandies' because large numbers of Pande Brahmins used to join the Bengal army. There were many reasons for this. Till the early nineteenth century, it was fairly common for British officers to have Indian women as lovers and sometimes, wives. The sahibs thereby understood Indian society better and interaction with Indian women encouraged white officers to empathize with their Indian soldiers. From the 1850s, white women began arriving in India in large numbers resulting in the severance of the social bond between British males and Indians. The British had experienced the military prowess of the *Dal Khalsa* during the Sikh Wars. Accordingly, after the annexation of Punjab, they began recruiting Sikhs instead of high caste men from Awadh and Bihar. The 'Pandies' felt threatened by this as their job prospects were narrowing with the increasing entry of the Sikhs in the Bengal army. The General Enlistment Act which was passed in 1856 further annoyed the sepoys. According to this act, the sepoys were obliged to serve Company interests even overseas. Caste taboos prevented the sepoys from crossing the seas. The feeling grew among the high caste soldiery that the white men were aiming to destroy their age-old *dharma*. As a last straw, the Company introduced Enfield rifles in place of smoothbore muskets. The rumour was that the cartridges of the new rifle were greased with the fat of cows and pigs. This was horrifying for both high caste Hindus in the Bengal army's infantry regiments and the Muslim landed gentry and their retainers who served the Bengal cavalry regiments.

Compared to earlier wars, the battles of the 'Mutiny' were more barbarous. The distinction between combatants and non-combatants vanished. Indians who functioned as bankers and *bhisties* for the Company were put to death by the rebels. At times, many Indian collaborators' limbs were cut off. The aim of the rebels was to deter other Indians from joining hands with the British. On 2 November 1857, when a *bhistie* of the Company's army went into a village near Lucknow searching for a well, rebel sentries stationed there cut off his hands, noses and ears. In return, the British troops burned that and seven other surrounding villages. This sort of indiscriminate violence against non-combatants was repeated during the 1970s in Vietnam by the American army.

The 1857 campaign was characterized by unprecedented brutality towards women. The henchmen of Nana Sahib, the rebel leader at Kanpur, killed British women at Satichaura Ghat and this incensed the 'master race'. From British reminiscences of the Mutiny, it is evident that they viewed the 'Pandies' as *untermenschen* who deserved to be exterminated. Most British officers came from the Victorian middle class. They were religious, small town men who had an 'extraordinary respect' for white women. Victorian males perceived the opposite sex as fragile creatures who needed to be protected, especially in an alien land, from mischievous 'blacks'. This created a lethal spirit of vengeance among British soldiers.

THE CRAWLING CAMEL

Britain's greatest commander of the twentieth century, Bernard Montgomery, has written that most great generals have humble origins. The privations that they face in their youth strengthen their determination. Colin Campbell, the Commander-in-Chief of Company's forces during 1857, was the son of a Glasgow carpenter. He had served under Wellington in Spain during the Napoleonic War and commanded a division against the Russians at the Crimean War. Campbell's motto seems to have been 'Slow and steady wins the race.' For his cautious conduct of war, Campbell was dubbed the 'Crawling Camel' by British soldiers who fought in British-India 1857.

In the summer of 1857, seared by the heat of mutiny, the beleaguered British in Lucknow took refuge at the Residency, which for about a century, had been the symbol of *feranghi* power in Awadh. Initially, Henry Lawrence, the Resident of Awadh, was in command. Then, a relief army under Henry Havelock reached Lucknow. However, the hunter became the hunted. Havelock's army itself was besieged by an ever-increasing number of rebels. And Lawrence died soon after Havelock came. After wresting Delhi from the rebels, the British high command debated whether to capture Kanpur or Lucknow. Before the British could think of relieving the Residency at Lucknow, they had to safeguard Kanpur, about 45 mi. away. The rebels, who were threatening Kanpur from central India, knew this communication hub linked eastern India with northwest and central India. In November 1857, Colin Campbell led an army into Lucknow, and after collecting the non-combatants from the Residency, retreated. However, Campbell left a rearguard near Lucknow headed by James Outram. In December 1857, James Outram, with a force of 4,400 infantry supported by a strong artillery park, entrenched himself in Alambagh, a walled enclosure about one and a half miles from the outskirts of Lucknow. Leaving aside the sick and wounded, Outram's strike force amounted to 2,000 men. Life in Outram's force was not only dreary, but also dangerous. Many thousands of rebels were scattered along the gardens on the bank of the canal which skirted the city. Besides musket shots, the rebels also fired artillery shells at the British camp. Campbell was vehemently criticized by the Delhi veterans for this withdrawal from Lucknow. They argued that in September 1857, the British had won in Delhi with a much smaller force, and Crawling Camel was overestimating the rebel's military prowess in his retreat.

In hindsight, we know that Campbell's decision was right. Time was on the British side. A delay would only strengthen the British position as more and more white troops were disembarking in Calcutta, and it was unnecessary for Campbell to risk more than he did. Further, when the British force on the ridge of Delhi moved to assault the Mughal capital, there was no rebel army threatening them at their rear. Instead, the chiefs of Punjab safeguarded the British rear. The situation at Lucknow was different. Tantia Tope threatened the British force all along the Lucknow-Kanpur axis. He was Nana Sahib's general, commanding Sindia's Gwalior contingent, which was superbly equipped with guns.

A commander is not worth his salt if his men have no faith on him. The Delhi veterans who disliked Campbell constituted a minority within his force. Sir Colin was especially liked by the Highlander soldiers recruited from the glens of Scotland. The Highlanders had a fierce reputation which they maintained during the Second World War. Their tenacity, bravery, ruthlessness—and tartan kilts—forced the personnel of a panzer division deployed in Normandy during June 1944 to marvel at them as 'ladies from hell'. Back in Lucknow, the 93rd Highlander Regiment's men with 'legs like young elephants', were dubbed *vilayati* Gurkhas by the rebel soldiery.

Campbell's portraits provide the image of a drunken man with uncombed hair, sleepy eyes and a pink face. In reality, Campbell was excitable and voluble. With clenched teeth, he listened to the plans made by his subordinates, muttering the odd 'ummh, mmps, hummm'. Gradually he would get excited and begin gesticulating wildly with both his hands, shouting, 'Oh yes, we will attack them here and here.' In contrast to the dynamic body language of Campbell, his Chief of Staff, General W.R. Mansfield remained silent during planning sessions. While Campbell was a straightforward man, Mansfield was less transparent and shrewder.

An army under siege needs adequate provisions and munitions continuously. The Sixth army under Paulas surrendered in Stalingrad in January 1943 because of the German high command's failure to get supplies to it in the winter of 1942. Colin Campbell was lacking in dash and the offensive spirit but his meticulous attention to detail was renowned. He took great care supplying the British outpost in Lucknow. One memorandum dated 15 December 1857 issued from Kanpur by Mansfield pointed out:

Two hundred gun bullocks have been despatched to James Outram, yoked to carts. He will have the goodness to apply them to the guns. A fortnight's provisions have been despatched for all James Outram's force, including Bunee, together with what stores of clothing, tentage, and boots it is in the power of Brigadier Inglis, commanding at Kanpur to give. . . . All accounts must be carefully kept by the respective corps and departments, and regiments. . . . Grain is now at Kanpur, about 11 to 12 seers to the rupee.

Every night about 450 soldiers escorted the convoys coming from Kanpur. Meanwhile, Campbell was also able to send reinforcements to Outram from time to time. Between 27 November 1857 and 14 February 1858, Campbell sent 2,000 men to Outram.

By 11 December 1857, Campbell had been able to defeat the Gwalior Contingent and the threat to Kanpur finally vanished. In the meantime, the rebels inside Lucknow realized that time was running out for them. So, on the morning of 12 January 1858, about 30,000 rebels took position to attack Outram's force. The rebels initiated the attack with shouts of '*Maro Angrez suar*' (Kill the English pigs). The core of Outram's defence depended on six 9-pounder guns. They opened up when the rebels were 500 yards away. Thanks to these guns, the attack was repulsed. Superior firepower as well as superior tactics gained the day for the British. The 9th Fusiliers attacked the rebels at their flanks and drove them away. Combined arms tactics was another feature of Outram's defence. The Fusiliers were supported with guns drawn by bullocks. By 4 p.m., the rebels had had enough and started retreating. The rebels tried again on 17 January 1858. But this attack was also driven back by the accuracy and range of Enfield rifles. Displaying extraordinary fire discipline, the 75th Infantry Regiment held back its fire till the rebels came within 150 yards and then opened a withering fire.

RETURN OF THE BRITISH RAJ

'. . . the accurate fire of our artillery, from which it could easily be seen he sustained considerable loss.'

—JAMES OUTRAM about the mutineers, 28 February 1858

The rebels finally realized that they had no hope of defeating the British in an open battle. The trap closed on them in March 1858 when on the one hand, Campbell's main army advanced towards Lucknow and on the other hand, the Nepal Maharajah Jung Bahadur's force descended on the city. While Campbell deployed 19,771 soldiers and 4,517 horses, Jung Bahadur assembled 15,000 Gurkhas. In desperation, the rebels resorted to static urban warfare. When the British relieving force entered Lucknow, they found the rebels had converted the whole city, including its suburbs, into a veritable fortress. The city of Lucknow had a circumference of twenty miles. The rebels manned two defence lines. The outer defensive arc included the suburbs around the river Gomti, while the inner defensive line was constituted around the principal buildings of the city.

As the British relief force advanced towards the doomed city, the rebels in the suburbs attempted to delay them. Taking advantage of the mango trees and long grass, the rebels started sniping at the British column. The standard British response was to send horse artillery supported by skirmishers to drive the snipers away. Outside the city limits, there were many ponds surrounded by forest. From inside the forest, the rebels opened musketry fire against the column of Company troops marching towards Lucknow. The horse artillery of the British advanced towards the forest and then fired grape shots. As the rebels moved out from the forest to cross the ponds, the Punjabi cavalry attached to Campbell's force charged them. The long lances of the troopers were able to pierce many retreating rebels and the water of the ponds turned crimson with blood.

The British troops marched towards Lucknow, and in this city buildings like Jelalabad, the King's Palace, Dilkhusa and Chattar Manzil had been converted to rebel strongholds. From the rooftops, windows, doors and loopholes poured forth intense musketry fire. The narrow, intricate, winding streets of Lucknow, jam-packed with buildings on either side, were similar to Delhi's streets. The confined built-up area within both the cities were transformed into heavily defended zones by the rebels.

Campbell's tactics were brutal. In fact, grand tactical manouevres are not possible inside a defended city. Like Zhukov in Berlin during April 1945, Campbell went for a slugging match, destroying each block of the city, occupying each and every house and fighting along the serpentine streets. In such attritional warfare, the invaders require firepower superiority. Campbell's force was firepower-heavy. His artillery train was manned by 1,613 men and 930 horses. The artillery was divided into a field artillery brigade, siege artillery brigade and naval brigade. The field artillery brigade, composed of relatively smaller guns, was used to support the infantry. The heavier siege artillery guns were used for counter-bombardment of enemy guns. The superheavy guns taken from the ship *Shannon* and organized in the naval brigade consisting of a hundred sailors were used for breaching the walls of heavily defended buildings. Debris had to be cleared and roads had to be built for the guns to be transported. Further, the siting of heavy guns required the construction of parapets with fascines and sandbags. The 50 European engineers who commanded 1,526 Indian sappers did all these complex jobs.

Inside Lucknow, the heavily defended La Martinere school building was taken by the Second Division under General Lugard on 9 March 1858. One despatch for the Governor General noted, 'It had been very heavily cannonaded. The action was principally one of artillery; the loss being trifling in consequence.' Like Zhukov, Campbell utilized his superior firepower in demolishing enemy strong points. He used 18-pounder iron guns to blast the walls. To destroy rebel defenders inside buildings, 8-inch iron howitzers and 24-pounder field howitzers were used. Walls were mined by sappers directed by the engineers. During the final phase of artillery bombardment, which occurred before the infantry assault, the British used their wonder weapon: the gigantic 68-pounders of the Royal Navy which were operated by the naval brigade. These monsters were used to blast the Kaiserbagh. Thanks to the heavy firepower at the disposal of Campbell, he was able to inflict huge casualties. Still, rebel opposition was intense, as proven by the fact that in the Company's force, the proportion of killed to wounded was nearly half.

The experience of city combat proved to be terrible for many. Several British soldiers were blown to pieces when gunpowder stacked in the streets by the rebels exploded. The bodies of soldiers near the explosions were blackened, shriveled, and charred just like the dead crews of a burnt out panzer. Soldiers who were somewhat removed from the epicentre of the explosions were horribly burnt and died agonizing deaths. Such casualties among the Company's troops hardened their response towards the opponents. The result was barbarization of warfare. Some rebels were defending a building and shooting at Company soldiers from the door and windows. The British soldiers rushed through the door shouting, 'Remember Kanpur'. Once inside the room, they bayoneted the rebel defenders. Then, the Sikh soldiers dragged out around 150 dead and wounded 'Pandies' and set fire to them. The wounded cried for a quick bullet wound to escape slow death by burning. Many British officers witnessed the ghastly scene with satisfaction. Nevertheless, there existed a lighter side to the soldiers' experience of the battle. Amidst the guns firing and hard campaigning with bitter and bloody memories, British soldiers' lives were punctuated by cricket and football matches. British Tommies who did not participate in the games spent their time sitting in the shade of mango trees and writing long love letters to their sweethearts back in Britain.

HISTORY TURNED UPSIDE DOWN

'This is splendid, no nonsense about it. We are fighting close up now, hurrying on the most rapid of sieges, working recklessly under fire.'

—LIEUTENANT ARTHUR LANG, Bengal Engineers, 1857.

James Outram in a despatch dated 28 February 1858 provided a portrait of the rebel army in Lucknow:

The outworks of a vast city swarming with hosts of mutinous sepoys; with Nujeebs—the undisciplined but well-armed soldiers of the rebel government; with many thousand city 'budmashes' the armed and turbulent scum of a population of 7,00,000 souls; and with numerous bands of those feudal retainers of the chieftains and great zemindars of Awadh, whose normal state for the last fifty years has been one of warfare.

The ratio of cavalry to infantry in Outram's force was 1:7, yet his force was able to defend itself against 15,000 rebel cavalry and 15,000 ill-disciplined infantry. The confrontation demonstrates the uselessness of cavalry in siege warfare. Urban combat, characterized by house to house combat and street-fighting, required artillery supported by a disciplined infantry. By February 1858, the rebel regular infantry in Lucknow had dwindled to only twenty-four regiments (Table 10.1). The rest of the troops consisted of ill-disciplined, irregular cavalry and infantry raised by the *taluqdars*. By this time, the rebels were also facing a serious shortage of cartridges and munitions. The British and allied Indian troops were liberally supplied with small arms and munitions of war. Not only did the rebels suffer from a deficiency

TABLE 10.1: Strength of the Rebel Army in Lucknow,
February 1858

Type of Troops	*Military Effectiveness*
24 Bengal Infantry Regiments	Discipline and firepower equivalent to the loyal sepoy regiments of the British forces. Deficient in firepower compared to the regular British regiments.
5 regular infantry regiments from Fatehpur numbering 5,000 men and 5 guns.	Somewhat inferior in discipline and firepower to the rebel Bengal infantry regiments.
13 Awadh Army Infantry Regiments	Equivalent in firepower and discipline to the Sikh and Pathan levies raised by the Company.
14 regiments of new levies	As above.
106 regiments of *Nujeebs*	Armed with matchlocks. Fit for only police duties.
25 regiments of regular and irregular cavalry	As above.
Levies of zamindars, *taluqdars*	A military liability for the rebel High Command. However, they could have proved their worth in guerrilla warfare.
Civilian, criminal elements, about 20,000	Useless mouths required to be fed; caused security problems in the rear area.
Guns =131	Most of the guns were old and indigenous. They were buried by the locals when Awadh was annexed and recovered during the mutiny. A majority of the guns proved to be unserviceable.

Total strength of rebel military in February 1858 was 95,500 soldiers (regulars and irregulars) and 20,000 indifferently armed civilians and criminals.

of shots and shells, but the bores of the guns manufactured by the rebels were also flawed. Often, the muzzle of a rebel's gun burst while firing. The breeches of many guns were also defective. The rebels failed mostly because of the lack of a military infrastructure to support their troops.

The resistance at Lucknow was led by the Begum of Awadh. Historians of the 1857 Mutiny have dwelt upon the role of the Rani of Jhansi but not as much on the enigmatic Begum who had the greater vision and was capable of leading men into battle. The Begum was the youngest wife of Wajid Ali Shah, the last Nawab of Awadh. Wajid Ali was an aesthete and a renowned gourmet, but he was fat and effeminate. He spent his time often wearing women's clothes and playing chess. The Begum hated her husband with a passion. After the annexation of Awadh by Lord Dalhousie, Wajid Ali moved to Calcutta but the Begum refused to go. Like Rani Jindan of the *Khalsa* Kingdom, the Begum came to power as regent of her young son Barjis Qadir.

The Begum realized the role of propaganda in mobilizing the masses. She issued a notice proclaiming joint Hindu-Muslim front for the protection of caste and religion. She used Hindu mendicants and Muslim religious men to inflame the passions of the soldiery, urging them to conduct a ruthless religious war against the godless *feranghis*. To motivate the soldiers to make more effort, she taunted them with sarcastic comments. After the fall of Delhi in late 1857, the defeated rebels came to Lucknow. The Begum understood that the addition of more troops would only increase her logistical burden. Soldiers with money were allowed entry and the rest were ordered to disperse in the countryside to disrupt the Raj's rural revenue-collecting administration. The Begum's strategy was to engage the British troops in Lucknow and to wear them down while Tantia Tope attacked them from the rear with the Gwalior Contingent. When Tantia Tope retreated after being defeated, the Begum waited in vain for a relief army to come and attack the invaders from the rear.

Despite the Begum's 'will to victory', it was very difficult, if not impossible, to maintain unified command over the disparate rebel force. Landholders like Jai Singh, Mahdi Husain, and others were unwilling to accept the authority of rebel officers who possessed professional expertise in matters military. The landholders considered the subedars and jemadars of rebel regiments socially inferior. To make matters worse, the regular rebel infantry and cavalry failed to coordinate brigade-sized attacks involving 5,000 or more soldiers. This was because the jemadars and subedars were trained to lead only ten to a hundred men; they were not trained in the higher management of warfare by the British when they served the Company. In Delhi,

Bahadur Shah was able to rely on a professional like Bakht Khan, the Subedar of the Bareilly Artillery Regiment. But the Begum had no such professional advisor. After the fall of Lucknow, when her lover Mammu Khan wanted to surrender, the Begum parted ways with him and commenting that her ex-lover was a corrupt cowardly donkey. Mammu surrendered, only to be hanged. The Begum, like a true heroine, refused to surrender and successfully escaped to Nepal.

With its defective command set up, firepower-inferiority and inadequate training, the rebel force was not suited to conduct battles or withstand sieges against the Company's firepower-heavy professionals. After the fall of Delhi, the rebels should have realized that their 'city holding strategy' was defective, and that they stood no chance against the siege guns of the Company. In fact, suitable preconditions existed for the rebels to conduct dispersed sporadic low intensity warfare against the road-bound British military columns. The conflict with the British not only took on a religious colour but also approached the character of a national liberation struggle. The green flag of Islam was raised in Lucknow. Indians inside the city who refused to join the side of the rebels were insulted and fined. The prostitutes of Lucknow and Kanpur eagerly supported the rebel cause. Not only did they provide financial aid to the rebel government, they also punished ineffectual rebel soldiers by the simple means of withholding their services. Such rebel soldiers were turned away from courtesans' quarters with shouts of 'No kisses for the cowards.'

The rebel cavalry was wasted in the city warfare of Lucknow. Though the rebels had the superior cavalry, horsemen could not be used profitably in defending houses and streets. The rebels failed to use the cavalry effectively to achieve mobility and surprise over the Company. Long-distance cavalry raids against British held territories could have been lethal. Such raids would have raised the tempo of operations against the slow-moving Company infantry and siege artillery. Long distance cavalry raids were used to devastate the enemy held countryside right until the early twentieth century when the introduction of machine guns, trucks, and aeroplanes made such attacks obsolete.

In 1857, the Company suffered from a grave manpower shortage. To counteract the 'Pandies', John Lawrence (brother of Henry who held the Lucknow Residency till his death) recruited Pathans and Sikhs who joined the Company's standard in large numbers. Whenever, they met white faces, Sikhs and Pathans would shout, '*Humne Matadeen ko bahut mara*' (We have killed lot of rebels). The Pathans had come to the British side at the prospect of plundering the rich cities of north India. The Sikhs had joined to take revenge on the 'Pandies' for invading Punjab in 1845. The rebels would have benefited by taking the war to Bengal. The hot and sultry climate of the lower Gangetic valley suited neither the Sikhs nor the Pathans, who were from a dry and cool bracing climate. If the rebels had carried out attritional guerrilla warfare in Bengal, then Sikh and Pathan enthusiasm to fight for Company's cause would have decreased. Neither the climate nor the marshy and swampy terrain of Bengal would have suited them. Bengal, being a British province, did not offer any prospect of plunder to the Sikhs and Pathans. Moreover, long range raids by the rebels in Bengal would have threatened the 'soft' unwarlike Bengali babus who, as clerks, were eagerly collaborating with the alien regime. Most of the Company's gun and munitions producing factories like Fort William, Cossipore and Dum Dum were in Bengal. The destruction of these arsenals or even the threat to these manufactories from the rebels would have tied down large numbers of white infantry, thus reducing the strength of the field army operating in the Ganga-Jamuna doab. Finally, most British reinforcements entered the north Indian theatre through Calcutta. Raids and threat of raids by the rebel cavalry in the lower Gangetic delta would have restricted the reinforcements to Calcutta instead of pushing them towards Colin Campbell's force. A fruitless attritional campaign throughout north India by the British might have encouraged the Afghans and the Sikh chieftains who were sitting on the fence to join the rebels.

CONCLUSION

The war of 1857 with its increasing violence against civilians, popular participation, and objective of total annihilation of the enemy marked, in a way, the genesis of 'total warfare' in South Asia. Increasing collateral damage became the trend for the future reaching its culmination during World War II.

Till the advent of Hitler's war, the Raj in India remained safe from the military point of view. The pacification campaign which continued for one year after the fall of Lucknow broke the back of the mutineers. After 1859, the Indians gave up the option of armed military struggle against the colonisers. Instead they took up the option of dialogue-based organized politics which reached its zenith under Mohandas Gandhi. British security managers at London and Delhi were confident of holding on to the subcontinent for a least another century. Their self-confidence was rudely shattered when in 1944, the soldiers of the Rising Sun arrived in northwest India along with Subhas Bose's phantom army.

11

—————

Mousetrap

Imphal and Kohima
March–July 1944

AFTER THE 1857 mutiny was crushed, the Raj in India restructured its military organization. Instead of *Purbiyas*, the British-led Indian army, also known as the Sepoy army, started recruiting Sikhs, Pathans and Gurkhas. The Sepoy army guarded India against the Indians for the Raj. During the First World War, the Indian army was used as an imperial reserve in the Middle East as well as in France. However, the British-officered Sepoy army faced its greatest challenge during the Second World War, when British-India was threatened for the first time. The traditional invasion route for India had been the North-West Frontier. But in 1942, India was threatened along the eastern frontier. It seemed that the Japanese steamroller would overcome everything in its route.

THE PHANTOM ARMY

'They [Japanese] were right in thinking that victory in Assam would resound far beyond that remote jungle land; it might, indeed, as they proclaimed in exhortation to their troops, change the whole course of the World War. Burma, for a space no longer a side show in the global struggle, would hold the centre stage.'

—FIELD MARSHAL BILL (WILLIAM) SLIM

Towards the end of 1943, Japanese intelligence assumed that the British-officered Indian army was being reorganized and readied for the reconquest of Burma. The Imperial Head Quarter at Tokyo ordered

Field Marshal Count Terauchi, commander of the Southern Theatre, to launch a preemptive strike to disrupt the British military preparations. It was hoped that if the supply dumps and railheads in North East India were captured then British preparations would collapse. The Chinese warlord Chiang Kai Shek's army and the American General Joseph Stillwell's American troops in south China were supplied by American planes stationed in east India. Aircraft had to cross the 22,000 ft. high Himalaya before landing in air strips in Yunnan province of south China. The pilots named this dangerous air supply route 'the Hump'. The Japanese hoped that the conquest of India's northeastern rim would prevent Americans stationed in Bengal and Assam from supplying Chiang Kai Sheik and Stilwell's armies in south China. A separate peace with China might then become possible. However, the Japanese were also ready to exploit wider strategic opportunities within India in case they presented themselves. And Netaji assured the Japanese that bigger political prizes would fall into their laps when the Nipponese and Azad Hind Fauj advanced towards India.

Subhas Chandra Bose was the angry young man of Indian politics. In the Indian National Congress, Bose had always been a hardliner. He believed that freedom could only be achieved through violent means. After differences on this issue with Gandhi, Bose floated his new political outfit named Forward Bloc. When the Second World War started, Bose was arrested. But he was able to escape his British captors, and after an adventurous journey which spanned Afghanistan, USSR and Italy, Bose finally reached Germany. He managed to meet Hitler. The *Fuehrer* convinced Bose that his presence in Japanese-occupied South East Asia would be fruitful for India's Independence. The German General Staff had a tradition of fomenting troubles in enemy countries by transporting revolutionaries. While Ludendorff provided Lenin with a sealed bulletproof train that conveyed the Red revolutionary to Czarist Russia, Hitler provided Bose with a submarine (U-180) that took the Indian leader to Japanese-controlled Indian Ocean. It proved to be a daredevil journey which seemed stranger than many war thrillers. On a rainy night (21 April 1943), when the ocean was rough, Bose was transferred in a dinghy from the German to Japanese submarine I-29 at a position 400 miles south-west of Madagascar. After Bose reached Tokyo, he convinced the Japanese High Command that he would command the army which Japan had raised from Indian prisoners of war. With this army, he asserted, a large-scale internal rebellion against the British inside India could be engineered. The dictator of Japan General Hideki Tojo and his henchmen were convinced by the ambitious plan chalked out by the fiery Bose. The army which Bose organized was known as the Azad Hind Fauj or Indian National Army (INA).

On Tojo's orders, Terauchi accommodated Bose's army within his own action plan. The Japanese had a predilection for complex plans. Lieutenant-General Shozo Sakurai's 28th Army composed of the 54th and 55th Divisions were to launch an attack at Arakan, which was code named HA GO. Each division was composed of about 20,000 soldiers. The aim was to draw the Allied reserves into Arakan. As soon as this was done, the Japanese would launch their main offensive, code-named U GO along the Imphal-Kohima axis. Lieutenant-General Renya Mutaguchi's 15th, 31st, and 33rd Divisions, along with an INA division, were ordered to smash the British 4th Corps and capture the twin cities of Imphal and Kohima.

The INA division had no combat value. Since it was a phantom army, its principal value lay in conducting psychological warfare. The Japanese high command and Bose decided to use the INA to seduce Indian soldiers deserting the British side. Bose and his Japanese sponsors believed that once the INA entered India, the masses would rise against their British oppressors. In case the rebellion was successful, the Japanese were ready to advance deep inside India. A hopeful Bose grandiosely named his programme '*Delhi Chalo*'.

The Burma-India theatre was within Admiral Louis Mountbatten's South East Asia Command. General Slim's 14th Army was designated by Mountbatten to stop the Japanese advance. The principal combat occurred at Imphal plateau in Manipur, some 6,000 sq. mi. in area and 3,000 ft. above the sea level.

JUNGLE STORY

'We will supply you by air. There will be no more retreat.'

—MOUNTBATTEN to Slim's troops

The battle started on 6 March 1944 when the 1,15,000-strong Japanese force confronted the 4th Corps of the 14th army. The combat was exceedingly savage because the Japanese proved to be tough fighters. In accordance with the *Bushido* code, every Japanese soldier took a personal oath to Emperor Hirohito to fight till death. Traditionally, the Japanese used to attack with the officer leading from the front, his sword drawn, shouting '*Banzai*'. Surrendering to the enemy was considered a dishonourable act. The families of Japanese soldiers who surrendered were maltreated by Japanese society. When left with no other option, surrounded Japanese soldiers committed *harakiri*. In the Burma campaign, on an average for every hundred Japanese soldiers killed, only one surrendered. When the Japanese evacuated their own field hospitals, they shot their wounded comrades. General Slim was shocked to see a wounded Japanese officer with his hands tied behind his back. He questioned the British soldiers accompanying the wounded Japanese prisoner about this. The British troops replied that the wounded man had tried several times to rip his bandages off. For the Japanese officer concerned, it was a matter of great shame that he had been taken prisoner by the British and treated by them for his injuries.

Besides their cultural conditioning, the Japanese soldiers were also egged on by their brutal penal system. The 33rd Division was the most dangerous Japanese division that the Allied encountered in Burma. Its commander, Lieutenant-General Nobuo Tanaka, issued the following order when the combat for Imphal was in progress:

Now is the time to capture Imphal—You men have got to be fully in the picture as to what the present position is; regarding death as something lighter than feather, you must tackle the task of capturing Imphal—In order to keep the honour of his unit bright, a commander may have to use his sword as a weapon of punishment, exceedingly shameful though it is to have to shed the blood of one's own soldiers on the battlefield. . . . On this battle rests the fate of the Empire. All officers and men fight courageously.

Only the autocratic regimes of Stalin and Hitler had issued similar barbaric orders to the Red army and the *Waffen* SS troops. Since Britain and America were democracies, the military officers of these two countries could not ask its officers to punish the defaulting soldiers with death. They had to rely on incentives like alcohol, cigarettes, condensed milk and films to motivate their soldiers.

Besides the Nipponese forces, the Sepoy army had to fight three 'M's—monsoon, mud and malaria. Marching through the leech infested jungle, getting completely drenched due to the continuous downpour, was a horrible experience for soldiers who fought along the India-Burma border. The area had virtually no metalled roads. With mud up to their knees, the soldiers had to crawl through slippery tracts while leeches clung to them from the grass and the bushes. Even a bonfire was not possible at night for the fear that it would attract the Japanese snipers' attention. The dark and dreary night resulted in a loss of spirit. But if the condition of soldiers of the Indian army was bad, then that of the Japanese was worse.

Japanese jungle fighting tactics though successful against the British in 1942, failed in 1944. Most of the British and Indian troops involved in the 1942 campaign were raw. When Japanese infantry columns equipped with light machine-guns, mortars, rifles and grenades infiltrated behind them and cut their lines of communications, the Allied troops panicked. They threw away their rifles and retreated pell-mell. In 1944, when the Japanese surrounded them, the Indian troops fortified their positions. The message which was hammered into the minds of the Indian troops was 'dig or die'. The Royal Air Force supplied these fortified positions by parachute-dropping.

During their Arakan offensive, the Japanese plan was to draw British reserves away from Imphal; this time, thanks to the Dakotas available, Slim was able to transport the 5th Indian Division from Arakan to Imphal when the Japanese advanced towards the latter town. The import of fresh troops considerably strengthened the Allied position. Gurkhas armed with *kukris* shouting their war cry '*Ayo Gurkhali*', met Japanese *Banzai* charges at the perimeters of the fortifications. The Gurkhas had a reputation for brutality. Once Slim came across a party of Gurkhas burying dead Japanese soldiers. Slim noticed a Gurkha on the point of chopping off the head of one Japanese soldier, wounded but alive. Slim shouted at the Gurkha to leave the injured man alone. The Gurkha turned to Slim, a little confused. He asked Slim if the Japanese soldier was to be buried alive instead.

The Japanese troops were under pressure not only to win but to win quickly. They had to finish the campaign before the monsoon broke. Once the rainfall started, the already rickety Japanese logistical apparatus running across river Chindwin would face total ruin. After ten to fifteen days, it was the Japanese who ran out of supplies. They had no supply system to back them up. Their High Command relied on captured Indian food dumps for provisioning their troops. Each Japanese soldier carried only three days' supplies on their backs. When the Indian troops inside their fortifications refused to budge, the Japanese had to retreat. While retreating, the absence of medical supplies and food, and foul drinking water, resulted in many thousands of Japanese soldiers dying. Scrub typhus and dysentery devastated them. The British wounded, on the other hand, were nursed at proper medical facilities. In many cases, seriously wounded British soldiers got a jeep ride and were then flown back to the hospitals in Calcutta.

The Japanese supply problem was aggravated by the Chindits. These were long range penetration groups air-dropped by gliders far behind the Japanese lines inside Burma. The Chindits ambushed Japanese supply columns and then hid in the jungles, causing havoc deep inside the Japanese rear area. Cargo carriers belonging to the British and American air forces maintained the Chindits through parachute drops.

Besides functioning as troop transporters and cargo carriers, the Allied air forces also provided close air support to Slim's ground forces. The Spitfires and Hurricanes of the Royal Air Force swept the once dreaded Japanese Zero fighters from the sky. British fighters flew at treetop level to provide fire support to advancing Indian troops. Besides machine gunning fleeing Japanese troops, the aircraft's cannons destroyed Japanese bunkers. In addition, Japanese troop concentration further behind was bombed round the clock by American Mitchell bombers. By the end of July 1944, Lieutenant-General Renya Mutaguchi had no other option but to retreat.

TWO YEARS TOO LATE

> 'The essence of all military planning is timing. A brilliant plan wrongly timed, put into operation too early or too late, is at best a lame thing and at worst may be a disaster.'
>
> —FIELD MARSHAL SLIM

For Subhas Bose and the Japanese, it was a tragedy that the attack against India started too late. By 1944, the Axis powers were on the run in all theatres of the war. *Generalfeldmarschall* Erwin Rommel had been thrown out from north Africa and the Allies had penetrated Europe, thus breaching Hitler's vaunted *Festung Europa*. And in the Eastern Front, the Wehrmacht was on a retreating spree, In the Pacific, the Japanese Carrier Fleet was in disarray and the American marines were winning one island after another.

The military situation had been radically different two years earlier. In early 1942, as the Japanese *blitzkrieg* unfolded in South East Asia,

British fortunes had reached an all time low. To the defeated and exhausted Allied troops, Japanese soldiers seemed supermen, invincible jungle fighters against whom the Allied troops stood no chance. At that time, the Japanese also enjoyed air and naval supremacy. The British fleet had escaped to the western Indian Ocean and the American fleet was yet to recover from the disaster at Pearl Harbour. The Indian Ocean was almost a Japanese lake. Admiral Chuichi Nagumo's aircraft carriers sailed into the Bay of Bengal and bombed Madras and Calcutta. The British position had weakened further after the Indian army suffered its greatest defeat in Singapore and subsequently in Burma. In 1942, the Indian army thus, lacked moral and material power to stop a Japanese advance. The Raj was further embarrassed when, at this point, Gandhi launched the biggest mass movement of his career. As the Quit India movement spread along eastern India, the General Head Quarter at Delhi was forced to remove troops from the India-Burma border to quell the internal unrest. About 52 infantry battalions were used for re-establishing law and order. At that time, there was virtually nothing to stop the Japanese army in Burma from moving into Bengal and Assam.

The summer of 1942 was desperate for the Allied powers in the West too. The *Wehrmacht's* Army Group South's advance in south Russia was continuing towards the Caucasus. Rommel's *Afrika Korps* was maintaining its inexorable advance towards Egypt. The *Afrika Korps*, Army Group South and the Japanese appeared likely to meet convivially in the Middle East. The Imperial General Staff in London and the Combined Chief of Staff in Washington agreed that if the Japanese decided to advance along the Indian Ocean, there was nothing to stop them. If the Middle East was lost due to an Axis junction, then the oil reserve of Persia, and the mineral, agricultural and manpower resources of India, would also be lost. Further, all communications with Australia and China would be severed. The war itself might be lost. The summer of 1942 was the Axis's 'finest hour'. But Hitler and Tojo came to the aid of the Allies. The city of Stalingrad instead of the Caucasus and the Suez Canal drew Hitler like moth to a flame. The Japanese Carrier Fleet sailed away from the Indian Ocean never to return. It met its watery doom in June 1942 at the Battle of Midway in central Pacific. Simultaneously, the German Sixth army was defeated at the epic struggle in Stalingrad (August 1942–February 1943). To cap it all, Rommel was hurled back at El Alamein in November 1942. The tide of the war was turning. This gave breathing space to the British in India.

By early 1944, the British had recruited a large number of Indian soldiers. The British and Indian troops stationed in India were trained in jungle warcraft by the Supremo (Mountbatten) and Field Marshal Slim. If one scans military history, then it becomes clear that extraordinarily popular leaders were also often handsome and charismatic. Alexander and Rommel are two examples. During campaigns, soldiers, lacking easy access to women, and living in a closed male society, start developing affectionate male (homo-social) bonding. This can mature into a sort of homosexuality. In other words, they can get attracted towards handsome men. Mountbatten in his forties was tall, good-looking and charismatic. Mountbatten's sex appeal was definitely a positive factor in raising the morale of his battle-weary troops. He used to visit the frontline troops frequently to give them pep talks. His charm and magnetism lifted the spirit of the troops. While the young Mountbatten radiated glamour, the 53-year old general Slim won the hearts and minds of his troops by displaying paternal care. His soldiers affectionately called him 'Uncle Bill'. Even when conducting the Battle of Imphal and Kohima, Slim made it a point to explain anti-malarial procedures to his troops regularly.

Malaria and dysentery had ravaged the Allied troops while they retreated from Burma in 1942. Even in 1943, as the Indian troops made forays into Arakan, for every single battle casualty there were 120 sickness casualties. Disease certainly lowered the morale of the men. The military administrators of the Indian army took steps to combat it. By 1944, there were only 20 sickness casualties for every battle casualty. The rate fell further to 6 : 1 in 1945.

By 1944, after massive aircraft production in the USA, the Allies achieved air superiority both in the European and the Asian theatres. With the introduction of Spitfires and Hurricanes, which escorted the cargo and troop-carrying Dakotas, Mountbatten's promise to his troops, 'We shall march, fight and fly through the monsoon', had come true. The Sepoy army which faced the Japanese at the onset of the 1944 campaign was very different from the under-equipped and untrained Allied army that had retreated from Burma in 1942. Hence, in 1944, when the INA appealed to Indian soldiers to desert the British cause, the sepoy's loyalty mechanism remained by and large intact. If the INA had appeared on Indian soil during the earlier British misfortunes and the Quit India movement, then large-scale desertion by Indian soldiers was a possibility.

When the Japanese launched U GO in early 1944, the dice was heavily loaded against them. Still, all was not lost. The situation at Kohima was dangerous for the British. Over 15,000 Japanese soldiers attacked a garrison of 3,500 Indian troops. The garrison was supplied from the railhead at Dimapur. The original order for the Japanese commander of the 31st Division, Major Lieutenant-General Kotoku Sato, was to capture the city of Kohima first, and then the railhead. However, he proved to be inflexible and failed to see that if his troops captured the relatively unguarded Dimapur railhead first instead, then the city of Kohima would fall. When pilots of the Royal Air Force located the Japanese divisional commander's command post, Slim asked them not to bomb it. Never before and never after this unique incident had a general requested his own air force not to hurt the enemy commander. In fact, the continued well being of the foolish Japanese commander was a boon for the 14th Army.

If a bold and audacious Japanese commander had been in charge of the 31st Division, then after masking Kohima with a regiment, he would have moved into Dimapur and far into the west. Since Jorhat and the Brahmaputra Valley were without any significant troops, the Japanese could have easily captured these areas. This would have made it impossible to supply troops and ammunition to British imperial troops at Imphal and Kohima and it would have triggered a disaster for the Allies in China. With the Brahmaputra Valley under Japanese control, the Allied air supply to Stillwell and Chiang Kai Sheik's forces in the Yunnan province of south China and north Burma (known as the Northern Combat Area Command) from Assam and Bengal would have ceased. Then, the Japanese 33rd Army under Lieutenant-General Masaki Honda could have easily moved north and destroyed Stillwell and Chiang Kai Sheik's armies. With Kohima gone, the disaster in the Northern Combat Area Command, and the Hump air route in disarray, the situation at Imphal would have been dire for the British. Imphal was already under attack by the Japanese 15th and 33rd divisions from the east and south. After the fall of Kohima, the Japanese would have been in a position to wheel in the 31st Division to take Imphal from the north. In such a situation Mountbatten, far away in his headquarters at Kandy, would have faced a bad situation. Mountbatten could not be relied upon to deal with tangled military situations. Known as Dickie among his friends and colleagues, he was not a military genius like *Generalfeldmarschall* Von Manstein. His rise could be partly attributed to his royal connections, sophistication and good looks. The serious-looking bespectacled Field Marshal Alanbrooke, who was Chief of the Imperial General Staff at London, wrote in his diary that 'Dickie' lacked many things and one of them was brains.

HOLLOW VICTORY

The butcher's bill at Imphal and Kohima was 60,000 Japanese soldiers. The British 14th army also lost 40,000 in killed and wounded. But while these losses could be replaced, the Japanese were not in a position to replace their losses. Worse, as the Japanese pulled out in the Arakan and north Burma, their losses mounted. The straggling Japanese columns recoiling from Imphal and Kohima back across the Chindwin also suffered grievous losses. In retreat, the Japanese lost another 55,000 soldiers. The back of the Nipponese war machine was finally broken.

Once the Japanese army was destroyed by the trap laid for them in Imphal and Kohima, there was no stopping Slim's armoured columns. The Sherman tanks and Lee Grants of the Indian armoured corps made a dash across central Burma. The race for Rangoon had begun. The disaster at Burma and the dropping of atom bombs at Hiroshima and Nagasaki forced the country of the Rising Sun to surrender unconditionally to the Allied powers. The British were again masters of South and South-East Asia. But, history was not repeating itself. The heyday of colonial rule was over. The victory at Burma proved to be a hollow one, because the very steps that the British took for gaining victory contained the seeds of decline within them. They started germinating as the World War drew to a close.

During the war, the British officers derided the Azad Hind Fauj as 'Japanese Inspired Fifth Columnists'. True, during combat, the 'JIFS' proved to be broken reeds. But after the war, the 'JIFS' came to haunt the British. To win the Second World War, the British had to expand the Indian army from a force of 1,50,000 men to about 2 million. But after the war, when the British decided to demobilize Indian soldiers in late 1945, the soldiers turned against the sahibs in utter disgust. After the First World War, when many Indian soldiers were demoblized, the Raj had provided them land in the Punjab Canal Colonies. But by the end of the Second World War, there was no such land to satisfy their local troops. The Raj lacked the financial resources to provide adequate compensation to these ex-soldiers.

The soldiers' grievances were intensified by the fact that in the INA, they had seen Indians occupying high posts. Such upward mobility was impossible in the British-controlled Indian army. Before 1939, the officer cadre of the Indian army was the white men's monopoly. After the British were forced to expand the Indian army during the Second World War, they required more officers. The shortage of white officers grew because of the continuous casualties the British army suffered while fighting the Axis armies. It was impossible to fill the officer cadre of the Indian army with white men. In desperation, the Raj was forced to recruit university-educated urban middle class Indians as officers. In 1945, there were about 8,500 Indian officers in the Indian army. These men were conscious of the discrimination they faced in pay and promotions, compared to British officers. As demobilization continued, the Indian officer corps felt threatened not only because future promotion slots were shrinking but also because the white men were on the point of monopolizing the available posts. Both, the brown privates and officer cadre were unhappy with their white masters. For the first time in the history of the British-Indian empire, disaffected brown sepoys could look to the Indian officers for guidance. All these developments forced Field Marshal Auchinleck, Commander-in-Chief of India, to inform Number 10 Downing Street in 1946 that the 'Indian army could not be relied upon.'

To cap it all, the British public too was weary of military service. Mothers and wives wanted their sons and husbands back. As demobilization continued in Britain, a greater danger threatened the Western democracies in Europe. After the demise of Hitler, Stalin emerged as the bogeyman of the West. With the onset of the Cold War, Britain was no longer in a position to import troops from Europe into India. Washington forced London to concentrate all her military assets in preventing Soviet tanks from crossing the Rhine. Further, British economy became dependent on financial doses from America injected through the Marshall Plan. All available British troops were concentrated in Germany and Greece. The consequences of six years of global warfare had finally sounded the death knell of the British Empire as Hitler had predicted. India was moving inexorably towards her Independence.

12

Mission Impossible? Kargil
May–July 1999

THE BATTLE OF KARGIL was fought in about the most inhospitable region in this country. Devoid of vegetation, the area is dominated by knife-sharp peaks towering at 10,000 or 15,000 ft. Besides being dangerous, it is also one of the coldest regions on this planet. The atmosphere is low in oxygen. Only specially equipped mountaineers could be expected to operate in this area. The battle was fought in this frozen region along a frontage of 200 km.

India maintains patrols to guard this harsh and cruel land. But every year, with the onset of winter, the situation worsens. Avalanches roar down, and about 60 ft. of snow is deposited on the ground. In the forbidding months between November and May, the patrols are withdrawn. In 1999, Pakistan decided to take advantage of this annual withdrawal of the Indian outposts. The 12th Northern Light Infantry started crossing the glacial frontier along Mashkoh Valley in February 1999.

THE *JEHADIS*

'The Indian Army is incapable of undertaking any conventional operations at present, [let alone] enlarging conventional conflict.'

—LIEUTENANT GENERAL JAVED NASIR, ex-chief of
Inter Services Intelligence, 1999

Pakistan's objective was both political and military. From the military perspective, occupying the heights at Kargil would enable Pakistan to bombard the strategic National Highway that connects the Valley of Kashmir with Ladakh. The National Highway is India's crucial link with Kashmir enabling the transportation of troops and supplies. The strategic situation in Kashmir had changed unfavourably for India with the emergence of the China-Pakistan alliance. It worsened with a part of POK being transferred to Beijing in the mid-1960s to allow China to construct a strategic highway linking Tibet with China's western provinces. New Delhi had to maintain many units in Kashmir for counter-insurgency operations against the *jehadis* who were trained and equipped by the Inter Services Establishment of Pakistan. The *jehadis* had superior weapons, and with their fundamentalist education, they were better motivated for battle than the police and paramilitary forces of India. Troops also needed to be concentrated in Ladakh to deter the Chinese. The supply lines for all these troops runs through the National Highway.

For Pakistan's Chief of Army Staff Pervez Musharraf, the Kargil campaign was a tit for tat. On 28 March 1999, he described the forthcoming Kargil operation as 'a reply to India's Siachen invasion of 1984'. The Siachen glacier is situated at the extreme north of the Line of Control (LoC). In the early 1980s, the Indian army found that the Pakistani army was creeping forward to occupy the Siachen heights. In a daredevil move, the Indian army preempted Pakistan and occupied the glacier. It was victory for India's military pride but proved to be financially costly. Everyday, the national exchequer spends Rs.1 crore for maintaining the personnel and equipment on that rugged glacier.

Pakistan had always perceived the Indian leadership as Hindu and hence, weak. The religious faith and 'racial' temperament of Hindus, they thought, made them cowards compared to the followers of militant Islam. The idea of 'softy Hindus' was propagated by Pakistan in order to negate its own inferiority in material resources. Pakistan was convinced by its own propaganda. During the 1965 war, the Pakistani establishment under Field Marshal Ayub Khan urged soldiers on with the rhetoric that one Pakistani soldier was equal to three Indian soldiers. This belief continues to persist. It is somewhat similar to the rhetoric cultivated by the Third Reich to counteract the massive superiority of the Soviets in material resources. Nazi propaganda emphasised that one Nordic German soldier was more than equal to three 'racially inferior' Slav soldiers.

By 1999, it seemed that Pakistani propaganda was to an extent true at least for the Indian political leadership. Successive Indian prime ministers were so frail and old they seemed fitter for retirement than leadership. Both Narasimha Rao and Atal Behari Vajpayee had public images of being 'weak pacifists'. To make matters worse, a caretaker government was in power in 1999. The Pakistani establishment believed that since the ruling party had no mandate from the majority, the government would be unable and unwilling to take any decisive step to check an invasion.

In order to strengthen his image of being a 'peace-loving poet', Vajpayee had taken the trouble to make a journey to Lahore in a bus to meet the Prime Minister of Pakistan, Nawaz Sharif. Nawaz Sharif was an ineffectual leader. When General Zia-ul-Haq decided to implement an eye-wash democracy, he had picked up Nawaz Sharif, the scion of a corporate house, along with some other stooges. At the end of the bus journey, even as Vajpayee was hugging Sharif, Pakistani troops were crossing the LoC. The intrusion had begun.

Pakistan was confident about its military power. In 1998, it had gone nuclear. Its nuclear arsenal encouraged Pakistan to aggressively support low intensity warfare in Kashmir. Despite the sorry state of the Pakistani economy, Islamabad was able to provide massive economic support to the *jehadis*. The money came from Pakistan's heroin industry whose annual turnover in 1994 reached $2.5 billion.

By 1998, however, the *jehadis'* armed struggle was dying out in Kashmir. A cleavage had emerged between *Kashmiriyat*—the cultural identity of the Kashmiri Muslims—and the mercenary Afghans and Pashtuns (Pathans) who posed as religious liberators who would cleanse the Valley of 'Hindu infidels'. The revival of tourism attracted local Kashmiri youth away from danger-filled insurgent movements towards commercial occupations. Pakistan hoped that the armed intrusion into Kargil would function not only as a morale booster for the insurgents—by forcing the Indian government to use up troops engaged in counter-insurgency duty—it would give greater scope to the militants. Finally, a conflict would result in Kashmir becoming an international issue. Pakistan's ruling elite assumed this would put India into a disadvantageous diplomatic position. All these developments, assumed the Pakistani strategic managers, would negate the numerical superiority of the Indian military. For the military balance between the two countries see (Table 12.1).

TABLE 12.1: Military Balance between India and
Pakistan in 1999

	India	*Pakistan*
Army	980,000	526,000
Corps	11	9

Divisions	4 Rapid Divisions
	18 Infantry Divisions
	9 Mountain Divisions &
	   9 Mountain Brigades
	1 Artillery Division &
	   3 Artillery Brigades
	18 Air Defence Brigades
	(2,000 Air Defence Guns)
	3 Engineer Brigades
	3 Armoured Divisions &
	   5 Armoured Brigades
	(3,314 Tanks & 1, 707
	Armoured Personnel
	Carriers & 4,175 Towed
	Artillery & 180 Self Propelled
	Guns)
		15 Mechanized Infantry
		Brigades 19 Infantry Divisions
		1 Artillery Division &
		   9 Artillery Brigades
		12 Air Defence Brigades
		(2,000 Air Defence Guns)
		7 Engineer Brigades
		2 Armoured Divisions &
		   7 Armoured Brigades
		(2,120 Tanks & 850
		Armoured Personnel Carriers &
		   1,590 Towed Artillery &
		   240 Self Propelled Guns)

Note: India's conventional superiority against Pakistan was not decisive since most of
its mountain divisions were earmarked for Indo-Chinese borders.

THE FOG OF WAR

'All warfare is based on deception.'

—SUN TZU, Chinese military theoretician, 500 BC

As the Pakistani troops ascended the ridges of Kargil, the 'fog of war' seemed to descend on the political and bureaucratic establishment in Delhi. Given the failure of democracy in Pakistan, and military control of civilian affairs there, Indian politicians have always been wary of finding themselves in a similar situation. Government civil servants took advantage of the situation. They obstructed smooth interaction between political leaders and the military. All military philosophers from Sun Tzu to Clausewitz emphasize that unity of command is a prerequisite for victory. However, civil servants, in order to maintain control over their private empires, prevented any single intelligence agency apparatus from coordinating the various agencies. This policy also had the support of all political parties, who followed the policy of 'divide and rule'. The result was the operation of various overlapping and competing departments attempting to procure information. Besides the Research and Analysis Wing, Intelligence Bureau, and the Border Security Force; Divisional Intelligence Units, Intelligence and Field Security Units of the army also collected information.

The first three institutions were manned by personnel from the Indian Police Service. They lacked the training and aptitude for collecting military intelligence. Adding to the inefficiency, there was no institutional mechanism for jointly processing raw data and then assessing their significance. Unlike in advanced countries, in India, the Directorate General of Military Intelligence was paradoxically in no position to collect strategic information. It had access to bits and scraps of only tactical intelligence gathered by the army's Field and Intelligence Security Units. Despite massive spending on defence, in the end, policy makers remained in the dark as the tragedy at Kargil unfolded.

Brigadier Surinder Singh, the commander of the 121st Mountain Brigade with four infantry battalions and one BSF battalion (numbering 3,000 men) was guarding the Kargil sector. Singh was under the 15th Corps which in turn reported to the Northern Army Command. Singh and his superiors were groping blindly when the *jehadi* thunderstorm hit Kargil. The Indian commanders were victims of an obsolete and stratified command system. The Indian army still follows the British command culture, which is hampered by its lack of the German *Auftragstaktik* command culture. In the German armed forces, junior, and mid level officers are encouraged to think and act. A decentralized command set up which allows a lot of flexibility and initiative to 'men on the spot' is the hallmark of *Auftragstaktik*. Such a command system allows the commander to act quickly before the enemy can react, thus enabling him to get inside the enemy's decision-making cycle. The result is that the enemy is both psychologically and physically disoriented. The Indian army, on the other hand, encourages the junior and mid-level officers to look over their shoulders for guidance from their desk-bound superiors who are far away from the scene of battle. Often the superiors fail to grasp the ground reality or by the time they take a decision, the situation has changed beyond recognition.

The defect of a rigid hierarchical command set up is that if a subordinate makes a mistake, it snowballs into a crisis by the time the news of the faulty decision reaches senior commanders. In early 1999, Brigadier Singh had the feeling that something was wrong in the Kargil sector. However, before he could send out patrols, he had to take permission from his bosses. Had he sent out patrols without authorization, and had any soldiers then died in a snow storm, then Surinder Singh would have been in trouble.

The permission never came, and the Indian military had no knowledge of the Pakistanis preparing *sangars* on ridges before it was too late. The Clausewitzian 'friction' inherent in conducting war increased as Singh's message travelled up the command hierarchy. Major General V.S. Budhwar, a tough-looking man with set jaws, who commanded the 3rd Infantry Division, ignored Brigadier Singh's pleas in March 1999 for more troops. Budhwar's superior, Lieutenant General Kishan Pal, the commander of the 15th Corps, in his Srinagar office believed that on 14 May 1999, 'the situation [in Kargil] was local and would be dealt with locally'. Confidence deviously rose as the distance between the commanders and the frontline increased. Kishan Pal's superior, Lieutenant General H.M. Khanna the Northern Army Commander, informed the Defence Minister George Fernandes Rommel-style on 12 May 1999 that only a 'handful of intruders' had entered and would be thrown out within forty-eight hours. At the top of the command echelon, the COAS General V.P. Malik believed all was fine. On 9 May 1999, Malik left India for a goodwill visit to Poland.

On the Pakistani side, the Force Commander Northern Area was in charge of operations. He reported to the Pakistan army headquarter at Rawalpindi. The intruders, armed with AK 47s and grenade launchers, also possessed snow scooters and night vision devices. About 1,700 regular Pakistani soldiers were involved in the operation, many of whom belonged to the Special Service Group. Pakistan intended to disguise the operation as a *jehadi* uprising to liberate Kashmir. The Pakistani regulars were, therefore, dressed in black salwar kurtas. Another aspect of Pakistan's *maskirovka* was to instruct its soldiers to speak in Pushtu, thus, encouraging Indian intelligence agents intercepting radio traffic to view the trespassers as *mujahideens* and not as Pakistani regulars. Some 1,300 bonafide *mujahideens* were recruited as porters and back up reinforcements.

BLOOD IN THE SNOW

'The weather cruellest, harshest and the nastiest. Disappointment to the lowest ebb of hope and courage. No mercy from *Allah* Almighty received yet despite five days rigorous treatment. Prayers. Cry in the desert.'

—Diary entry 12 April of an unknown Pakistani soldier
belonging to the 12th Northern Light Infantry

Malik returned on 20 May and at last, the Indian army launched an attack which was grandiosely named 'Operation Vijay'. The intruders had spread over about 9 km. The Indian army's tactic was to bombard possible enemy posts with heavy artillery and follow that by an infantry assault. It seemed an impossible task for the infantry. Heavy self-loading rifles were slung around their shoulders and haversacks containing rations were strapped to their backs. To these loads were added pitons and ropes with which to climb, often crawling along narrow precipices in blinding snowstorms. As they struggled up, *jehadis* perched on the peaks shot at them with rifles and machine guns. The area was also strewn with anti-personnel mines. Indian soldiers defused some 8,500 mines after the Pakistanis finally retreated. To prepare the infantry for high altitude combat, the authorities set up two training centres at Sonmarg and Karu, the latter 25 kilometres from Leh. Officers from the High Altitude Warfare School trained combatants for a week before they were moved to Kargil.

Both sides relied greatly upon indirect fire by heavy artillery. Several 120 mm. mortars and 105 mm. mountain guns situated far back within the Pakistani side of the LoC gave support to the invaders. In the first week of June, through one day in the Batalik sector, Pakistani artillery fired 2,000 rounds. The 56th Mountain Brigade of the Indian army which was deployed at Drass found the area pockmarked with craters.

The Indian artillery forced the intruders to take cover as the jawans advanced. As the Indian assault infantry came close to the *sangars* and cement bunkers constructed by the intruders, the artillery fired smoke shells to temporarily blind the Pakistanis. The plan was that the Indian infantry would form up and then launch close quarter attack under cover of the smoke. The Indian infantry's 'encircle and choke' tactics were an attempt to surround ridges held by the enemy and then eliminate them. But all lines of communication between the intruders and Pakistan could not be severed because the Indian troops could not cross the LoC—they were forbidden by a strict government order. Indian troop concentrations were meanwhile repeatedly hit by Pakistani guns firing from 20 km. behind the LoC. The long-range gunnery of Pakistan, directed by the Pakistani troops who sat atop the Kargil ridges as gun observers, was deadly accurate.

In order to minimize casualties to the infantry climbing uphill, the Indian army requested air support. It took five days for the government to take the decision. When the army requested air support, Prime Minister Vajpayee dithered. Nevertheless, his hand was forced by George Fernandes and the second 'iron man' in the cabinet, Home Minister Lal Krishna Advani. The IAF operation, named Safed Sagar, aimed at local domination of the battlespace. All-weather Mirages imported from France were used for reconnaissance. Heavy helicopters like the Mi 17 bought from Russia provided fire support to the Indian ground troops. The IAF tried to drive the Pakistanis into pockets which they then identified for Indian artillerymen. Indian heavy guns shelled the pockets containing Pakistani soldiers. In addition to close fire support, IAF helicopters also dropped small teams of soldiers on top of the mountains. Such teams guided the infantry along the peaks. The aim was to surround enemy-held peaks by capturing the neighbouring peaks.

The IAF at Kargil faced the same problems that the Soviet air force faced in Afghanistan in the 1980s. The terrain of Afghanistan and Kargil are similar. Snow-capped mountainous ridges frequently cut by narrow, winding, glaciated *nullahs* are the chief features of both the Afghanistan and Kargil landscape. The pilots of high-speed fixed wing aircrafts found it difficult and dangerous to manoeuvre in those narrow valleys. One false move and the aircraft could crash into a rock face. The treacherous wind made the aircrafts spin out of control. Stinger missiles that the *mujahideen* launched proved to be deadly for the low flying Indian helicopters providing fire support to their ground troops. The intruders at Kargil fired four Stingers at Indian Mi 17s and downed one gunship. This loss prevented the gunships from hovering low enough to provide accurate fire support to the Indian infantry. Cloudy days also reduced the effectiveness of air reconnaissance because the IAF lacked night vision devices and infrared sensors.

Nonetheless, India decided to utilize her superiority in conventional armoury indirectly. The Western Fleet of the Indian navy was activated and put to sea in Operation Talwar. The Western Fleet received reinforcements from the Eastern Fleet. Operation Talwar was a sort of deterrent deployment to confine the much smaller Pakistani navy within Karachi harbour. Pakistan understood that any further escalation of the conflict would be counterproductive because she was dependent on oil imported through tankers along the Arabian Sea.

After ten days of war, Pakistani Prime Minister Nawaz Sharif's nerves were in tatters. The resolute defence by India's political and military establishment had come as a shock. China's stance too, was not at all encouraging to Islamabad. Actually, Beijing itself was concerned about the rising tide of Islamic fundamentalism in her western provinces. Pakistan lost hope of China preventing India from transferring mountain divisions from Ladakh and Arunachal Pradesh to Kargil in case of a long-drawn-out attritional war. The Pakistani troops, meanwhile, were at the end of their tethers. By early June, their food and ration stocks had dwindled sharply. In the first week of June, the Pakistani soldiers perched in Kargil asked for intervention by the Pakistan Air Force (PAF). The PAF remained in a state of high alert at Skardu but refused to intervene. Both the political and military establishments of Pakistan were well aware of the qualitative and quantitative edge that the IAF possessed over the PAF. The military junta of Pakistan accordingly, refused to allow the war to enter into the third dimension.

By August, snow storms brought the armies to a halt in Kargil. Battle would have been impossible in such weather. In July a 'negotiated settlement' between India and Pakistan allowed the intruders safe passage, providing a face-saving formula for both sides.

MORE KARGILS?

'I am tired of lifting dead bodies.'

—An Indian soldier belonging to the
56th Mountain Brigade at Drass

Kargil was India's first television war just as Vietnam was America's. Initially, the American middle class was very enthusiastic about a hardline approach towards North Vietnamese communists. The American middle class remained complacent about the conflict as long as the body bags emerging from cargo planes were not those of middle class white Americans. But as the war continued, the army faced manpower shortages. When the Pentagon conscripted university-educated young males as temporary officers for service in Vietnam, anti-war demonstrations started. The urban middle class did not want its children dying squalid deaths in the swamps and jungles of Vietnam. By the late 1960s, the American middle class had turned away from the war with the USA having suffered some 55,000 dead over a decade. Pictures of gory battlefields and body bags being loaded onto the cargo planes turned the American middle class against the war, forcing Washington to sign a humiliating treaty with the 'commies'.

At Kargil, the jawans fought bravely because the junior officers displayed 'heroic command' and led from the front, thus, suffering high casualties. Still, the Indian army's junior command set up was not flawless. After the war ended, in September 1999, forty army personnel (including jawans, junior commissioned officers, and majors) were charged with cowardice, desertion and command failure. Indian losses—474 men killed and 1,109 wounded—were lower than Pakistan's. Pakistan lost 700 men including 71 officers. Despite this, if Pakistan, in accordance with the policy enunciated by Sartar Aziz, its Foreign Minister at the time, had initiated several more limited incursions with *jehadis*, then, things would have been nastier for India. A predictable effect of a long-drawn-out battle would be the shortage of officers. The Indian army's officer corps is largely composed of lower middle class men. Jawans are usually the offspring of small farmers. During the Kargil campaign, the Indian army was short of 13,500 officers. Continued Kargil-like engagements would have resulted in losses to the seasoned commissioned officer corps of the Indian army. India could not have moved officers *en masse* from the mountain divisions facing China either. The only alternative then may have been to tap the university-educated urban middle class through conscription, which is fraught with difficulties. Not only are short service conscripted officers less effective, conscription may have resulted in the Indian middle class turning against the war.

Were Pakistan army personnel to occupy Kargil-like heights equipped with Stingers in large scale, the Indian infantry would probably have to fight without the material and psychological advantages of air support. Flying conditions in those areas make air combat difficult, stressful and dangerous. Sooner or later, the Indian military would pressurise the government to cross the LoC, which would certainly lead to full-fledged war. During the Kargil crisis, both the Indian and Pakistani governments had alerted their nuclear delivery vehicles: a point to be kept in mind.

Kargil is significant not for its objectives, scale or number of casualties but for new features that might reappear. Compared to the other battles described in this book, Kargil could be termed a 'Limited Battle' fought under a nuclear shadow. Rather than annexation of enemy territory or annihilation of the enemy army, Pakistan's principal aim was to precipitate a third-party intervention in the dispute over Kashmir. Battles of this kind are also termed catalytic war.

Conclusion

Towards Armageddon or the
End of Battle?

'War is decided only by battles, and it is not finished except by them.'

—FREDERICK THE GREAT

A NEW VIEW ON the origin of decisive battles has emerged in recent years in the Western academe. V.D. Hanson and Geoffrey Parker claim that the West invented the concept of decisive battles. It was the Greek farmers of the polis who first came up with the idea of conducting a decisive confrontation in a demarcated area, and in a single afternoon, to gain a decision. Hanson and Parker trace the origin of modern warfare back to ancient Greece. They draw a linear connection between hoplite infantry carrying spears and the American soldier armed with a self-loading rifle. Parker continues that technological superiority from the beginning of civilization has aided the West in the successful conduct of decisive battles; and technological pre-eminence has been possible due to the economic superiority of the Western world. W.H. McNeill points out that the triumph of Western warfare from the late Middle Ages onwards arose from the West's free market economy which generated greater resources than the command economies of Asian states. In a way, the views of Hanson and Parker do not differ much from the interpretations of Charles Callwell and G.B. Malleson who, in the nineteenth century, theorized that the 'savages' had no notion of decisive battles. This, according to Malleson and Callwell, was due to the racial inferiority of the Oriental people.

That modern warfare and capitalism feed each other is a sustainable view; but the Eurocentric view regarding the origin of decisive battles and technological supremacy is less convincing. Long before the great hoplite battles like First Mantinea (418 BC), and the Second Coronea (394 BC) were fought, the Aryan tribes conducted a decisive battle known as Dasarajna (1900 BC) which in a single afternoon on a riverbank established the supremacy of the Bharata tribe. Before AD 1800, the West did not enjoy any appreciable superiority in hardware either. Between the fall of the Western Roman Empire during the late fifth century and the rise of gunpowder weapons in the seventeenth century, it was the steppe nomads, with composite bows and iron stirrups, who enjoyed the upper hand in the military balance with settled agrarian societies.

The rise of Postmodernism and the resultant Cultural turn has its effect on military history writings also. Social historians in the 1980s truned away from the study of leaders and political organizations to non-statist aspects. Academic focus turned the spotlight on the marginal groups and on the nameless and faceless common men and women. John Keegan championed this approach in 1976 with his publication of *The Face of Battle*. After doing research on military history for more than 20 years, I conclude that the bottom up perspective does not throw much light. As far as the Indian case is concerned, we do not have any account by the common soldiers till the mid nineteenth century. Sitaram's memoirs is probably spurious. The court martial records give snapshots of what the common soldiers had to say under duress. For the First World War, we have some letters by the sepoys and sowars. Some Indian officers' memoirs exist for the two World Wars. The rank and file's view are available from mid twentieth century onwards. Moreover, the privates' perspective tells us one common thing across the centuries: war is hell. They do not explain why they were fighting in a particualr spot and why one party emerged victorious. The 'fox hole' perspective does not really explain causality. I believe that macro questions are important in history. And only top down perspective can answer the macro issues. Further, women both elite and subaltern have played a marginal role (in supporting cast at best) in battles. Like Joan of Arc, Indian military hsitory have a Rani of Jhansi and the Begum of Lucknow. Unfortunately or fortunately (depending on one's perspective), battles remained a male preserve. This monograph by focusing on commanders, strategy, tactics and technology has unabashedly followed the history from top approach and rightly so.

The history of battles shows both continuities and discontinuities. The battlefield remains a deadly place filled with abominable stench, blood, dust and gore. This is because the race between lethal killing technology and life-saving technology is a continuing one. When combatants at Jhelum and Tarain faced spears and swords, the *vaids* could only offer the wounded the option of amputating their limbs with sharp-edged knives—without anaesthetics. Till the early modern age, the surgeon's tools did not differ much from those of a butcher. Rapid advances in medical technology occurred in the nineteenth century when bandages, painkillers and quinine appeared. But the mechanics of killing were also improving. Cordite, rifles and steel cannons were designed to kill more men quickly and easily. The Second World War with its air-dropped bombs, machine guns and quick-firing cannons began a new era of killing. In the same period, however, many wounded soldiers were saved by the blood transfusion machines carried by field ambulance units. The wounded were also evacuated by air. In Kargil, for example, many Indian infantrymen were saved from sure death when helicopters carried the injured to the 15th Corps hospital in Srinagar. Combatants with more serious injuries were flown to Chandigarh and Delhi.

Despite the rapid progress in life-saving technology, the lust for battle has been declining. The Roman military theorist Vegetius rightly pointed out that civilized men engaged in culture and business would not offer themselves for sacrifice to Mars. History shows that the higher the economic surplus a society generates, the less the motivation among its citizens to face death at war. The Macedonians who were considered to be the most uncultured among the Greeks were able to conquer Athens and then destroy the richer and more cultured Persian empire of Darius. When Rome was poor, its legionaries fought the Gauls. But when it became the 'mistress' of the Mediterranean world, no Romans would join the legions and Rome instead had to depend on the mercenary German tribes for soldiers, which in the long run had disastrous consequences. Reading Eurasian history, we can see that nomads repeatedly defeated the rich and literate agrarian societies of China, India and Persia. Whether it was Attila or Chengiz Khan, their armies at a basic level represented the hunger for three Ws: wine, women and wealth.

In Indian history, the semi-educated, landless and jobless Afghans from a conservative theocratic society repeatedly came and won—for example, the soldiers of Mahmud Ghori, Babur and Ahmad Shah Abdali. Even Kargil in a way was possible because Osama Bin Laden's *mujahideens* became jobless once the Soviets pulled out of Afghanistan. But this is not to say that the poor and the illiterate always win against settled and civilized societies which have the upper hand in technology and organization—two crucial ingredients for success in warfare.

Despite mind-boggling technological progress in surveillance equipment and social upheavals, some things in battle are constant. One unchanged element is the failure to procure proper intelligence about the enemy. Both Paurava in Alexander's time and General V.P. Malik in Kargil, lacked proper intelligence regarding enemy movements. Both these commanders were surprised by the enemy in an unexpected place. The presence of tactical reserve is an unchanged requirement whether at the Battle of Second Tarain or at the Battle of Kargil. Combat effectiveness required and still requires heroic command at the lower levels. Whether it was the centurions and decurions of the Roman army, the jemadars and subedars of the East India Company's Sepoy army, or the lance naiks and sergeants of the present day Indian army, how well the privates fight still depends on these faceless and nameless junior leaders.

Nevertheless, with time, the face of battle has been changing. Battlefields have expanded in length and breadth. While Paurava's army occupied 5.5 mi. during the Battle of Jhelum, the Marathas under Sadashiv Rao Bhau at Panipat were spread along 7 mi. During Imphal and Kohima, Slim's XIV army was scattered over a hundred miles. Now, the battlefield extends to the skies. A single commander can no longer control all his forces in person. The widening battlefield forces the top commanders to delegate command. This in turn reduces the importance of heroic command among the top echelon of the leadership. But that does not mean courage among the top military leadership has become redundant. According to Clausewitz, courage is of two types; physical courage required in the battlefield against the enemy and mental courage necessary to formulate plans under multidimensional pressure. As the fog of war descends, implementing a plan and holding on to it with conviction requires great courage.

This book challenges linear determinism in history, itself the product of the Enlightenment. The evolution of battles also questions lineal development. From 326 BC onwards, the scope and intensity of battle increased. The size of the battle zone, as well as the number of combatants involved, and non-combatants killed also increased. But in 2001, the US army at Afghanistan deployed less troops compared to the number of troops they inducted at Omaha and Utah, beaches of Normandy in 1944. Similarly, in 1971 more than 1,00,000 Indian troops were engaged in East Pakistan compared to 5,000 at Kargil. In some battles, numbers have been replaced by more powerful weaponry and different methods of warfare.

Though this volume deals with big battles, it does not mean that guerrilla warfare is unimportant. In fact, most of my counterfactual scenarios show that guerrilla warfare is not merely the weapon of the weak but if integrated within the operational framework of a regular army, it holds great promise for conventional armies. It is difficult to predict with exactitude the nature of future battles.

Clausewitz writes, 'In war, as we have already pointed out, all action is aimed at probable rather than at certain success. The degree of certainty that is lacking must in every case be left to fate, chance, or whatever you like to call it.' To conclude, the only certainty about future battles is the utter uncertainty about its nature.

Bibliographical Essay

IN ORDER TO PLACE these twelve great battles within a wider matrix of military history and for a supplementary bibliography, look up my *From Hydaspes to Kargil: A History of Warfare from 326 BC to AD 1999* (New Delhi: Manohar, 2004). The present book dealing with twelve great battles is based on numerous works dealing with general military history as well as books focusing on specific topics. My articles, 'The Historiography of the Colonial Indian Army' (*Studies in History*, vol. 12, no. 2, 1996, pp. 255–73) and 'Mars in Indian History' (*Studies in History*, vol. 16, no. 2, 2000, pp. 261–75) provide an academic analysis of monographs and articles written on Indian military history.

Some classics cut across space and time. One such book is Field Marshal Bernard Montgomery's *The Path to Leadership* (1961, repr., London: Fontana, 1963), which explains the nature and function of leadership. Montgomery also brings out the distinction as well as the commonality between military and political leadership. For a brilliant conceptual discussion on 'heroic command' in the battlefield, John Keegan's *The Mask of Command* (1987, repr., Harmondsworth: Penguin, 1988) remains invaluable. Though West-centric, Keegan's formulations help to analyse non-Western military leadership as well.

In order to get an idea of the evolution of military thinking from the Stone Age to the nuclear one, see Gerard Chaliand's edited volume *The Art of War in World History from Antiquity to the Nuclear Age* (Berkeley: University of California Press, 1994). Mark McNeillys *Sun Tzu and the Art of Modern Warfare* (New York: Oxford University Press, 2001) shows how the Chinese military theoretician's principle of avoiding decisive battles has been used by many military leaders throughout history. Thomas R. Phillips' edited volume, *Roots of Strategy: A Collection of Military Classics* (1940, repr., Dehradun: Natraj, 1989), offers a translation of the original writings of five great practitioners of warfare. The giants included are Sun Tzu, Vegetius, Marshal Saxe, Frederick and Napoleon. One must refer to Carl von Clausewitz, the pundit of decisive battles and a virulent critic of attritional warfare. Clausewitz, *On War* (edited and translated by Michael

Howard and Peter Paret, 1976, repr., Princeton: Princeton University Press, 1984) remains the best edition available. Clausewitz's strategy based on *Kesselschalachts* is challenged by B.H. Liddell Hart. Liddell Hart's *Strategy* (New York: Frederick A. Praeger, 1954) is essential reading. An empirical analysis of attritional strategy in the twentieth century which plays down the importance of battle is available in Correlli Barnett's *Britain and her Army: A Military, Political and Social Survey* (London: Penguin, 1970). *Guerrilla Warfare* (1961, repr., London: Cassell, 1963), which Liddell Hart edited, helps to understand guerrilla strategy.

The only Indian scholar before the modern era who provides a conceptual understanding of the role of battles in India's national security is Kautilya. Here, I am not entering into the debate about whether Kautilya is the sole author of *Arthashastra* or if a band of ancient scholars wrote the magnum opus. *The Arthashastra,* edited, rearranged, translated and introduced by L.N. Rangarajan (1987, repr., New Delhi: Penguin, 1992) is handy.

From theorists, we move on to the practitioners of military history. Herodotus in *The Persian Wars* (tr. George Rawlinson, Toronto: Random House, 1942) gives an account of the beginning of interstate war. This is the first book of military history. After Herodotus, the story of battles among the Greeks was continued by the Athenian Admiral Thucydides in his *History of the Peloponnesian War* (tr. Rex Warner, 1954, repr., London: Penguin, 1988). Thucydides' successor as a military historian was Xenophon, who was also a commander. Xenophon's *The Persian Expedition* (tr. Rex Warner, 1949, repr., London: Penguin, 1972) was the prelude to Alexander's invasion of Asia. A nineteenth-century German historian Hans Delbruck's *History of the Art of War: Warfare in Antiquity* (tr. Walter J. Refroe, Jr, 1975, repr., vol. 1, Lincoln and London: University of Nebraska Press, 1990) supplements Herodotus's account of the genesis of warfare in ancient Eurasia. Delbruck gives special emphasis to the Macedonian war machine. A flavour of Roman warfare is provided by *The Civil War* (tr. Jane F. Gardner, 1967, repr., Harmondsworth: Penguin, 1984) by Julius Caesar, who describes some of the greatest battles that he fought in his life.

Depicting battles remains the most popular genre within military historiography from the ancient to the modern era. Though G.B. Malleson could be criticized for his 'racist' views, his *The Decisive Battles of India* (1883, repr., Jaipur: Aaviskhar, 1986) remains a minor classic. Jadunath Sarkar's *Military History of India* (1960, repr., New Delhi: Orient Longman, 1970) is the only academic analysis we have of the ancient and medieval battles of India. With Sarkar's mastery over Persian sources, his analysis of some of the medieval battles is penetrating and insightful. Major General J.F.C. Fuller's three volumes about battles crucial to the rise of the West is informative. I found his *A Military History of the Western World: From the Earliest Times to the Battle of Lepanto,* vol. 1, (1954, repr., New York: Da Capo, 1987) very useful. However, John Kegan's *The Face of Battle: A Study of Agincourt, Waterloo and the Somme* (1976, repr. Harmondsworth: Penguin, 1978), following the 'history from below' approach gives the best account of what happened on 18 June 1815 at Waterloo. V.D. Hanson's recent book, *Carnage and Culture: Landmark Battles in the Rise of Western Power* (New York: Doubleday, 2001) supports the theory that the West invented decisive battles and thereby constructed empires in the extra-European regions. It is an empirical account of a dominant model in military historiography.

Whether the West invented decisive battles or not, Western military supremacy in the extra-European world from 1700 onwards is unquestionable. Geoffrey Parker's *The Military Revolution: Military Innovation and the Rise of the West, 1500–1800* (Cambridge: Cambridge University Press, 1988) changed the landscape of military history. His book is a masterpiece, describing the managerial supremacy of Westerners in matters military. Parker's edited volume, *The Cambridge Illustrated History of Warfare: The Triumph of the West* (Cambridge: Cambridge University Press, 1995) despite being a saga of triumphal march of the West against the 'rest' is worth reading. The best overview of the varieties and lethality of non-Western military systems which challenged the 'triumph of the West', is Jeremy Black's *War and our World: Military Power and the Fate of Continents, 1450–2000* (1998, repr., New Haven: Yale University Press, 2000). Nevertheless, Parker's achievement lies in integrating the history of battles with governmental and technological changes. The technological determinist view regarding Western warfare is put forward by J.F.C. Fuller in his *Armaments and History: The Influence of Armament on History from the Dawn of Classical Warfare to the End of the Second World War* (1945, repr., New York: Da Capo, 1998). William H. McNeill in *The Pursuit of Power: Technology, Armed Force, and Society since AD 1000* (1982, repr., Oxford: Basil Blackwell, 1983) provides a heady brew of technological progress and free market economy to explain the military rise of the West. Despite his economic reductionism, Paul Kennedy's majestic *The Rise and Fall of the Great Powers: Economic Change and Military Conflict from 1500 to 2000* (1988, repr., London: Fontana, 1990), cannot be bypassed. And for the complex interaction between British victories in battles fought on land and their supremacy in naval warfare, look up Kennedy's *The Rise and Fall of British Naval Mastery* (1976, repr., London: Fontana, 1991). For a flavour of writings by anthropologists, sociologists, historians and journalists on various aspects of modern warfare including battles, see Lawrence Freedman's edited volume *War* (Oxford: Oxford University Press, 1994).

Military history writing remains a problem. The biggest problem lies with the sources. From the dawn of civilization both in India and elsewhere, victors wrote the histories. And not all the victors have penned their activities. Unfortunately, neither Alexander nor Mahmud Ghori have left any memoirs. We are lucky to have Babur's autobiography. The edition used in this book is *Baburnama,* vols. 1 and 2, tr., A.S. Beveridge (1921, repr., New Delhi: Saeed International, 1989). Babur comes alive in his narrative. His pages are interspersed with his views about fruits, birds, trees, wine and certainly tactics. For the Second Battle of Panipat, we have to depend on the history written by the courtier historian of Akbar, Abul Fazl, in *The Akbar Nama,* tr. H. Beveridge, vol. 2, (1939, repr., New Delhi: Saeed International, 1989). We have no alternate sources that challenge the victor's viewpoint presented by Babur and Abul Fazl. As with other decisive historical events in colonial India, most of the accounts of the 1857 revolt are written by the victors. The memoirs written by the defeated rebels have almost all perished. Most of the Indian participants, being illiterate, have left no written accounts. A glimpse of some Indian accounts of 1857 is provided in my 'Company Bahadur against the Pandies: The Military Dimension of 1857 Mutiny Revisited' (*Jadavpur University Journal of History*, vol. 19, 2001–2). The trend of the victor's dominance over history-writing continues even in the twentieth century. There are few English translation of Japanese accounts of the Battle of Imphal and Kohima. There is nothing on the Japanese side to challenge Field Marshal Slim's account of his victory in Burma, *Defeat into Victory* (repr., Dehra Dun: Natraj, 1981).

While eyewitness accounts of most of the pre-eighteenth century battles are lacking, as an exception, we have eyewitness accounts of the First and Third Battles of Panipats. Both Babur and Kasi Raj Pandit were present at these two battles. Kasi Raj Pandit's *An Account of the Last Battle of Panipat and the Events leading to it* (tr. H.G. Rawlinson, London: Oxford University Press, 1926) is more trustworthy than Babur's account of the First Battle of Panipat. Babur, being a protagonist who was also the victor, probably bragged about his followers, the Mughals. But Kasi Raj, a desk-bound obese

Brahmin diplomat in Shuja-ud-Daulah's service had no particular axe to grind. The point remains that Kasi Raj also belonged to the victor's party. Every eyewitness account is also partial because the author can see only part of the battlefield. T.S. Shejwalkar, in *Panipat: 1761* (Poona: Deccan College Postgraduate and Research Institute, 1946) tries to correct some of Kasi Raj's bias basing himself on letters written by Maratha participants at the battle.

Modern historians of India have neglected biographical studies. Buddha Prakash's *History of Poros* (Patiala: Publication Bureau, Punjabi University, 1986) is a modern reconstruction of Paurava's role at the Battle of Jhelum. But Prakash's account depends on anecdotes and he attempts to portray a romantic picture of a 'heroic' Paurava. Though dated, Stanley Lane-Poole's *The Emperor Babur* (1899, repr., Delhi: Sunita, 1988) is a standard biography depicting the rise of Babur. M.L. Bhargava's *Hemu and his Time: Afghans versus Mughals* (New Delhi: Reliance, 1991) is the only biographical account of someone who came very close to defeating the Mughals. Bhargava has done good work on the basis of the limited sources available to him. The standard biography of Hemu's nemesis, Akbar, remains Vincent A. Smith's, *Akbar: The Great Mughal, 1542–1605* (repr., Delhi: Sultan Chand, 1962).

Victor Davis Hanson's illustrated book, *The Wars of the Ancient Greeks* (1999, repr., London: Cassell, 2000), helps in understanding the rise of hoplite warfare. Godfrey Hutchinson in *Xenophon and the Art of Command* (London: Greenhill, 2000) analyses the beginnings of generalship in the Greek military system, which was refined by Alexander before invading India. Gustav Oppert's *On the Weapons, Army Organisation and Political Maxims of the Ancient Hindus, with Special Reference to Gunpowder and Firearms* (Ahmedabad: The New Book Order Company, 1967) traces the genesis of organized violence in India. Oppert is an expert in the use of Sanskrit sources. However, his view regarding the use of gunpowder weapons by the ancient Hindus needs to be taken with a pinch of salt. A.K. Srivastava's *Ancient Indian Army: Its Administration and Organisation* (New Delhi: Ajanta, 1985) is of some help in understanding the evolution of *Chaturanga Sena*.

Several Muslim historians belonging to the medieval era have chronicled the conquest of Hindustan from the Arab invasion of Sind till the decline of the Delhi Sultanate. Their historical narratives have been translated by John Dowson and H.M. Elliot. I have used *The History of India as told by its Own Historians,* vol. 2 (1867–77, repr.).

We must thank J.S. Grewal and Indu Banga for editing and publishing some of the orders of the *Khalsa* government in *Civil and Military Affairs of Maharaja Ranjit Singh: A Study of 450 Orders in Persian* (Amritsar: Guru Nanak Dev University, 1987). Several of these documents provide a detailed account of the state of military modernization in the *Dal Khalsa*. Many Europeans who were employed by Ranjit Singh had left their memoirs. John Martin Honigberger was a physician-turned-military bureaucrat. His *Thirty Five Years in the East: Adventures, Discoveries, Experiments, and his Historical Sketches relating to the Punjab and Kashmir in connection with Medicine, Botany, Pharmacy* (1852, repr., New Delhi: Asian Educational Services, 1995) portrays the tension within the *Khalsa durbar* between the modernizers and the traditionalists. About the British side of the imperial military operations, one of the most useful books remains Charles Gough and Arthur D. Innes's *The Sikh and the Sikh Wars: The Rise, Conquest and Annexation of the Punjab State* (1897, repr., Delhi: Gian Publishing House, 1986). Technical details about British tactics of assault on entrenched Sikh camps are available in Colonel Lewis in 'Campaign on the Sutlej: 1845–6', *Papers on Subjects connected with the Duties of the Corps of Royal Engineers*, vol. XLIX (1849). To understand the Company's superiority in siege warfare from Seringapatam in 1799 till the 1857 Mutiny, the best piece is 'Siege Artillery in the Nineteenth Century' (*Journal of the Society for Army Historical Society*, vol. LX, no. 243, 1982) by B.P. Hughes. Regarding the Siege of Lucknow, for those unwilling to visit the National Archives of India, a shortcut is available. Several important documents from the Military Department Proceedings had been published by one of the most famous imperial historians of the 1857 Mutiny, G.W. Forrest, in his *The Indian Mutiny: 1857–58, Selections from the Letters, Despatches and other State Papers Preserved in the Military Department of the Government of India*, vol. 3 (1902, repr., Delhi: Low Price, 2000). The journal of the Bengal Engineer, Arthur Moffat Lang (who was only 22 in 1857), available in the Oriental and India Office Collection provides a picturesque account of the military struggle. Some pieces from his journal have been edited by David Bloomfield and published as a volume titled *Lahore to Lucknow: The Indian Mutiny Journal of Arthur Moffat Lang* (London: Leo Cooper, 1992). While Forrest lists the dry official documents, Lang's letters to home portray the human aspect of the tragedy that unfolded in Lucknow. Lastly, P.J.O. Taylor's (General Editor), *A Companion to the 'Indian Mutiny' of 1857* (Delhi: Oxford University Press, 1996) is a reference book including everything and excluding nothing regarding the 1857 Mutiny. This volume is a must for all students of the Mutiny.

While studying any twentieth century battle, for example Imphal and Kohima, one is overwhelmed by the availability of sources. Besides the Nipponese, the Fourteenth Army also had to battle the jungle, monsoon and malaria. George Forty's *XIV Army at War* (Surrey: Ian Allan, 1982) includes many eyewitness accounts of how the Allied personnel overcame these problems. Most of the histories of the Second World War neglect India and the Indian army. To understand the pivotal role played by India within Allied strategy, see the Cabinet Papers and War Office Papers available at the Nehru Memorial Museum & Library, New Delhi. The INA files transferred from the Ministry of Defence to the National Archives of India help us to understand the Azad Hind Fauj. Netaji's activities in Germany are covered by Rudolf Hartog in his book, *The Sign of the Tiger: Subhas Chandra Bose and his Indian Legion in Germany, 1941–45* (New Delhi: Rupa, 2001).

I have studied the Battle of Imphal-Kohima within the broader framework of global warfare. That the Allied victory in the Second World War was not inevitable is put forward by Richard Overy in *Why the Allies Won* (1995, repr., New York: Norton, 1996). The importance of the Middle East and the Allied weakness in this sector are emphasized by J.F.C. Fuller in *The Second World War: 1939–45* (1954, repr., New York: Da Capo, 1993). Soviet military weakness in the Caucasus during the summer of 1942 and an assessment of Mountbatten are given in Alex Danchev and Daniel Todman's edited volume, *War Diaries of Field Marshal Alanbrooke: 1939–45* (London: Weidenfeld and Nicholson, 2001). John Keegan in *Six Armies in Normandy: From D-Day to the Liberation of Paris* (1982, repr., London: Pimlico, 1992) ably covers the Normandy theatre. Keegan's *The Price of Admiralty: The Evolution of Naval Warfare* (1988, repr., New York: Penguin, 1989) provides the most interesting account of the Battle of Midway. Richard Overy's *Russia's War* (1997, repr., London: Penguin, 1998) is informative about the Russian theatre. Lastly, for Hitler's *Gotterdammerung*, Antony Beevor's *Berlin: The Downfall* (London: Penguin, 2002) is the best.

From Surprise to Reckoning: The Kargil Review Committee Report (New Delhi: Sage, 1999) is the official account of the Kargil fiasco. In accordance with the administrative culture in India, a retired Indian Administrative Service officer chaired the Kargil Review Committee. The report naturally overlooks the criminal negligence and inefficiency of the civilian bureaucracy in mismanaging the intelligence operation. The weekly national magazines covered the Kargil operation in detail. Retired Admiral and military theorist Raja Menon's article 'View to a Clean Kill' (*Outlook*, 7 June 1999) is profitable. The Kargil campaign also resulted in a batch of fresh and relatively young journalists rushing to the battlefront and reporting from the death zone. Some of the war correspondents' stories, like Sunil Narula and Ranjit Bhusan's 'Drawn into Battle' (*Outlook*, 7 June 1999), Rajesh Joshi's 'Life in the Line of Fire' (*Outlook*, 14 June 1999) and V.K. Shashikumar's 'Choking the Enemy' (*The Week*, 13 June 1999) are useful. Shantanu Guha Roy's 'The Army wants You' (*Outlook*, 21 June 1999), points to the chronic officer shortage problem that is lurking in the Indian army even during peacetime. If not handled properly, officer shortages will have a negative multiplier effect on the army's performance in the near future. Nitin A. Gokhale and Murali Krishnan in 'War and Witch Hunts' (*Outlook*, 2 October 2000), narrate General V.P. Malik's attempt to shore up the command system. Lieutenant General Harbakhsh Singh's autobiography *In the Line of Duty* (New Delhi: Lancer, 2000) is profitable in pointing out the absence of *Auftragstaktik* in the Indian army's command system. My article 'The Battle for Kargil: Post-Modern War in South Asia' (Kanti Bajpai, Afsir Karim and Amitabh Matoo, eds., *Kargil and After: Challenges for Indian Policy*, New Delhi: Har-Anand, 2001) explains battle tactics at Kargil. The battle of Kargil to an extent was a gunner's war. A synoptic account of the artillery-oriented battles that occurred in the First World War will be found in the fourth chapter of Peter Browning's *The Changing Nature of Warfare: The Development of Land Warfare from 1792 to 1945* (Cambridge: Cambridge University Press, 2002). Numerous Kargils might result in a sort of 'Vietnam of the Indian army'. The American army officer corps' experience in Vietnam is covered in a critical manner by Richard A. Gabriel and Paul L. Savage in *Crisis in Command: Mismanagement in the Army* (1981, repr., New Delhi: Himalayan Books, 1986).

The present book attempts to challenge linear determinism in history by analysing some of the big battles fought in India. Among many others, the best proponent of determinism remains E.H. Carr. His *What is History* (1961, repr., Harmondsworth: Penguin, 1986) is still worth reading. In response to Carr's methodology, counterfactual scenarios are provided in this book. If any reader is interested in ifs and buts regarding battles outside India, see, Robert Cowley's edited volume *What If: Military Historians Imagine What Might Have Been* (1999, repr., London: Macmillan, 2001). The American scholar Robert L.O' Connell in his book *Ride of the Second Horseman: The Birth and Death of War* (1995, repr., New York: Oxford University Press, 1997) charts an optimistic trajectory about the 'death of battles' in the near future.

Glossary

Afrika Korps	German military units in north Africa under Rommel
Akhtar	Regimental insignia on the *payat*
Altmash	Reserve behind the centre in the Mughal order of battle
Amil	Revenue official
Amir	Muslim chief
Ancien Regime	Pre-revolutionary regime in France
Arabas	Carts used by steppe nomads for conveying guns to the battlefield
Asva	Horse
Auftragstaktik	Decentralized command set up of the German army
Autarky	Self-sufficient economy
Banjaras	Grain dealers attached to the armies of pre-modern India
Banzai	Japanese war cry
Bargirs	Irregular cavalry maintained by semi-autonomous Maratha chieftains
Beldars	Pioneers of the Maratha army
Bennechavadi	The bullock department in Tipu's kingdom
Bhang	Intoxicating drink made from hemp
Bhistie	Indian water carrier
Blitzkrieg	Lightning war conducted by the Germans
Bushido	Japanese soldiers' code of conduct
Campoo	Infantry brigade in the Maratha army

Chagan	Polo
Chaturanga Sena	Army of the ancient Hindus consisting of horses, elephants, chariots, and infantry
Chauth	One-fourth of the produce extracted by the Marathas from enemy as well as allied territories
Corps	Conglomerations of divisions. Two or more Corps constitutes an army. Two or more armies make an army group
Daftar	Department
Dal Khalsa	Sikh army of the *Khalsa* kingdom
Dasta	Cavalry regiment in Ahmad Shah Abdali's army
Dhows	Premodern Muslim ships
Division	Each division has about 15,000 to 20,000 soldiers. Each division has several brigades. Each brigade is composed of several regiments. Each regiment has two or more battalions
Falconets	Handheld firearms carried by medieval Muslim soldiers
Farman	Order issued by the government
Fauj	Muslim army of the medieval world
Faujdar	Commandant of a locality
Feranghis	Europeans, especially British; literal meaning Franks
Festung Europa	Fortress Europe
Fortuna	Goddess of luck
Furusiya exercise	Military exercise of the Mamluks
Gada	Wooden mace covered with spikes and used by a *paik*
Ganimi Kava	Scorched earth policy conducted by Maratha light cavalry
Generalfeldmarschall	Field Marshal of the German armed forces
Gotterdammerung	Twilight of the Gods

Harawal-i-Manqula	Deep penetration strike force which moved ahead of the main Mughal field army
Hastis	Elephants
Hircarrahs	Indian news writers
Hoplon	Hollow round concave shield carried by a hoplite
Hoplite	Disciplined heavy infantry of ancient Greece wearing bronze armour
Howdah	The seat on the back of an elephant
Howitzer	Cannon with a short barrel pointing upward and used for plunging fire
Huzurat	*Peshwa's* household cavalry. They were recruited and paid directly by the *Peshwa*
Ishtihar	Proclamation
Jawan	Infantry soldiers
Jemadar	Non-commissioned Indian officer in the Company's Army
Karkhana	Factory
Kesselschlacht	Double envelopment of the enemy's flanks leading to Pocket or Cauldron battle resulting in slaughter
Killadar	Commander of a fort
Kukri	Curved Gurkha knife
Lithobolos	Siege machines of Alexander's army
Malik	Muslim chieftain
Mamluk	Slave soldier
Mangonel	Stone-throwing engine of the medieval Muslim Army
Manjaniq	Siege engine of the medieval Muslim army
Maskirovka	Deception in matters military; a Russian term
Matadeen	Pandy
Materialschlacht	Battle of materials in which the side with greater economic resources wins through sheer attrition of the opponent's economic assets

Muqaddam	Officer in charge of the advance guard of the Turkish Army; later this term denoted a revenue official
Najibs	Muslim cavalrymen from western Uttar Pradesh
Nasaqchis	Military policemen of the Durrani army
Nullah	Dried-up stream
Osthismos	Frontal push by hoplites
Paiks	Infantry of ancient India. The medieval armies of India continued to employ them albeit in a secondary capacity
Palki	Traditional Indian carriage carried by two or more Porters
Paltans	Disciplined infantry of the East India Company
Panches	Elected representatives of the Westernized Sikh infantry regiments
Pandies	Brahmin soldiers in the Company's Bengal army
Panzer	Armoured fighting vehicle of the Germans
Payats	Regimental flags of the Turkish army
Peshwa	Prime Minister of the Maratha Kingdom and leader of the Maratha confederacy
Phalangites	Infantry soldiers in the *phalanx*
Phalanx	Linear arrangement of the hoplite infantry armed with *sarissa* in successive lines
Polis	City-state of ancient Greece
Purbiyas	High caste soldiers (Brahmins, Rajputs and Bhumihars) from Purab, the East, i.e. Bihar and Awadh
Rathas	War chariots
Rathins	Drivers of war chariots
Safed Sagar	White Sea
Sanghar	Temporary fortifications constructed of stone and Wood
Sardars	Chieftains
Sarissa	Lengthened pike of the Macedonian *phalangite*

Satrapies	Provinces of the Persian Empire
Sena	Hindu army
Senapati	Commander-in-Chief of the ancient and medieval Hindu army
Shutaranals	Camel swivel guns
Sipah Salar	Commander-in-Chief of the Turkish army
Sowar	Cavalry
Subedar	Indian infantry officer in the Company's army
Taulqama	Mounted archers of the Mughal army whose job was to attack the flanks and rear of the enemy army
Ucqi	Contingent of archers placed at the flanks of the Mughal army
Wehrmacht	German army under the Third Reich
Zamburaks	See *Shutarnals*

Bibliography to the
New Edition

Aquil, Raziuddin and Kaushik Roy, eds., *Warfare, Religion and Society in Indian History*, New Delhi: Manohar, 2012.

Barua, Pradeep P., *The State at War in South Asia*, Lincoln/London: University of Nebraska Press, 2005.

Brekke, Torkel, ed., *The Ethics of War in Asian Civilizations: A Comparative Perspective*, London/New York: Routledge, 2006.

Callahan, Raymond, *Triumph at Imphal-Kohima: How the Indian Army Finally Stopped the Japanese Juggernaut*, Lawrence, Kansas: University Press of Kansas, 2017.

Cooper, Randolf G.S., *The Anglo-Maratha Campaigns and the Contest for India: The Struggle for Control of the South Asian Military Economy*, New Delhi: Foundation Books, 2005.

Garza, Andrew de la, *The Mughal Empire at War: Babur, Akbar and the Indian Military Revolution, 1500-1605*, London/New York: Routledge, 2016.

Gates, Scott and Kaushik Roy, *Limited War in South Asia: From Decolonization to Recent Times*, London/New York: Routledge, 2018.

Gates, Scott and Kaushik Roy, eds., *Critical Essays on Warfare in South Asia: 1947 to the Present*, vol. 1, *Conventional Warfare in South Asia*, Surrey: Ashgate, 2011.

———, *Critical Essays on Warfare in South Asia: 1947 to the Present*, vol. 2, *Unconventional Warfare in South Asia*, Surrey: Ashgate, 2011.

———, *Critical Essays on Warfare in South Asia: 1947 to the Present*, vol. 3, *The Nuclear Shadow in South Asia*, Surrey: Ashgate, 2011.

Katoch, Hemant Singh, *The Battlefields of Imphal: The Second World War and North-East India*, Oxon/New York: Routledge, 2016.

Keegan, John, *A History of Warfare*, 1993; repr., New York: Vintage, 1994.

Lavoy, Peter R., ed., *Asymmetric Warfare in South Asia: The Causes and Consequences of the Kargil Conflict*, 2009; repr., Cambridge: Cambridge University Press, 2010.

Olivelle, Patrick, tr., *King, Governance, and Law in Ancient India Kautilya Arthasastra*, annotated translation, 2013; repr., New Delhi: Oxford University Press, 2014.

Prasad, S.N., ed., *Historical Perspectives of Warfare in India: Some Morale and Materiel Determinants*, New Delhi: Motilal Banarasidass, 2002.

Roy, Kaushik, *Brown Warriors of the Raj: Recruitment & the Mechanics of Command in the Sepoy Army, 1859-1913*, New Delhi: Manohar, 2008.

———, *The Oxford Companion to Modern Warfare in India: From the Eighteenth Century to Present Times*, New Delhi: Oxford University Press, 2009.

———, *The Armed Forces of Independent India: 1947-2000*, New Delhi: Manohar, 2010.

———, *War, Culture and Society in Early Modern South Asia, 1740-1849*, Oxon and New York: Routledge, 2011.

———, *Hinduism and the Ethics of Warfare in South Asia: From Antiquity to the Present*, New York/Cambridge: Cambridge University Press, 2012.

———, *The Army in British India: From Colonial Warfare to Total War, 1857–1947*, London: Bloomsbury, 2013.

———, *Military Manpower, Armies and Warfare in South Asia*, London: Pickering and Chatto, 2013.

———, *Military Transition in Early Modern Asia: Cavalry, Guns, Governments and Ships*, London: Bloomsbury, 2014.

———, *Warfare in Pre-British India—1500 BCE to 1740 CE*, London/New York: Routledge, 2015.

———, *Sepoys against the Rising Sun: The Indian Army in Far East and South-East Asia, 1941-45*, Leiden/Boston: Brill, 2016.

———, *India and World War II: War, Armed Forces, and Society, 1939-45*, New Delhi: Oxford University Press, 2016.

———, *Indian Army and the First World War: 1914-18*, New Delhi: Oxford University Press, 2018.

Roy, Kaushik, ed., *War and Society in Colonial India*, New Delhi: Oxford University Press, 2006.

———, ed. and tr., *Tale of an Indian Warrior: Durgadas Bandopadhyay's Amar Jivancharit*, with an introduction, London: Anthem, 2008.

———, *War, Technology and Society in South Asia: 500 BCE–2005 CE*, New Delhi: Viva, 2010.

———, *The Uprising of 1857*, New Delhi: Manohar, 2010.

———, *Warfare and Politics in South Asia from Ancient to Modern Times*, New Delhi: Manohar, 2011.

———, *The Indian Army in the Two World Wars*, Leiden: Brill, 2012.

Roy, Kaushik and Peter Lorge, eds., *Chinese and Indian Warfare—From the Classical Age to 1870*, London/New York: Routledge, 2015.

Roy, Kaushik and Gavin Rand, eds., *Culture, Conflict and the Military in Colonial South Asia*, London: Routledge, 2018.

Singh, Upinder, *Political Violence in Ancient India*, Cambridge, Massachusetts: Harvard University Press, 2017.

Thapliyal, Uma Prasad, *Military Costume and Accoutrements in Ancient India*, New Delhi: Manohar, 2012.

Index

Abdali, Ahmad Shah 5–6, 71, 73, 167
     cavalry 74–5, 79
     lines of communication 80
Abhisares 22
Adolphus, King Gustavus 84
Afghanistan 8, 27, 30–1, 33–4, 41–2,
     45, 48, 53, 56–7, 60, 71–2, 80,
     107, 125, 130, 144, 161, 168–9
Afrika Korps 149
Aibak, Qutub-ud-din 29, 44
air-land battle 7
Ajatasatru, ruler 16
Akbar the Great 5, 61–3
Alam II, *Padshah* Shah 87, 94
Alanbrooke, Field Marshal 152
Alexander's conquests 39
     Battle of Arbela (or Gaugemela) 16
     Companion Cavalry 35
     defeat of Paurava's camp 14–24
     of Greece 8
     of *Indika* 8–9
     nocturnal adventures 14–15
     secret of Alexander's victory 20
     strategies 14–15, 22–3
Al-Hindi, Al-Muttaqi' 29
Ali, Haidar 6, 94–5, 98, 103
Ali, Ustad 51
Ali, Wajid 139
Ambhi, King 9
ambushes 11
amils 97
Anglo-Sikh Wars 128, 130
Angre, Admiral Kanhoji 84
Army Group South 149
Asoka's invasion of Kalinga 30

asramas 39
Assaye battle 109–11
     aftermath of 111–13
     tactics 109–11
atavika bala 24
Auchinleck, Field Marshal 153
Auftragstaktik command culture 55,
     158
Aurangzeb, Emperor 84, 86
Axis powers 2, 148
Azad Hind Fauj or Indian National
     Army (INA) 145, 150, 152–3
Aziz, Abdul 51

Babur, Zahir-ud-din 5, 47–8, 59, 167
     fortifications 50
     frontier raids 48–9
     mobile cavalry 49
     tulghama contingents of 51–2, 54
Bahadur, Maharajah Jung 134–5
Bahadur, Raja Beni 89
Baillie, Lieutenant-Colonel William
     103
Baird, General David 102
Balas 30
banjaras 110
Bareilly Artillery Regiment 140
bargirs 106
Barnett, Correlli 2
Beg, Dost 57
Beg, Muhammad Jani 55
Bengal 68, 71, 82–4, 86–8, 93, 97,
     103, 116
Bengal army 94, 130
Bengal Battalion 91

Bengal European Battalion 89–90
Bhau, Sadashiv Rao 71–3, 77, 81,
    168
Bhonsle, Raghuji 110
Bhrta Balas 30–1
Bihar 9, 16, 60–1, 63, 69, 84, 86, 93,
    122, 130
Bikramaditya, Raja 64
Bombay army 100
Bombay Detachment 91
Bombay Presidency 84, 86, 99, 103,
    110
Bose, Subhas 142
bow 17–19, 23, 25, 29, 35, 48, 52,
    57–8, 166
    armed mounted archers 5
breaching batteries 100
Britain, Battle of 4
British military
    artillery 92
    cavalry 111–12
    sepoy regiments 120–1
    supremacy in south India 105
Budhwar, Major General V.S. 159
Bussy, Marquis de 72, 103
Buxar battle, 1764 6, 83–94
    effect of 94
    final showdown 89–91
    force of firepower 91

Calcutta 92, 94, 132, 139, 141,
    148–9
Caldwell, Captain 102
Callwell, Charles 165
Campbell, Colin 131–5
    tactics 135–6
campoos 108–13
Cannae battle, 216 BC 79
capturing forts, art of 6
Carnac, Major John 84
Carr, E.H. 4
Chaldiran battle, 1514 51
Chand, Raja Jai 40
Chandra, Hem 60–2

Afghan-Hindu regime of 62
army 63, 65
fall of 67–9
managerial capacity 61
tactical novelty 63, 67
Chaturanga Sena 12–13, 32
Chauhan, Prithviraj 27, 33, 77
    leadership in Battle of Tarain
    33–8
Chausa battle 59
chauth tax 71
China-Pakistan alliance 155
Chindits 148
city holding strategy 140
Clausewitz, Carl Von 1, 4, 68, 76,
    169
Collins, Colonel 110
Cornwallis, Charles 103
Count de Suffren 103
Creveld, Martin van 1
curikabandhanam 39

Dal Khalsa 6
Das, Raja Bhagwan 64, 68
Dasarajna battle 166
Delhi 33, 41, 49, 53–5, 57, 59,
    61–3, 65–8, 72, 94, 108,
    132–3, 139–40, 149, 155,
    157, 167
Delhi, battle, 1556 63–4, 66–7
Delhi Chalo programme 145
Delhi famine, 1556–7 61
Delhi Sultanate 29, 48, 53
Dharmayuddha 10, 26, 28, 41
    code of 13
Durrani army 70, 72, 76–9

East India Company 2, 81, 95
    combating techniques of 104
    against *Khalsa* army 119–24
    lal paltans of 86, 113, 119–20, 128
    maritime supremacy of 99
    military bureaucrats of 86
Eisenhower, General Dwight D. 23

Ermattungstrategie 2
European military activities 83–4
  combat technique on land 84
European military mercenaries 118

Fabian strategy 1
Fabius, Maximius 1
The Face of Battle 166
Farquhar, Lieutenant 102
Fazl, Abul 61, 66
feranghis 6
feranghi shots 57
First Anglo-Mysore War, 1767 95,
  130
First Battle of Panipat, 1526 50–7,
  123
    destruction of Lodhi Sultanate
    53–7
First Mantinea battle 165
fortification 6
Fort William 84, 86, 92, 141
free market economy 85
French maritime supremacy 103
Fuller, Major General J.F.C. 3
furusiya exercise 30

gadas 10
Gafur, Sayyid 98, 102
Gardi, Ibrahim Khan 72
Gardi infantry 75
General Enlistment Act, 1856 131
German armed forces 158
German siege of Leningrad (1942–3)
  62
Ghaznavid Empire 27
Ghazni, Mahmud 32, 41, 45
Ghori, Mahmud 27, 29, 36, 43, 167
  campaign in India 30
  corps de elite of 35
  integration of 'missile power' 36
  Muslim army 33
Gilbert, Major-General Walter 120
Gosains 88–9
Gough, General Hugh 120–1

Greek military. *see also* Alexander's
  conquests
  cavalry 12, 15–16, 18, 20
  Companion Cavalry 16–17
  hoplite armies 11–12
  phalanx/phalangites 11–12, 24, 33
  tactical superiority of 24
guerrilla warfare 1, 79, 81
Gupta cavalry 39
Gupta Empire 39–41
Gurkhas 133, 135, 143, 147

Halim, Muhammad 101
Hanson, V.D. 165
harawal-i-manqula 65
Hardinge, Lord 120–1
Harris, George 100
Havelock, Henry 132
Highlander soldiers 133
Hindu Shahi dynasty 41
Hitler 23
Holkar, Jaswant Rao 115
Holkar, Malhar Rao 72, 78
  cavalry 74
Honda, Lieutenant-General Masaki
  151
Honigberger, John Martin 119
hoplite infantry 11–12
hoplite warfare 11
howitzers 105, 115, 128, 136
Humayun 59–60
Husain, Mahdi 139
Hussain, Mir Muhammad 101

Imphal-Kohima battle (1944) 5, 7
  British imperial troops at 148–52
  Japanese defeat 152–3
  jungle story 145–8
India-Burma border, soldiers'
  experiences 146–7, 149
Indian military
  Chaturanga Sena 12–13
  use of *hastis* or elephants 13
  weaponry 18

Indika 8–9
Indo-Aryans 9
inter-*jana* warfare 11–12
iron weapons 11
Islamic civilization 28–9
Islamic *Kutayuddha* 28
Ismail, Shah 51

Jafar, Mir (Nawab of Bengal) 88–90,
    93
Jagir grants 96
jalajils 37
janapadas 10–11
Janjira, Siddi 84
Japan 144–5
Japanese Inspired Fifth Columnists
    (JIFS) 152
Japanese soldiers 145–8
Jats 72
jawan 160, 163
jehadi uprising 159
Jennings, Captain 93
Jhelum battle (Battle of Hydaspes)
    8–9, 35
    lessons of 24–5
Jindan, Rani 126

Kargil region 154
Kargil war, 1999 4–5, 7, 126, 167
    impact on political and bureaucratic
        establishment 157–8
    military balance between India and
        Pakistan 157
    operations and engagements
        159–64
    Pakistan's objective 154–6
Karnal battle, 1737 78
Kautilya 13, 24
Kennedy, Paul 2
Khalsa army *(Dal Khalsa)* 118–19
    against East India Company
        119–24
    excellence of 128–9
    gunners 121, 123–4

infantry 128
    problems in Westernized 119
    right brigade 122
Khan, Abdulla 66
Khan, Afzal 63
Khan, Alam 56
Khan, Attai 81
Khan, Bahadur 49
Khan, Bairam 62–4, 69
Khan, Bakht 140
Khan, Banghas 74
Khan, Dera Ghazi 119
Khan, Dundi 74
Khan, Field Marshal Ayub 155
Khan, Hafiz Rahmat 74
Khan, Ibrahim 75
Khan, Iskander 66
Khan, Kuli 89
Khan, Lal 65
Khan, Mubariz 60
Khan, Munim 63
Khan, Shadi 64
Khan, Shah Ali Quli 67
Khan, Shah Pasand 74, 78
Khan, Shaibani 48, 51
Khan, Tardi Beg 63
Khan, Wali 77
Khan, Wazir Shah Wali 74
Khanna, Lieutenant General H.M.
    159
Khwaja, Mahdi 49
Kriegsfuhrung 3
Kukuldas, Khusrau 51
Kutayuddha 28

Laden, Osama Bin 167
lal paltans 86, 113, 119–20, 128
Lawrence, John 140
Limited War 7
lithobolos 20–1, 57
Littler, Major General John 120
Lloyd, Henry 13
Lodhi, Bahlul 48
Lodhi, Daud Khan 49

Lodhi, Ibrahim 48
  force 50
    military responses 48–9
    relations with nobles 56
Lodhi, Sikander 48
Lorenz, Konrad 123

Macedonian army 8–9, 13–16, 19–22, 25–6, 41, 167
Makhlis, Qasim 63
Mal, king Suraj 72
Malik, General V.P. 159, 168
Malleson, Colonel G.B. 3, 165
  The Decisive Battles of India 3
Mamluks 29
manjaniqs 41
mansabdari system 5
Mansfield, General W.R. 133
Mao Tse Tung 1
Maratha army
  cavalry 76–8, 93, 111, 115
  collapse at Panipat 6
  Commanders, at Panipat 75
  fort-based strategy 115
  guerrilla warfare 81
  modernization of 106–9
  tactic of destroying villages 115
Maratha confederacy 2, 4–5, 70–1, 77, 81, 105, 109, 115–16, 118
  Peshwa's huzurat cavalry 74
maritime power 96
Marshall, S.L.A. 124
Marshall Plan 153
maskirovka 159
Maula Balas 30
Maurice of Nassau 85
Maurya, Chandragupta 24
Mauryan Empire 24
McLaran, Brigadier J. 123–4
McNeill, W.H. 165
Midway battle, 1942 149
military-fiscalism 96
Military History of India 3

Military History of India (Jadunath Sarkar) 3
military situation, 1942 148–9
military transformation of West 83–4
Mirza, Muhammad 51
modern warfare 96–7
Mongols 2, 28, 45, 54
Montgomery, Field Marshal Bernard 65, 131
mortars 57, 147, 160
Mountbatten, Lord 150
Mouriset 99
Mughal military intelligence 54
Muhammad, Sultan 61
mujahideens 159
Musharraf, Chief of Army Staff Pervez 155
Mutaguchi, Lieutenant-General Renya 148
mutiny of 1857 131–4
  resistance at Lucknow 137–41
Mysore
  agrarian structure 97
  irrigation dams and tanks 97
  military-fiscal infrastructure 96
  risalahs 98
  sandalwood trees 97
  sericulture 97
  stud farms and animal husbandry department 96

Nagas 88–9
Nagumo, Admiral Chuichi 149
Nanda Empire 9
Napoleon's technique of launching Imperial Guards 69
Narihalla River 97
night attacks 11
Nizami, Hasan 44
Nizami, Taj-ud-din Hasan 29
nomadic tribes and settled agrarian communities, conflict between 9–11

On War 1
Operation Barbarossa 125
Operation Talwar 162
Operation Vijay 160
osthismos 12
Ottoman Turks 62
Outram, James 132, 137

paiks 10, 13–14, 31–2
Pakistan 126, 154–7, 159–64, 169
Pal, Lieutenant General Kishan 159
Pal, Raja Sulakshan 45
Pandies 129–30, 137, 140–1
Parker, Geoffrey 165
Patna battle, 1760 87
Paulas, Field-Marshal Friedrich 73
Paurava (Porus), king 9, 14–15
    army mobilized by 14–15
payats 37
Pearl Harbour disaster 149
Peloponnesian War 2
Perambakam battle 103
Persian Empire 8
Peshwa 71, 73–4, 80–1, 106, 110,
    115–17
Phadnis, Nana 76
phantom army 142–5
Philip of Macedon 12
Pindari cavalry 74
Plassey battle 87
polis 11
Pollilur/Polilore battle 103
Poona 71–2, 104–6, 110
proleterianization of warfare 84
Punjab 9, 13–14, 20, 43, 49, 53–4,
    61, 63–4, 69, 71, 79–80, 101,
    119, 127–8, 130, 133, 141,
    152
Purbiya soldiers 122

Qadir, Ghulam 89
Qasim, Mir (Nawab of Bengal) 88
Qasim, Muhammad 66
Quit India movement 149, 151

Quli, Shah Ali 67
Quli, Ustad Ali 57

Rai, Govind 33
Rai, Jujhar 61
Rai Pithaura 27
Raja, Woodeyar Maharajah Chik
    Krishna 95
rajans 10
Rajput confederacy 33–4, 37–8, 41,
    44, 77
Rajput military conduct 32, 34
Rajput warriors 27
    cavalry 34
    impact of second battle of Tarain
        43–6
    against Muslims 27–38
Rani of Jhansi 139, 166
Rao, *Peshwa* Balaji Baji 70–1, 80–1
    huzurat cavalry of 74
Rao, Raghunath 71
Rao, Vishwas 78
ratha (chariot) 12, 25, 32
real warfare 10
rebel army 137–41
Reihardt, Walter 88
Residency system 128
Rohillas 76–8, 89
    infantry 75
Rommel, *Generalfeldmarschall* Erwin
    148
Royal Air Force 148
rules for combat 10

Sakurai, Lieutenant-General Shozo
    145
Sanga, Rana 49
Sanjukta, queen 38
sardesmukhi tax 71
sarissa 12
Sarkar, Jadunath 3
Sato, Major Lieutenant-General
    Kotoku 151
schlacht 3

scientific war 6
Scottish Highlanders 133
Scythian nomads 9
Scythians 16–17
Second Anglo-Mysore War (1780–4) 95, 103
Second Battle of Panipat, 1556 59–69
  artillery and horse archery 68–9
  rapid deployment force 69
  tactic of attacking 63, 67–9
Second Battle of Tarain (AD 1192) 3–4, 33–8, 167–8
  barbarization of warfare 30
  equestrian engagement 33–8
  net effect 43–6
  Prithviraj's command vehicle 36
  Rajput confederacy 38–9
  Turkish cavalry 35
  Turkish horse archers 35
Second Coronea battle 165
Second World War 2, 167
Seleucus 25
Senapatis 37
sepoys 85, 110, 120–1, 146, 166
Seringapatam's construction and its weaknesses 101
Shah, Adil 60–1
Shah, Islam 60
Shah, Khwarizm 34
Shah, Nadir 70, 81
Shah, Sher 59–60
Sharif, Prime Minister Nawaz 162
Shivaji 56
shock troops 35
Shuja-ud-Daulah, Nawab of Bengal 82, 88–93
  army of 89–91, 93
  against Company force 89–91
shutarnals 78
Siachen glacier 155
Siege of Seringapatam, 1799 95, 100–4
Sikhs 6–7, 80, 108, 117–29
Sindia, Daulat Rao 109–10, 113–16

Singh, Brigadier Surinder 158
Singh, Maharaja Ranjit 6, 118
  Westernization programme 118–19
Singh, Raja Gulab 126–7
Singh, Tej 119–20, 125
Sirhindi, Abdullah 33, 37
Skandagupta, emperor 38–9
skirmishing cavalry 35
Slim, Field Marshal 150–1, 168
Smith, Harry 124, 128
Smith, Major General Harry 121
smoothbore muskets 131
Sreni Balas 31
Stalin, Joseph 153
Stevenson, Colonel 110
stirrups 32
strategic bombing 4
Subuktagin 36
Sulaiman, Muhammad 63
Sultan, Tipu 6, 94–8
  diplomatic failures 104
  fortifications and infantry 98–9
Sun Tzu 3
Suri, Sikander 59, 63
Sur or Suri dynasty 59

Tabakat-i-Nasiri 42
taccavi 97
taktika 3
taluqdars 137
Tarain or Tararoi 33
tawachi 55
Taylor, Brigadier Charles 123
Ten Kings battle *(Dasarajna)* 9
Third Anglo-Mysore War (1790–2) 100, 104
Third Battle of Panipat, 1761 4, 90
  Afghan army 74–5, 79, 89
  battle 73–9
  consequences 81–2
  Maratha army 74–6
  prelude to 71–3
  significance 82
Thucydides 2

Tope, Tantia 133, 139
Treaty of Bassein 109
tulghama contingents 51–2, 54
    tactics 66
Turkish cavalry 35, 40
Turkish horse archers 35
Turks
    of Central Asia (Tatars or
        Turkomans) 28–9
    in India 45

Umayid Caliphate 29
Uzbeg, Abdullah 63
Uzbeg, Sikander Khan 68

Vardhan, Harsha 31
Vegetius 167
Vira charitas 32

Viswanath, Balaji 81

Wallace, Brigadier-General William
    120
War of American Independence
    (1775–83) 103
Washington, George 103
Wellesley, Henry 109
Wellesley, Major General Arthur 109,
    114–15
Western maritime powers 85
Western warfare 98
White, Captain 98

Xerxes' (Persian Emperor) invasion of
    Attica 8

zamburaks 90